The Path

From Illusion to Freedom

by

William J. Cozzolino

Raissa Publishing

The Path

From Illusion to Freedom

Copyright ©1997 by Raissa Publishing
All Rights Reserved

Library of Congress Catalog Card Number 97-67353

ISBN 0-9658163-0-3

Manufactured in the United States of America
First Printing 1997

Published by
RAISSA PUBLISHING
Port Angeles, WA

Produced by
PPC BOOKS
Westport, CT

For Matthew Aaron

Contents

Foreword	i
Preface	iii

Unit One, Knowledge

Dream Time	3
The Movie Experience	7
Holographic	10
The Paradigm	18
The mind and Mind	21
The mind and the Computer	23
The mind is a Powerhouse	30
Paradigm Limits	35
The Magic of Agreeing	38
Consensus Reality	42
Out There	44
Maya	48
The Path in the mind	53
The One	63

Unit Two, Integration

Horizons	69
Balance	71
Falling	84
Meditation	89
Karma	106
Reincarnation	112
The Script	116
Worthiness	121
The Movie Will End	129
Transition	135

Unit Three, Return of the Sky Heroes

The Transpersonal Realm	147
States of Awareness	171
A Master	176
Working Together	182
Lucid Dreaming	189
A Shaman's Way	200
Remembering	210
The Quality of Faith	211
You Are	217

Foreword

In the sixteenth century, Galileo invited his colleagues in science to climb the steps of a tower and see for themselves the observations he had made in the night sky. Galileo, I am sure, hoped for a positive response from his peers. To him, the sky was filled with the obvious and, if they would just look, they would surely see. They would be convinced, as he was, that it is the sun—not the Earth—that is the center of the solar system.

Galileo didn't get the response that he thought he would. Even after he offered solid scientific proof, his findings were rejected out of hand because they disagreed with established "truth." Not only were his findings rejected, but he was threatened with torture and even death when he persisted. He was forced to recant.

For many years, historians believed that it was the bullheadedness of the establishment that caused such a reaction to new scientific knowledge. Today, we know much more about how our mind functions. We know that the mind plays a powerful role in selecting information that it will allow into our awareness. It develops a paradigm so powerful that sensory information from our environment is shaped to fit our beliefs and expectations. In cases where the sensory information is drastically different from what we believe is possible, that information is virtually eliminated from our conscious awareness. We simply do not perceive it. It may appear as bullheadedness, but we all have these filters, and that is why we perceive the world differently. Our personal beliefs make it difficult for us to understand the beliefs of another. The learned social values of our society make the values of others appear misguided or wrong. These are cultural differences, and they are the main cause of a divided world. It's difficult for us to believe that if we had been raised in one of those other cultures, we would hold dear the very beliefs we now consider wrong. And our paradigm extends well beyond social values. We have "schools of thought" that prevail from the foundation of our personal relationships to the halls of higher learning. Once established, these schools of thought are hard to penetrate—and even more difficult to change.

Galileo had to contend with an established school of thought. He was not the first person to discover the principles of the solar system. Other civilizations had already developed an understanding of cosmology. They attained that understanding in ways that Galileo's peers did not understand, and so their knowledge was rejected as religious superstition. Helicocentrism is the school of thought the evidence Galileo presented gave support to. It was one that his peers were well aware of, but one that they viewed as morally and spiritually wrong.

In the following pages, you will climb the steps of a tower of knowledge. You will be confronted with observations that may not fit with your perception of the world. These perceptions—like those of Galileo's—are not new. Your reactions—like those of Galileo's peers—may be shaded by your current paradigm. What you read may be difficult to understand because it conflicts with what you already know. Or, it may fit right in with your concepts about the world around you. In either case, you will learn that an emotional feeling of right or wrong is a natural result of the way our minds deal with new ideas.

You should know that the tower you are climbing is not a tower of new knowledge. These observations are but reflections of ancient understanding. We are beginning to see these old perceptions concerning reality emerging in the light of our state-of-the-art science. As we unravel the mysteries of the physical universe, we find that they have been unraveled before—a long, long time ago.

Let us begin our climb.

Preface

My entire life has been one of seeking answers for the conundrums of life. I suppose everybody could say that, but for me it has been more than a passing fancy. Although I occasionally attempted to lead a "normal" life, my Heart always led me back to this quest. My profession as a hypnotherapist kept me ever aware of the power of the mind, and my journeys took me to the far reaches of the world in search of answers. Answers came, but the Question remained in my Heart. The Question is that which remains after the mind is satisfied. The mind asks the questions, but the Question lives deeper in our being, well beyond the thoughts of our mind.

In 1982 a Master walked into my life. She didn't appear during some esoteric ritual or deep prayerful state. It happened, without fanfare, during my usual everyday activity. And she didn't proclaim herself a Master. After a brief introduction and a pleasant exchange, she simply asked: You have questions?

Yes, I had questions, and I asked them. I was taken aback by her answers at first. Her Chinese dialect and imperfect English did little to add to her ever cheerful attitude. As far as I was concerned, there was much to understand, much to do, and much that should be changed in the world. As far as she was concerned, everything was as it should be. We had not yet gotten to the Question.

Slowly, over a period of years, my Master led me to understand the nature of the reality in which we live. Many of our meetings were attended by others with the same lingering Question. Whether I would seek her out or she would just show up, there was always the same brief exchange of greetings followed by: You have questions? She always seemed to know that someone did.

The book you are about to read is the result of her teachings and of my many years of research and study. I must admit, though, that my work was a meaningless tangle of notes and research papers until my Master began to unravel them. Once we covered all the questions that I could muster, we were left with the Question. It still remains, and as you will learn, should always remain.

I have attempted to present these teachings in a manner to which the everyday Westerner can relate. My Master has given her blessing to this effort, but cautions that mental understanding is useless unless we develop the ability to listen to our Heart. The Heart is where the Question resides. The mind, it seems, is the only thing standing in the Path to freedom.

Unit One

Knowledge

Dream Time

Student: How did this reality begin?
Master: Reality has no beginning, and no ending. What you call reality is and always has been a potential of The One, and there are many realities. For you, this reality began when your mind began giving attention to a possibility of The One that was the focus of your desire and intent. What you call your reality was but one of many experiences available to you. Realities are nothing more than experiences isolated within limited awareness. Experiences become limited when you lose awareness of the potential of The One within them. When many agree on the same limited experience, and when the many lose awareness, reality becomes a shared illusion. The illusion is not in the experience. The illusion is in the conflict, in the separation.

Most belief systems include a story of creation. Shamanism is among the most ancient belief systems known, with a rich oral tradition dating back to before recorded history. Throughout the world, Shamanic tradition tells of a time when reality was more fluid, more flexible, and more like a dream. Called by many names, a common thread of all these traditions is seen in what the Australian aborigines call "Dream Time." Dream Time is their story of the creation of the world and all its inhabitants. Their tradition explains that the world was created by The Sky Heroes during Dream Time. But it also explains that creation is not a one-time process. The world continues to be created each moment. The Sky Heroes of old are still here, and they are found still at work creating their world. The tradition of Dream Time reflects what we will explore in this book. I retell the story in the light of my Master's teachings, bringing it into modern times in words that reflect Shamanic teachings throughout the world. It goes something like this:

The Sky Heroes were awakening from their dream into the world of created illusion. While in transition, they recalled being immersed in a vast potential of awareness. But their memory lasted only for an instant, and that fleeting moment of total awareness quickly faded into the background as they focused their attention on their creative abilities. Their desire was for self-expression, and they were in agreement on the chosen theme. They thought it would be a great idea to participate together in an illusion, in a dream. It would be like making a movie, but it would only exist in their minds. Most of them just wanted to create and direct their dream movie. They did not all want to be actors.

Combining their efforts of thought and creativity, they began to build the set and write the script for their movie. They created it from the energy of which they were a part. The set they created was beautiful, with plants and animals, majestic mountain ranges, vast oceans, and great plains. They had a wonderful time, and thought they had created the best dream movie ever. They selected, from among themselves, actors that would follow a script. The actors would rely upon each other to make the movie whole.

These Sky Heroes dreamed and created for quite awhile, agreeing upon constant changes in the flow and the plot. It held a certain fascination for them. The dream movie was very fluid, very flexible. All it took to change it was an agreement and the combined focus of their attention. Because it was easily changed, they agreed to change it often.

Most of them remained aware that they were dreaming, but occasionally, some would become so involved in the dream movie that they would lose themselves in it. Those who remembered always helped the others to return to the awareness that their creation was just a dream—and that they were the dreamers.

Soon, the dreamers who had become actors wanted to take larger roles in the dream movie, so they created costumes for themselves. They tried many different costumes before they found the right ones. Then they got into the costumes and played their parts in their movie. While involved in their dream movie in their costumes, they were able to temporarily set aside the awareness that they were the creators and directors of their movie. This allowed their participation to become more realistic. But they always came back to full awareness after each act.

But soon, some of the dreamers became so deeply involved in the parts they were playing that they wanted to play them better. They even began to tell others how to play their parts. They began limiting their options, and made fewer and fewer changes. Their focus of attention on the dream movie became so strong that they forgot to return to full awareness when their parts had ended. They forgot that their dreamed experience was just a projection of their mind. Rather than return to the energy that they were a part of at the end of each scene, they would simply step off stage and wait for an opportunity to return again. Worst of all, they forgot that they were the creators of their dream movie. They began to believe that they were just actors. They began to call their dream movie "reality."

Some of the actors became scientists. They began trying to find out what the dream—the dream that most of the actors now called physical reality—was all about. The scientists believed that they could understand their reality by looking deep into the physical makeup of it. They thought that the dream was holding itself together by some power hidden deep inside it. They talked about their beliefs and shared them with other actors. Soon many actors became scientists and spent their time studying the dream movie of reality.

Other actors believed that the dream was created for them, and that the power holding it together was coming from an outside source. These actors became theologians and philosophers. They spent their time thinking and talking about the nature of this power, and came up with many different ideas. There was much disagreement among these actors, so they divided themselves into groups. Each group believed they had found the source of the power holding the dream together. Once they believed they had found the source of their dreamed reality, they devoted a great deal of effort convincing others to believe as they did. Soon, many actors became members of these groups and devoted their time convincing others that they had found the source of the dream movie of reality.

And a few of the actors—a very few—remained aware that they were both the creators of and the actors in the dream movie of reality. They knew that the entire dream is made up of the energy of which they were a part. They tried to tell the others, but most of the actors wouldn't listen to them. They had become too involved in their reality to listen.

This is how the Sky Heroes of long ago became actors in the movie of reality today. But they are still Sky Heroes—even though they don't remember. They are still creating their dream movie of reality—even though they believe they are just actors. Scientists, theologians, and philosophers are still trying to understand the dream. And today, the actors who are scientists are coming very close to discovering the source of the dream.

The Sky Hero scientists long ago realized that everything in our reality, everything that we experience with our five senses, is in constant motion. They discovered that every physical thing is constantly changing from a state of order and organization to a state of disorder, and they declared this to be a natural tendency. They called this discovery the law of entropy. It's one of the laws about physical reality that is true. Everything in the physical world is changing from a state of order and organization to a state of disorder and disorganization. Like water in a glass. It evaporates. Order to disorder. Every physical "thing" is doing it.

Yet, living things seem to defy this law. They seem to organize themselves. Scientists said: Life organizes itself, so there has to be order somewhere, let's look deeper. They began taking things apart. They found smaller and smaller things and began taking them apart, too. They found the atom. They thought that the atom was the smallest thing in their physical reality, the building block for all physical things. They had a big problem, though. Atoms don't organize themselves. In fact, they decay. The scientists kept looking anyway.

Even though scientists could observe decaying atoms, they could not take them apart and look at them. So they began blasting them apart and looking at what was left. Scientists found new "things" when they did this, but these new things they found were not following the "laws" that the scientists had found earlier. They were acting differently than the bigger things. The scientists found that there were more little parts in an atom than they first thought possible, and that these smaller parts were made of only energy. They found ways of observing and testing these little parts of energy.

The scientists found that the very, very little parts could disappear from one place and appear in another place instantaneously, without any energy exchanged. They call this the "quantum leap." Scientists found out that energy would appear in a physical world as whatever they were looking for. They called it the "observer effect." They discovered that the deeper they looked into the physical world, the less things and the more energy they found.

And now, scientists have discovered that there are no things at all—that the physical world is made up of pure energy. They have discovered that they, as they focus their attention on their experiments, are actually interacting with this energy. They are effecting it by thinking about it. The boldest of these scientists now declared that the world is made up of energy, not matter, and that their expectations in a scientific experiment have an effect on this energy. They now realize that they are influencing the energy, and therefore the physical world, by their thoughts.

These bold scientists are looking into the physical world on the subatomic level—the level of the dream where there is little difference between a thought and a thing. They are finding out that what they have been looking at in the physical world is just a dream, just an illusion. They are beginning to realize that they—that all of us—are effecting the dream by the way they are looking at it and thinking about it. These scientists, with their persistent efforts in the face of an ever-changing reality, have done more to help us understand our dream movie than any "belief" could ever have done.

The dream is again becoming more flexible. Dream Time is returning, and many of us are beginning to realize that we are the creators of our own reality. The Sky Heroes are again awakening from their dream.

The Movie Experience

Student: Why is it that we remember most of what happens during the day but little of what happens when we dream at night?

Master: Are you sure that you are dreaming while you are sleeping, or is it possible that you are awake in your dreams, and dreaming while you think you are awake?

Student: This is not a dream. This is reality. I'm sitting here talking to you, and you're not a dream. I'm quite sure that I know the difference between being awake and being asleep. Things happen in dreams that aren't real. You can do things in your dreams that you could never do while you're awake.

Master: What is it that you can do in a dream that you cannot do while you are awake?

Student: Well, lot's of things happen in dreams that can't be real, I mean, you can even fly through the air in your dreams.

Master: And this is not possible while you are, ah, what you call, awake?

Student: You mean levitation. I suppose it is, but when it happens it's an exception.

Master: There can be no exceptions in an absolute reality. Exceptions only happen in dreams. Perhaps you have not yet awakened from your dream.

That there can be no exception in an absolute reality is a scientifically logical statement, and it's a fact. Although the question was asked by another member of our group, the answer my Master gave remained with me. She is saying that the physical universe we have learned to trust as reality may be nothing more than a dream. To conclude that our reality may be only a dream seems a bit of a stretch, but there are exceptions in our reality. Our reality is not absolute. Can we take this challenge seriously? Is it possible that our reality might be just a dream? Can we devise a test to prove that we are not dreaming? While you think about that, let's consider how reality is presented to us by our mind. We could say that reality is like a movie. It's happening out there, and we are watching in here. Sometimes we are involved and participate—sometimes we just watch. It's all happening on a view screen—the view screen of our awareness.

We go into the cinema expecting an experience. Experience is the purpose of being there. It can take a while, however, for the experience to begin having an effect on us. When we first enter the cinema, we are immediately aware of the change in lighting. Yes, it's darker in there, but it's light enough to find our way to our seat. Our seat? We've already begun a process of participating in experience—of finding a place for ourselves. Once seated, we go through a routine of observation. We may notice the younger crowd is a little noisy. There are couples that have come together to be together; they are easily spotted by the attention they give to each other. The ceiling, the walls, the seats, the floor, all have a fascination of their own as we give our attention to them. We may hear the sound of an airplane overhead, perhaps even a horn honking outside. We notice how comfortable or uncomfortable the seat is. Does it recline? We try it. If we are early and have a long wait, we may drift off and think about things we have to do, or things we have done. Our thoughts, our attention, can take us out of the cinema and into world of imagined reality while we are waiting for our movie experience to begin. Wherever our attention is, we see a movie in our mind. Our focus of attention creates a movie on the view screen of our awareness.

Then the lights go down, the curtain draws back, and the projector lights up the screen. With this change, our awareness undergoes a shift. All those things we were experiencing just a moment ago are filtered out. All the other information is still there—the thoughts we were pondering, the lovers in the back row—and it is still processed in our mind. But we're not aware of it. It's all filtered from our awareness by a natural process in our mind. Our awareness of our surroundings dims as we focus our attention on the presentation—on the movie. It has to. We would have no experience if we remained fully aware.

We may be taken into the movie. A good one will cause our mind to filter out the fact that we are even in a cinema, and our reality unites with the action of the movie. We laugh. We cry. We have a sense of good and bad, right and wrong. We may cheer for the hero and boo the villain. We lose touch with our normal sense of time. The individual frames of film flow over the projector lamp giving the illusion of unbroken motion. Somewhere in our mind, we still have the facts. This is a roll of film produced earlier, but we are experiencing it as if it is a current event. This is a movie, and we are watching it. There is no motion in the individual frames of film. But these facts are hidden from us for the time. Again, they have to be. We cannot have the experience of the movie if we retain the awareness that it is but celluloid frames passing before the light of the projector.

All the events that led up to the movie are contained in a larger experience, that of going to the cinema. And that experience is contained in yet a greater experience, that of who we are—our family, our friends, our work, our play, our best and our worst. All this awareness is set aside, virtually eliminated from the view screen of our awareness so that we can experience the movie.

The mind is the mechanism that produces our experience, and the process it follows in creating experience—any experience—is automatic. A host of experiences are available to us in the cinema, even while the movie is running. We could, for example, spend our time focused on the person next to us and never partake of the movie. Look around. There may be lovers in the "movie of life" doing just that right now.

The entire experience of the movie becomes available to us because our mind has the ability to filter out information that does not fit in with our current sensory experience. This process is active all the time. The mind presents us with a "movie" while we are awake and while we are asleep. This movie appears on our "view screen" of awareness. In our waking state, we call this movie "reality." In our sleeping state, we call it a "dream." But both movies are a presentation of our mind on the view screen of our awareness.

While awake, our mind relies on incoming sensory information and experience to create our movie, and it presents the movie on our *conscious* view screen. While we sleep, we are isolated from most incoming sensory information, so our mind creates it according to our dreamed experience. We still see, hear, taste, touch and smell in our dreams.

During sleep, our mind presents the movie on our *unconscious* view screen. Even though things can happen in dreams that do not usually happen in our waking life, our expectations remain the foundation for our dreamed reality. We have a body in our dreams. And our dream world, though often altered, remains a place for us to experience the dream. The dream continues while we focus our attention on it—and fades away when our attention shifts.

The process of creating the dream movie and our movie of waking reality is the same, and both movies appear as if they are "real." This is why dreams seem so vivid, and why what we call "reality" can seem so real. Again, the mind uses the same mechanism to produce both movies, and it operates automatically. And both movies remain on our view screen, and are our realities, until our attention shifts.

We will discuss the process in depth, but for now, know that all experience, be it a "dream" or "reality," is created in the same place and by the same method—in our mind.

Holographic

Master: All that is, is of The One. There is no separation, no time as you know it, and no limitation in The One. All that is, is of The One.

Many of us believe that everything in our world is of the same source, but it is difficult for us to create a model for our belief in our mind. Although we believe it, we cannot comprehend it. We are surrounded by physical things that appear separated from each other and we from them.. But modern science now tells us that those "things" in our world are really made up of energy, and they say that all energy is connected.

Holographic images are seen everywhere today. When held in sufficient light, the images have a fascinating three-dimensional effect that shifts its shape as we move the image back and forth. This effect is accomplished by the way the image is produced. An understanding of the holographic process will help us better understand the world of energy we live in.

A laser is a beam of nearly pure light energy. A holographic image is made by splitting a single laser beam into two beams. One of the beams is reflected off the object being recorded, and the reflected light is then projected onto a special holographic film. The second beam is allowed to merge with the light reflected off the object by the first beam. The beam that is reflected off the object being photographed contains the information to reproduce that object. The beam that is allowed to merge with the first is still very pure light energy. The two beams meet before they reach the film, and at that point they interfere with each other to create "interference patterns" of light. (*Figure 1*)

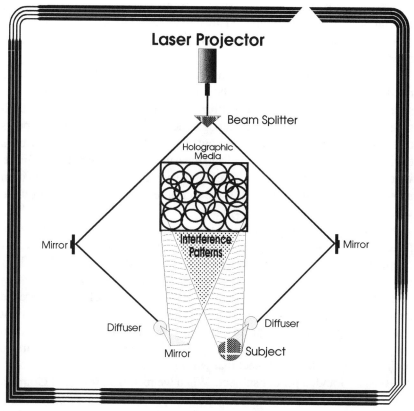

Figure 1

Holographic Recording

The image arriving on the film looks nothing like the original object. Rather, the image resulting from the holographic process is captured in interference patterns. Interference patterns occur whenever waves of energy collide with each other.

Let's look at it another way. When we toss a pebble into a still pond, we see a series of waves spreading away from the point where the pebble hit the water. These waves are energy patterns created by the pebble. By freezing the image of these rings of waves and measuring them, we can learn much about the pebble. We can determine how large it was and at what angle it struck the water. Information about the pebble is contained in the waves it created.

Imagine the rings of waves that are created when we toss two pebbles into the pond. A series of rings expands from each pebble and meets, or interferes with the rings created by the other. We can determine the individual nature of each pebble by observing the waves *where they meet*—or interfere with each other.

Now, imagine the waves that are created on our pond when we toss a handful of pebbles into it. Many individual rings of waves are created, one series of waves for each of our pebbles, and the waves interfere with each other where they meet. Even though the surface of the water appears disturbed, it contains information about our handful of pebbles. If we freeze the image of the rings on the pond and measure the waves where they meet, we can find out much information about the adjoining pebbles. Information about the pebbles is contained in the interference patterns created by the waves where they meet.

The holographic process captures information as a record of interference patterns much like the patterns created by the pebbles on our pond. Remember, the first of the two beams is pure laser light that is reflected off the subject. The second beam is pure laser light that interferes with the first beam before it reaches the holographic film. They result is interference patterns of light energy. It is these patterns of interfering waves of light that appear on the undeveloped holographic film, and these patterns contain the information necessary to recreate the subject. We can record an image in this manner with any subject that will reflect light.

Let's use Grandpa for our subject. When we record an image of Grandpa with this method, all we see on the undeveloped film are these interference patterns. These interference patterns contain all the information required to reproduce an image of Grandpa.

We can reproduce the image of Grandpa right in the air by projecting a single laser light back onto the film. When we do this, the image of Grandpa is created by the laser light passing through the interference patterns on the film and it appears in the air. Remember, the information for the image of Grandpa is in the interference patterns of light energy recorded on the holographic film, and the laser light shining onto the film decodes this information to produce the image. We can't see an image of Grandpa on the film. We see only the interference patterns created by the holographic recording process. (*Figure 2*)

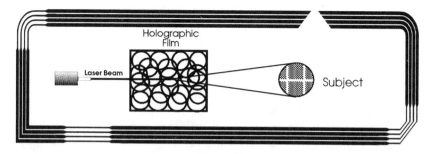

Figure 2

Holographic Projection

Once again, you can't see the image of Grandpa on the film. All that is on the film is the interference patterns of light that contain the information of Grandpa. Just as on our pond, even though there are no pebbles left on the surface, information for each pebble is recorded in the interference patterns they created.

Okay, you say, that's no big deal. After all, we can't see the image of Grandpa on our regular film until it's been developed.

That's true, but let's do an experiment. Let's take a photograph of Grandpa made with our holographic process and one made with standard photography. Now, before the images are developed, we get our scissors and cut both negatives in half. When we develop the two halves on standard film, we have the two halves of the image, half of Grandpa on one side and half on the other. When we reproduce an image by shining a laser beam through *either of the two halves* made with the holographic process, *we have a complete image of Grandpa*—a complete image is recorded on each half of the film. How is this possible?

Recall again the pebbles on our pond. The characteristic of each wave is a product of an individual pebble. We can tell how big the pebble is and at what angle it struck the water by measuring the wave that it created. But the patterns that are created where the waves meet, or interfere with each other, contain information about many pebbles. We can calculate the nature of these pebbles by measuring their intersecting waves. We are working with physical waves when we measure our waves in the pond, and interference patterns that were created *after the pebbles struck the water.* But we are working with light energy in the holographic process. In the pond, the interference patterns in the waves are created by those pebbles that are in the immediate area, and are created on the water as the pebbles hit the water.

The interference patterns in the reflected laser light are contained in the light itself. The laser beams interfere with each other *before they hit the film.* The light does not strike the film like a pebble on our pond, but rather, spreads out over the entire film. Every intersection of rings—or every interference pattern—contains all the information necessary to replicate the entire image of Grandpa. The rings are energy patterns, and they are infinite on the negative. If we cut off just one tiny corner of the negative, the information to reproduce an image of Grandpa is still there. Now, because we are recording energy patterns on a physical media—the holographic film—the image becomes dimmer in the tiny corner of film. But Grandpa "exists" on the film as a record of interference patterns. Theoretically, there is no place on the film where the information for the entire image of Grandpa is not recorded.

We can record more than one image on a single piece of holographic film. To do this, we need only to change the angle at which the light is reflected off an object and onto the film. We can just twist the film a bit to the left. After we have recorded the second object, we can adjust the angle and record still a third, using the same holographic film. Although we are limited by our technology, there is theoretically no limit to the number of objects that can be recorded with the holographic process.

When we project these images into the air, we can select the individual image by again adjusting the angle of the film. Adjusting the angle will cause the image of Grandpa to fade and the second image to appear. Twisting further causes the second image to fade and the third to appear. Remember, all the information for all the images is recorded in the interference patterns of light on the film. It is the angle of the projection laser light that causes an individual image to appear in the air. As with the single image, all the information for all the images is recorded everywhere on the film.

Finally, we can record different images on top of one another. To accomplish this, we simply insert a new subject without adjusting the angle of the film as we did previously. When the recorded image is projected, it is a combination of both images. It looks like neither individual, but has the characteristics of both. We can get some very strange results by doing this. We can record Grandpa, and then Uncle Harry. The projected image is a combination of both. We can actually see characteristics of both of them in the projection, yet it looks like neither of them.

Keep in mind that the images recorded with the holographic process are interference patterns of light energy, and that all the images exist everywhere on the film.

Think of our early scientists looking into the physical matter of reality as looking at the *projections* resulting from the holographic process. They were looking at objects, at things that appeared around them where they could be observed and studied—like laser images in the air. You may think that it would not take scientists long to discover that these images are reflections of light, but remember, the scientists are reflections of light, too. Being of the same substance as their experiment, they have no objective platform from which to observe. The result is a reality that appears as solid and real as the observer.

It was once thought that atoms were the foundation of all matter, the smallest of all the "things." Atoms resembled the solar system. The nucleus of the atom was like the sun, and the electrons revolve around the nucleus like the planets. This model of physics was initially called the "atomic theory" and evolved into "particle physics." Scientists kept looking for the smallest "thing" in the physical makeup of matter, and it looked as if the atom might qualify. But as scientists looked deeper and deeper into the makeup of the atom—into the "subatomic world"—they made some startling observations.

The deeper they looked, the less "things" they saw. You can smash a rock apart and you still have rock. It acts like a rock should act, only on a smaller scale; what is left over is still rock. But when scientists began smashing atoms apart, they found that they did not end up with smaller parts of atoms. What was left over was often something that did not even act as if it belonged to the physical universe. What the scientists found did not follow the laws of physics that they had been using all along. It acted more like energy than matter. Its "parts" were communicating with each other even though they were separated by great distances, and they were communicating instantly and appeared to be everywhere at once, like the rings on our holographic film. It began to appear that the physical universe may not have any "things" in it after all. Just as the Earth was not the center of the solar system for Galileo, the atom is no longer the fundamental structure of matter for modern physicists.

Remember, scientists began studying *things* in our physical world. We have compared these things to holographic projections. When they traced these projections, these things, back to the source, they found nothing but energy. They discovered that this energy is holographic, that the tiniest bit of it contained the information for the whole. Scientists named this world of energy the "quantum" state. It is a world in which only energy exists—and it exists holographically. When we speak of the quantum world, we are referring to a world of energy that is totally connected throughout time and space.

Again, the energy of the quantum world is holographic. This means that the smallest portion of this energy contains all the information of the whole. The physical world is a reflection of this energy—like our projected image of Grandpa. But on the film, the smallest bit of film contains, in its energy patterns, the information for the whole. And in our physical world, the smallest bit of matter contains, in its holographic energy, the information for the entire universe.

And the scientists discovered another startling fact. The holographic energy of the quantum world does not appear as a physical thing until we are observing it. Until we focus our attention on the holographic energy of the quantum world, it exists only as potential, only as energy. This is also true of our holographic film. Until we focus a laser light and adjust its angle on the film, there is only potential. The holographic film contains, as our holographic energy world does, the potential for all the images recorded on it, and they are recorded in every "place" on the film.

Remember, our holographic film contains all the images recorded on it, and that they are everywhere on the film. What causes only one of the images to appear when we project an image? As you have learned, it is the *angle* of the laser light shining on the film. We select the image we desire by adjusting the angle of the laser light.

Our holographic world of energy also contains all possible images, everything that is or could be, recorded everywhere in the energy of it. What causes only one image at a time to appear in our physical world? Again, it is the angle of our laser beam, only this time it is the laser beam of our attention. Just like our experience in the cinema, where we focus our attention, our reality appears.

One of the earliest examples of this was a result of observations made with light. Light is energy. Light can be detected in our consensus movie in two ways. It can be detected as a "particle" or as a "wave." It contains the information to become either a particle or a wave in its holographic energy. Light cannot be detected as a particle and a wave at the same time. It appears only as one or the other, depending upon *what we are looking for*.

For a long time, scientists tried to determine if light was really one or the other. The scientists of old did not like things that shifted shape. But even so, what they found is that whenever they set up an experiment to prove that light is a particle, they could prove it. And whenever they set up an experiment to prove that light is a wave, they could prove that, too. So they came to the conclusion that light is neither a particle nor a wave until it is observed.

Until the moment of observation, light exists as energy with the potential to become either a particle or a wave. This energy holds the sum of both possibilities in energy form, just as our holographic film contains both Grandpa and Uncle Harry in the same energy patterns. Scientists looking for either a particle or a wave narrow the possibilities by focusing, or adjusting their attention on their experiments. As a result of their expectations, and the focus of their attention, the holographic energy of light becomes either a particle or a wave.

Albert Einstein developed mathematical principles that tell of a relationship between light and matter. He and other scientists applied this simple and elegant math to the world of matter, and it worked. However, it worked too well. What the scientists of today know is that there is not just a relationship between matter and light, but that matter is light, and light is energy. Light is the energy we use in our holographic recording process, and is the one constant in the physical world. All physical matter is, in some way, patterns of interacting pure light energy. Our scientists now know that it is energy, not matter, that is the foundation of the physical universe, and that energy appears as matter only when it is looked for it as a "thing." They also know that this energy is holographic. It is everywhere and interconnected. It's at the moment of observation that energy becomes available to the five senses. And it becomes just what we are looking for.

Once again, our entire physical world is a hologram of pure energy. It is a hologram without the limitations of time and space. Like our holographic film, every image recorded is available in the energy of the hologram, and is available everywhere. In our physical world, this includes everything from the smallest part of a physical atom to the black holes of space.

In our demonstration with Grandpa and Uncle Harry, it is the angle of the laser beam projected onto the holographic film that causes an individual image to appear. This image appears in three a dimensional shape projected into our physical world. Likewise, it is the focus of our attention that causes the holographic energy of the quantum world to appear as an image in our physical reality. And it is the focus of our attention that determines what image appears.

And remember the words of the master: All that is, is of The One.

The Paradigm

Student: Is there a time when the secrets of the universe will be revealed?

Master: There are no secrets in the universe. The One is not hidden. The One is obvious anywhere you choose to look. You need only look with the Heart.

Student: We are looking. We're trying to learn and understand all we can about the world we live in.

Master: You are looking with your mind. Your mind does not allow you to see clearly. Your mind decides, before you look, what you will see. You must learn to look with your Heart.

A paradigm is a pattern, or an example. Patterns and examples have boundaries that represent something. A pattern for a dress defines what the dress will look like when it is finished. In making a dress, we lay a pattern on the material and cut away all the material that is outside the pattern. When we have finished, the material is not just in the shape of a dress, it is in the shape of our pattern for a dress.

In giving an example of an automobile race, I may say that all the cars are lined up facing the same direction, and they travel around an oval track as fast as they can, each driver trying to remain ahead of the others. This definition gives you an example of how an automobile race, as I define it, might take place. Patterns and examples tell us what things should look like and how they should work.

Remember, a paradigm is a pattern, or an example. The examples of the dress and the automobile race might give you the impression that paradigms are already established, and that we just select one that fits what we are involved in. But paradigms are *self created* and *totally personal*. What type of dress came into your mind when the example was given? Did you think of a long flowered dress taken in at the waist, or a short skirt? What kind of cars were in your automobile race? Were they 500 types, or formula ones? Do you have any idea what I was thinking when I gave the examples? Each of us has established a paradigm based on our past *experience* and *knowledge*. Although we may agree on the basic outline of a paradigm, every one of us is unique, and our individual paradigms reflect it.

A paradigm is activated by *attention*. The moment you read the previous examples, your paradigm was activated. This happens every time you focus your attention. When you read the word "dog," your paradigm eliminates all the cats and cows in your memory and places a dog on your conscious view screen. Whoops! Right then, cats and cows entered your awareness. But that was only because you read the words "cats and cows." They came within your *attention*. If the words hadn't been there, your paradigm would not have allowed them into your awareness.

You may get the impression that a paradigm only *limits* what we will accept, like when it filtered out elephants and snakes, but it does more than that. The moment you became aware of a dress pattern, your paradigm kicked in and processed all the dresses you have in your memory. The dress that appeared on your conscious view screen was a combination of all the dresses, but it included more information than just dresses. It may have included the table you use to cut out the pattern, the sewing machine your mother had, a pin cushion, or any number of a host of memories that simply fit into the image of a dress in the making.

The paradigm draws on information from our mind, gathers it together, and *refines* it to fit our understanding of reality. There could have been many different types of cars in your race. You have everything from Volkswagens to Limos in your memory. But your paradigm selected only those that fit your concept of an automobile race. In addition, it selected a track that you may be familiar with, a position from which to watch the race, a checkered flag, pit crews, and any information you have in your mind that relates to an automobile race. Again, your paradigm is *selecting and refining* information from your mind to give you the experience you hold in your attention.

Paradigms live in our minds. You have just drawn on information stored in your mind, filtered and refined it through your paradigm, and responded to the examples of a dress and an automobile race—and some dogs, cats, cows, elephants, and snakes. All this was a response of your mind, through its paradigm, to the words I chose to write and the examples I decided to give. You may think that you have reached as far into your mind as you can, but you have just scratched the surface.

Your mind, you see, is not in your brain. Your brain is a physical thing. You have just learned that all physical things are, in essence, pure holographic energy. Where, then, is your mind?

Many scientists believe that awareness is a function of the brain, and that what we call the mind can be found by studying the brain. Almost any book you read on the workings of the brain uses the terms "brain" and "mind" interchangeably. But remember, the quantum world is a world of pure holographic energy, a world where physical things appear only when this energy is observed. Yet, it is with the *physical senses* that we *are defining the laws of quantum physics*. We have learned to trust these senses, and to believe that what we are experiencing in our awareness is a result of our physical observations.

But, if the physical matter of the brain and the product of our physical senses exists under the same rules that all physical matter in the quantum world exists, as pure energy, it must *first have been observed.* Some attention, some form of awareness has to be present *before it can become a physical thing*. The brain and the senses, being physical, are the result of attention and expectation. The brain and the physical senses must, by the very laws that they have defined, be limited. So to say that the senses and the mind, or awareness, are functions of the brain is absurd considering our understanding of how physical matter relates to the quantum world. Consciousness cannot be a function of the brain. *The mind cannot be in the brain.* The brain, like anything we observe or study in our physical world, must be the reflection of attention and expectation on a level beyond the physical. Our mind is not in the brain. Our mind is energy. It is, as with all in the energy of the quantum world, everywhere and interconnected.

When my Master speaks of the mind, she is not talking about the brain. She explains that the brain is simply a physical organ and, like any other organ of the body, it has a function. The function of the brain is to reflect the images that our mind is presenting to us. It is much like the movie screen in the cinema. The mind, by the same comparison, is the projector. The mind is energy, and as such, is holographically connected to all energy that is. Because of this, it has access to all potential and possibility.

The mind can be looked upon as a projector with the *ability* to present any or all images in holographic energy, but with *programs* that limit and refine the information and the resulting images it presents. The programs of our mind limit our awareness of the world around us, the holographic energy of the quantum world, in order to give us the experience of our movie of reality. These programs are the *paradigm* through which our mind selects and refines which frames of holographic potential will appear on our view screen, the view screen of the brain, and which will not.

Our mind is energy. We have, in our mind, access to all the energy of the holographic world. But we also have expectations of what our movie of reality should look like and how it should work. These expectations are the foundation of our paradigm. These expectations cause our paradigm to filter the holographic potential and refine it to meet our view of reality.

Remember, our mind is energy, and all energy is holographic. When we focus our attention on a dress, an unlimited number of possibilities become available to our mind. These possibilities include not only the dresses that we have seen and experienced in our movie of reality, but *every possibility for a dress that exists*. Again, our mind is energy. We have, in our mind, access to the entire potential of holographic energy.

Paradigms *limit* other possibilities. The pattern for a dress limits the final product. We will not produce a shirt by following the pattern for a dress. Our paradigm for an automobile race does not result in a boxing match. In this way, our paradigm is a filter. It filters our holographic awareness and selects what we become aware of.

But the process of filtering is just one function of our paradigm. Our paradigm *refines and shapes* information in our memory, as well as the holographic potential of the quantum world, and presents it in a way that *meets our expectations*. It is important to remember that our paradigm is not just a filter. Our paradigm selects and refines the holographic information in our mind. It does this in response to our attention, and accomplishes it in a manner that meets our expectations. Our mind then projects the results onto our view screen of conscious awareness. This presentation of our mind becomes our reality.

If this is true, we should be able to access holographic potential with just a change of attention. Well, we can. But first, we will have to take a closer look at the paradigm and our mind.

The mind and Mind

Master: All that you experience is a product of your senses and is a result of your mind in action. It is your mind that makes this thing you call reality seem so real. Your mind is very limited. It gives you awareness of only those things that meet your expectations. You must learn to listen to your Heart.

We have learned that all physical things are a reflection of pure energy, and that this energy is interconnected. It is holographic. This means that the potential for all is contained in the smallest portion of energy. This being true, the potential for the whole is contained in the smallest physical reflection of this energy, the smallest physical piece of matter. Energy, and the physical universe that is a reflection of this energy, cannot be divided. All is energy—and energy is holographic. Remember, when we speak of the quantum world, we are referring to the world of holographic energy. This includes all things we know as physical, including our brain. We know that our mind is not in our brain. Our mind is energy. We have a challenge, though. We do not perceive the quantum world in our movie of reality. Remember, our mind is the projector of our movie of reality and our paradigm is limiting our perception to meet our expectations. We see things as separate and isolated from one another. And this is all accomplished in our mind.

We are, for the purpose of understanding only, going to divide the mind into *functions*. This allows us to understand the manner in which our mind limits our awareness. Remain aware, though, the mind is holographic energy and is not divided. Our division is only for the purpose of understanding. We will call these functions "Mind" and "mind." Again, we are not talking about the brain. The brain is simply the "movie screen" of our reality. It is reflecting images that are created in and projected by the energy of our mind. Remember, also, that we are developing a map that will lead us to an understanding of the function of our mind in creating our reality and, as is the case with any map, there are different paths to the same goal.

Let's look at the functions of the mind. We will say that the mind—with a small "m"—has the function of running programs and presenting us with our movie—like the projector in the cinema or the laser light in our experiment. Recall how we recorded many images on our holographic film by changing the angle at which the images were recorded, and how adjusting the angle of the film when reproducing the recorded images caused one image to fade and the next to appear. The programs of our mind can be thought of as a laser projector. Like the angle of the projection laser, the programs limit what we become aware of and therefor what we experience. Again, these programs are the *paradigm of our mind*. They filter and refine the holographic potential—the energy that contains all—and present us with only the awareness and experiences that are consistent with our expectations. These images are projected onto our movie screen of reality. We call this movie screen our "conscious awareness" or "conscious view screen." We have also learned that changing our attention changes our awareness and our experience. Attention, then, can be thought of as that which changes the angle of the laser projector of our mind.

Mind—with a capital "M"—has the function of networking or linking to the total of all minds. It is the holographic component of our awareness. It can be compared to a computer that is networked to all other computers. Some call the network of Minds The One, and it is commonly called The

Heart, The Higher Self, The I AM, or a host of other names. The name we give to Mind does not matter, but we should remain aware that neither the mind nor Mind are separate in any way, they just have different functions. The separation only appears to be there because our mind is refining the holographic potential of Mind to fit our current sensory experience.

Recall your cinema experience, where you are involved in a movie and the information from your surroundings is filtered out of your awareness. And in the cinema, every bit of sensory information is still being processed by your mind. Its programs filter, refine, and project onto your conscious view screen only that information that fits in with our current experience or the focus of your attention.

The mind—with a small "m"—is that function of Mind—with a capital "M"—that provides us with reality and experience. The mind is the home of our paradigm. The product of the paradigm is what we are consciously aware of, even though Mind is always present. Should you choose to call it Mind, The Heart or The One, it's always in the background, always aware of all. Mind is alive and aware of all potential all the time. Mind, The One, is that *in us* which is just behind the programs—the paradigm—of our mind.

The mind and the Computer

Student: It's our mind that allows us to understand our world and ourselves. How can our mind be the cause of our limitations?

Master: Your mind is not the cause. Your attention is the cause. You are now giving your attention to this conversation. In doing so, your mind is limiting your awareness.

Student: But I can't talk to you without thinking about it.

Master: Are you aware of what is going on around you while we talk?

Student: Not just then, but I can be just by thinking about it.

Master: And you can still speak with me?

Student: Yes, of course.

Master: Are you aware of what is happening outside while we talk?

Student: If I don't pay attention to our conversation, I won't be able to interact with you.

Master: Perhaps if you gave less attention to what is going on in your mind as a result of our conversation, you would become more aware of what is being said.

Student: You mean don't think about it?

Master: You may think about it, but do not limit your thoughts so much. Allow your mind to drift, to expand. Listen to the answers being given without words by those around you, by the growing of the trees, by the flowing of the water, by the wind.

A further understanding of how the mind constructs our movie of reality can be made by comparing the mind to a computer. A computer is an extension of the mind, a reflection of the mind in a mechanical world. Although in no way as powerful as a human mind, a computer is a product of the mind and, because of this, there are similarities. But there also are important differences.

Let's compare the movie on the conscious view screen of our mind with a program on a computer monitor. We know that our mind can run many programs at a time, but there is usually only one that holds our attention. For example, your "Reading This Book" program is running now, and it's the program on your view screen. Your mind, in this way, is similar to a computer that is running a program. But there is much more activity taking place in your mind during the presentation of a program than there is in a computer.

A computer can store a host of inactive programs in static memory. It can have programs on a hard disk storage device or on other storage media. All the inactive programs are in a static state. They are doing nothing until they are loaded into the computer and accessed by the keyboard or through a programming command. They exist as little bits of information on a media of some kind.

When we want to run a program, we load it by typing a command or clicking on an icon. Much activity takes place when we do this. Lights flash, and sounds come out of the processor. Soon we see our program on the monitor. The computer doesn't show us all the internal activity that is taking place to create what we finally see on the monitor. It waits until it has everything in order, and then it lights up the monitor. The computer filters out all the activity that is not necessary for us to use and enjoy our program. If all that activity were presented on the monitor, the computer would slow down to a crawl. Computer experts know that we are not interested in all that activity, and that it may even be confusing or overwhelming for us. It was nice of them to provide us with such a simplified view screen.

The mind can be compared to the holographic process. Remember, we are not speaking of the brain, but of the energy that is our mind. Information is stored in the energy of the mind. Your mind is a living, holographic, energy media, and it can never be "off." Unlike the computer that is limited to one program at a time, your mind is running all the programs it has ever created—and it's running them all the time. There are no inactive or static programs in your mind. Your "How to Ride a Bicycle" program is running all the time. Your "How to Tie a Shoe" program is running all the time. The "Smell of Baking Bread in Mother's Kitchen" program is running all the time. Every program—and all your memories—are alive and buzzing in the holographic energy of your mind all the time. But if these billions and billions of programs were simultaneously presented on your conscious view screen, you would be confused and overwhelmed. So your mind has a built-in program that is active throughout your life. This program filters out all information and all programs that do not fit in with what you are currently experiencing in your sensory world, or where your attention is. This is why your "How to Tie Your Shoe" program is not on your conscious view screen right now. Not, at least, until sensory information brings it to the surface. It happened for a brief instant as you read the words, "How to Tie Your Shoe." Just briefly, though, for it did not fit in with your "Reading This Book" program. This ability of the mind to select which programs are presented in your conscious awareness allows you to experience a nice comfortable program of reality.

You select different programs by placing our attention on them. Again, your attention can be compared to the laser projection light or, in this case, a computer keyboard. Remember, changing the angle of the light causes one image to fade and another to appear. Typing a command or clicking on an icon causes the same thing to happen in a computer, one program fades and another appears. Changing the angle of your attention causes one program or memory in your holographic mind to fade and another to appear.

As we have learned, the mind is also processing incoming sensory information all the time. It processes all the sight, sound, taste, touch, and smell information that is available to our senses. The feeling of your body in a chair, the smell of a room, and the visual information that you are not "aware" of is all being processed by your mind. If it were presented to you all at once, all that information would be overwhelming on your view screen of consciousness. So, unless it fits in with your current sensory experience, it is filtered out.

Right now, as you are reading this, your mind is filtering out incoming sensory information and all the other programs that do no fit your reading experience. You can access other sensory information. All you have to do is to place your attention on something else. Is there anyone else in the room with you? There it goes. Did you know that one foot feels a little bit different from the other? There it goes again. That's the way it works. Each time you focus your attention, your mind runs another program. Simple, isn't it?

A computer can only present us with information as it was recorded, and can only present us with the information we request. Your mind is not so limited. Think of the telephone number of your best friend. Most of us can think of the number but, it is not just the number that appears on our conscious view screen. Just the number is the information requested, but what we get is other information based on experience. You may see a face, have a feeling, or remember that you have not returned a call. Your mind presents the information you requested along with all associated information. It cannot process isolated individual bits, and there is a reason for this.

Remember, information in our computer is stored in "bits." Each bit of information is stored in a specific location. If we were to punch a hole in a physical location, a bit of information would be lost. Recall the pattern of waves on our pond. When we cut out a section of that pond, we remove the information of the surrounding drops. But your mind has no specific location for any bit of information. Your mind is like the holographic film. Every bit of information, every program you have, is recorded everywhere in the energy of your mind as our images are on the holographic film..

Remember, your mind is energy, and all information for all programs in your mind is stored holographically. Just as on the holographic film, all the information for all the programs and memories that you have is available in every "location" in your mind. But, every time your mind records incoming information it stacks it on top of associated information. It does this in the same way that we combined Grandpa and Uncle Harry on our holographic film. Remember, we are talking about the energy of the mind, not the physical matter of the brain. Now, Grandpa and Uncle Harry may not be combined in your mind on top of each other, but they are relatives, so there is a link. But the telephone number of your friend is very closely related to a wealth of information about him or her, and there is a combination of information. In fact, everything about your friend is very, very close to *all* the information about him or her. You get a combination of information whenever you think of them.

You cannot go into the mind and extract a telephone number from a specific location. Once again, unlike a computer, the mind doesn't store the number in a specific location. Think holographically now. The information recorded is as a combination of memories that are holographically recorded, not individual memories. Those that are associated are combined, just like Grandpa and Uncle Harry. When you recall a telephone number, you are presented with a selection of information that fits in with the request and results in something like a mini-movie experience. Take a moment to close your eyes and say aloud the name of a few individuals that you know well. You are presented with a wealth of information just by saying their names.

Here is another example. When you run your checkbook program on your computer and request your balance, the computer presents you with only that information. Your mind, as you view the balance, presents you with that information along with associated information. When your balance is below what you expect, you may worry, wondering where the problem is. This is an automatic process in your mind. You cannot stop it. Even when your balance is higher than you expect, you may think you have forgotten to pay a bill. Your mind never gives you just the facts. It always includes associated information. This is because your mind is energy—and energy is holographic. All your memories are holographic and interconnected.

A computer is not able to provide us with this kind of information. Computers do not store information holographically, so information in programs not currently active is not available. Even when we access a history program and call up "Native American History," what the computer presents to us is information from that location only. The information is a result of a program that tells the computer to get data from specific areas and perform a specific task with it. This program was written by someone, and is limited to the interpretation of the writer. The computer must provide us with information in this way. If an interpretation is presented during the program, it came from the individual who wrote the program, not from the computer.

Again, your mind is not limited to specific programs. It is holographic energy, and energy has no "location." Every time you place your attention on your home, you are presented with a wealth of information related to it. You see and hear things related to your home experience. When you place your attention on your job, you experience your workplace and co-workers, and perhaps even the sounds of the workplace. Your mind may even replay an emotionally filled experience that happened at work. Any time you focus your attention, your mind searches for and presents you with related information.

And it is performing the same operation now, presenting you with your current sensory experience. Every word you read is presented with associated memory. Your mind is searching for things that holographically relate to what you read. Every concept you read in this book is compared to concepts already stored in your mind. To you, this seems perfectly normal. It is, after all, the way your mind has been working all your life. Your reality is not happening in your head—it's happening in your mind. Why, then, does your reality appear "out there?"

It's another function of your mind. When your mind presents you with information related to your current sensory experience, it gives you the impression that what is happening is happening "out there," and that you are "in here" watching it. When the information is a response to a memory, as when you think of your workplace, it's presented as if it were happening in your mind. The feeling of out there is eliminated from your experience. But there is no difference in the way your mind accesses and processes the information about your workplace whether you are thinking about it or when you are there. When you are thinking about it, your mind relies on memory and gives you the feeling that you are not there, that it's just a thought. When you are there, your mind relies on both sensory information and memory, and gives you the illusion that the information is coming from the outside. But you are experiencing both movies on the same view screen of consciousness—and both movies are a result of the same programs in your mind.

When you were a child, your mind had not fully developed the ability to add this illusion of external reality, and your imaginary world was often as real as your physical reality. In the process of developing a paradigm of adulthood, your mind began to accept the consensus opinion that there was a difference between dreaming and reality. The feeling of "in the mind" and of "out there" became stronger. As an adult, you can have a nice daydream and rest comfortably in the fact that it's not real, that it's just happening in your mind. Yet your mind is performing exactly the same function while daydreaming as it does when processing sensory information. There is physiologically no difference in the processing of information. Your *mind* adds the feeling that the movie running on your view screen during daydreaming is happening only in your head. It gives you the impression that what you are experiencing is not really happening—that it's just a daydream. When processing sensory information, your *mind* adds the illusion that your experience exists "out there." This added illusion provides you with what you call "reality." It is here that your mind decides, as a result of your paradigm, what is real and what is an illusion. It has nothing to do with reality at all. Again, the movie of your accepted reality and the movie of your thoughts, daydreams and nightly dreams originate in the same place. You never realize that there is no difference in the movies. This is a natural process. Nothing would appear "real" to you if you knew that it was just happening in your mind.

We also know that computers can be linked together, or networked, electronically. When you network your computer, the information and processing power of many other computers is available on your computer view screen. It is Mind that is naturally "networked" to all Minds, and has access to all the information and programming available anywhere or anytime. We have labeled this networking a function of Mind, but just as a reminder, there is no separation in our natural energy state. Again, we are holographic energy, and as we have learned, all energy is connected. We are not aware of our holographic connection on our view screen of reality because it does not fit in with our current sensory experience.

But our paradigm is not perfect. Occasionally, holographic information slips through. When this happens, our mind refines this information and presents it in a way we expect to experience it in our reality. Our paradigm is often not as effective for those who are emotionally close to us in this movie of reality. Occasionally, we may experience an awareness of information that transcends our paradigm. Here is an example of how the mind shapes information to fit our expectations. It often happens that someone who is "on our mind" will call us and say: I was thinking of you all day, and just thought I would give you a call. Our response might be: You know, I've been thinking of you, too. What a coincidence! What we call a coincidence is evidence of the holographic nature of our mind.

Our paradigm changes as we grow and learn. The majority of us involved here in our movie of reality are not sensitive to this holographic information. We have learned to filter it out completely. A few, however, have learned to rely on it. But it is always there in everyone, available with just a readjustment of our attention. Remember, our mind is naturally networked to all of the potential of Mind. Just like networked computers, every program and all information is available at every single monitor—every single mind.

Computer experts have established a system that allows anyone with a computer and a telephone to gain access to a vast storehouse if information. This system is called "The World Wide Web." With the proper software and a telephone connection, your computer can now access programs that contain entire college libraries, current stock market activity, street maps of any city in the country, or a radar image of the weather in any state, just to name a few. You can communicate with millions of people around the world, typing messages back and forth in real time with individuals or groups having the same interests. You can even create your own "web page," which places you or your business on the web for others to access. Thousands of pages are added daily, and with improvements in technology, it is becoming easier and easier to access information on the web.

In beginning this section I said: A computer is an extension of the mind, a reflection of the mind in a mechanical world. When you think about what is happening with computer technology and the web, it seems that somewhere in our minds we have a drive to be connected. But computers do not connect holographically. Remember, a computer is only a *reflection* of the mind. A single computer is a creation of our own minds, and what it presents on its view screen is limited not only by our own paradigms, but by the limitations we have built into its creation. The connection we achieve with computers is, then, a limitation within a limitation. We are able to access only the *interpretations* of others, only after they have been filtered through *their* paradigms, and only after they have been displayed through a *limited mechanical device*. In addition to these limitations, we again filter and refine the information through *our* paradigm as we view it on our computer monitor. We are, in fact, allowing our mind to perform the same function with a computer that it does in a movie at the cinema. We are allowing it to present a reality that we can become involved in, a reality that was created by others. And it is as easy to become involved in the illusion of this mechanical connection as it is to become involved in a movie at the cinema—or our current movie of consensus reality. In fact, computer connections are rapidly becoming a part of our limited movie of reality.

The connection made in Mind is not so limited. Mind is holographic. Connections made in Mind are, as you have learned, rich with *all associated information* and *without interpretation*.

But our paradigm is in place, filtering and refining this information to fit our expectations. Let's take a look at how effective the mind is in filtering and refining the holographic potential in Mind.

The mind is a Powerhouse

Student: If I just allow my mind to wander, I won't even have any questions.
Master: You will have questions, but you will also have answers.
Student: I'll have the answers to all my questions?

Master: Answers arrive with the question. All that is, is of The One. The One is Balance. It is not possible to ask a question without the answer appearing. There is the Balance. But while your Heart already knows the answers, the attention of your mind is on the question. Here the limitations begin.

Student: So the answers to every question are always with the question?

Master: It must be so. Balance is. The answers are in the very energy of the question you voice.

Student: So if I asked, "What's my son doing right now?" The answer would automatically be here?

Master: That is correct. This is because of the Balance of The One.

Student: And this is true of any question I ask?

Master: Any thought you hold in your Heart contains the whole of that thought. Nothing is hidden in The One. Consider this carefully, and hold it in your Heart. Nothing is hidden in The One.

We have compared the mind to a projector and a computer, and the brain to a movie screen and computer monitor. Once we are involved in a movie or a computer program, the presentation becomes our reality. The more involved we become, the more active our paradigm becomes. Our involvement is a result of our attention. Again, giving attention is like adjusting the angle of a projection laser or deciding which cinema we will attend. Our reality appears or fades away as a result of our attention. Our mind gives us no indication of what is going on behind the scenes, or the process by which our reality is created. Experiments in hypnosis indicate how effective the mind is in filtering out that which is not consistent with our current experience and refining information to create an experience for us. Let's look at an example that has been demonstrated many times.

We have two volunteers we will call Jane and Sally. Jane is a very good hypnosis subject. When we give Jane a suggestion under hypnosis, that suggestion becomes her reality for a time. So we give Jane the suggestion that Sally has left the room when, in fact, Sally is still sitting here. We tell Jane that Sally has been called out of the room and, when she awakens, she will not see or hear Sally. What we have done is create a new paradigm through which the mind of Jane filters and refines sensory information. Remember, our mind filters information through our paradigm, and refines it to meet our expectations.

When we awaken Jane and ask her where Sally is, she tells us that Sally has left the room and is no longer here. Jane cannot "see" Sally sitting here, nor can she "hear" what Sally is saying. When we talk to Sally, Jane thinks that we were talking to ourselves, playing a trick on her, or having an "illusion." She actually feels and believes that Sally is no longer in the room. Remember, Jane is experiencing a reality that is not consistent with what is happening in her physical surroundings. Her mind is refining information that is "real" to the rest of us. To compensate for this, Jane's mind reinforces the illusion that what she is experiencing is perfectly normal and that everyone else is experiencing something out of the ordinary. To her, it is we who are suffering from an illusion. This phenomenon is called "negative hallucination." Until recently, its function has been a mystery. We now have the technology to find out just what is happening inside Jane's brain. So let's hook her up to instrumentation and find out where Sally disappeared.

Using electronic instruments that record electrical activity in the brain, we can see that Jane's eyes are indeed "seeing" Sally. We can observe visual information transmitted down the optic nerve and processed in the visual center of the brain. But the visual image of Sally is filtered out of Jane's conscious movie. A similar thing happened to us in the cinema when we became involved in our movie experience. We became unaware of the others in the cinema and focused our attention on the movie. Someone could get up and leave the cinema, and we would not "see" them. Our attention was focused on the movie. But, if they were to stand in front of us, blocking our view of the screen, we would surely notice them. This is consistent with our paradigm for the cinema, but Jane is not in the cinema. Jane has an entirely restructured paradigm. Not only is the visual information of Sally filtered out of Jane's movie, but her mind is refining her visual information so that it is consistent with what she would expect to see if Sally were not there. She "sees" the whole chair that Sally is sitting in—and the wall behind her. She is presented with a reality on her conscious view screen that meets her expectations—expectations provided by the suggestions of the hypnotist, and it is real and normal to her.

It's easy to understand that Jane's mind can create the empty chair and fill in the wall from the information in her memory, and just as easy to say that it's just an illusion. She does have knowledge of what the chair and wall should look like. Her mind could construct these things from memory, just as it would in a dream. But what if we were to place something behind Sally that Jane has never seen, like a dollar bill? Would Jane be able to "see" it through a physical body? Would she be able to identify it as a dollar bill and read the serial number? From a physical standpoint, this is not possible. But from what we know about the holographic nature of the mind, the information of the dollar bill is limited only by Jane's paradigm, and she has a new paradigm.

The mind and Mind are one, and Mind holds all the potential of The One. Information of the dollar bill is held in Mind. Sally has access to that information through the new paradigm implanted by the hypnotic suggestion. The suggestion focused her attention on the holographic information in Mind and nullified the paradigm of her everyday physical reality. Her mind now refines the information of the dollar bill and displays it in her reality in a manner that fits her paradigm. She "sees" the dollar bill, the refined information of Mind, through the physical body of Jane, the filtered information of Mind. The dollar bill appears naturally within her paradigm, and she is able to identify it easily.

The experiment is an example of how holographic information of Mind is always available, but it also shows how powerful the mind is in creating our reality. Through our paradigm, it filters and refines the holographic potential of Mind and presents us with a reality that meets our expectations. This creation is so powerful that we seldom question it and often rely on it as if it were absolute fact.

We may ask ourselves how much of what we experience in our movie is created by the mind to present us with experience that meets our expectations? How much of our reality is a result of our programming? How much of it is just what our mind is projecting to fit our paradigm?

The answer is simple. Every aspect of the movie of reality that we are experiencing right now is a projection of our mind. The mind combines sensory information and holographic awareness, filters and refines it through its paradigm, and presents it as reality. Only about fifty percent of the actual visual information that is gathered by our eyes is presented in our reality. The rest is filtered and refined through our paradigm and projected onto our view screen by our mind. That is why we can see someone who has changed their appearance in some subtle way and not even notice the change. A friend may have shaved his mustache, and it can be days before we notice it. We continue to see him as we expect to see him. Or we can look for something that we have habitually left in a specific place, something that someone has moved. We may look directly at the item during our search and never "see" it. Our mind is still looking for it through its paradigm. The same is true of the audio information. We often hear what we expect to hear. What we remember is often nothing like the words spoken. A precise record of an actual conversation is recorded in our mind, but it is filtered and shaped by our paradigm before it's displayed on our conscious view screen. Our mind presents us with a movie that meets our expectations—one that fits our paradigm.

The mind, in fact, has no method of differentiating between "illusion" and "reality." The mind just runs programs and produces a movie consistent with our expectations. Our expectations are the result of past experience. Our mind gathers information from any source—including the vast potential of Mind—to make our movie a valid "experience" within its paradigm.

Repetition and expectations often produce the same hallucinations that hypnotic suggestion did in our experiment. As an example, people living on country roads with little traffic are often involved in a particular type of accident. The kind of accident happens when someone approaches an intersection, perhaps as their driveway joins with a road, at the same time each day and seldom sees another vehicle. They stop and look both ways, time after time, and there is never another vehicle on the road. This may continue for a year or more. The process becomes so routine that the mind supplies an image of an empty road even when another vehicle is present. You may think that they just didn't "notice" the other vehicle, but their mind actually filters the image of it from their conscious view screen and fills in the empty road.

When an individual involved in such an accident is under hypnosis, they are able to report two different movies in response to what questions we ask. When asked: What did you *see* when you looked down the road? They respond that the road was empty—no vehicles were on it. This is the movie that their mind presented them, and it is a real and valid experience. When taken back in hypnosis to the time and place of the incident and asked: What is on the road? They recall the other vehicle. Their mind still holds the memory of the actual physical events *before they were filtered and refined*. They have two different movies recorded in their mind. Remember, even though our mind is supplying us with a movie of reality through its paradigm and keeping a record of it, it is still recording all incoming sensory information.

It continues this process even while we sleep. The program that our mind is running to produce our nightly dreams is the same program it runs to produce our daily reality. Even though we experience things in our dreams that we would not consider normal in our waking reality, our dreams are a product of our paradigm. The program is so effective that dreams *are* our reality until we awaken. Once we awaken, we reflect on the fact that what has just happened occurred while we were asleep, that it happened in our mind, so we call it a dream.

Information that fits well into our paradigm is the foundation of our movie. What we experience now in our movie creates expectations for the future. Our mind develops its paradigm experience by experience. Information available to our mind that is outside its paradigm is that which *transcends* our individual personal experience. It can be called "transpersonal awareness," and is not made available to our conscious view screen simply because it has no place in our current movie.

But transpersonal awareness is a personal thing. Each of us has a different paradigm. What is transpersonal awareness to me may be perfectly normal within your reality. As an example, a good police detective follows his hunches. Remember, a hunch is holographic information beyond the limitations of consensus reality, and for many, it is transpersonal awareness. But hire a psychic? Forget it. A hunch is perfectly normal for him. He has shaped the holographic information and given it a name that fits his paradigm. Even though the results he achieves time and time again by following his hunches prove that he is accessing information from beyond the physical senses, his paradigm will not allow him to believe it.

Have you ever had the feeling that someone was looking at you, and in turning to look, find that someone was? How did you know? It was a feeling, sometimes called a hunch. Where did the information come from? It could not have come from your physical senses. You were looking the other way. This is another common example of transpersonal information making its way into our movie of reality.

Experiments with hypnosis do not always produce such results. Successful results are achieved only with a very good subject and often require a great deal of work creating a paradigm acceptable to them. This is true of all the hypnosis experiments presented in this book. But it does not mean that these abilities are not available to everyone. Remember, we are holographically one in Mind. What it does mean is that some of us have developed paradigm limits that are very strong—ones that even a good hypnotist cannot circumvent.

Paradigm Limits

Student: Then the purpose of the mind is to limit all that information, all those answers?

Master: This is not the purpose of the mind. Your mind allows you to experience your thoughts. Your thoughts, and your mind, are also of The One.

Student: Is every single thought I have of The One?

Master: All that is, is of The One. Every thought you have has its origin in The One. You are of The One. There is only The One.

Student: Than everything that I can imagine is a possibility?

Master: All that you can imagine is possible. What you can imagine is only that which has the potential to be, and that potential is of The One. A thought is a thing. If a thought were not possible, it would not have the potential to become a thing.

We know that our paradigm filters and refines the holographic potential of The One to meet our expectations. With hypnosis, we can strengthen or weaken the paradigm. How powerful is this paradigm in our everyday life? To find out, we look again to the results of experiments with hypnosis.

The average person has a fairly good knowledge of simple addition. We tend to think that this knowledge is an asset to our ability to function in this movie of life. But it's really one of the boundaries of our paradigm, the edge of a pattern beyond which our mind does not allow information to enter our awareness. The boundary exists in our belief that each time we are confronted with an addition problem, we must consciously go through the addition process. The *conscious process of addition* is what we learned, and this program is activated every time we see an addition problem. The mind tells us that we must perform the process consciously, as we learned. But this is a paradigm limit. It does not allow information, such as another way to gain the answer to our problem, to surface on our conscious view screen. It is the point at which our mind begins to filter information and require us to perform a learned process to achieve the results we expect. It is here that our mind has reached its *paradigm limit*.

When you think of adding all the seven-digit numbers on one page of your telephone book, the task seems overwhelming. This is because your paradigm limit reminds you that you must go through the process of addition consciously—as you learned in school. But is it necessary to perform an addition process consciously?

Given the proper instructions, individuals in a state of hypnosis can glance at such a column of numbers and give the total instantly. They do so without having to perform the process of addition *consciously*, and complete it faster than any computer. Once we have learned the process, our mind performs it *instantly* each time we confront an addition problem. But it does not allow this information to surface in our reality because it has also learned that we *expect to perform it consciously*. Do you keep a checkbook? Your mind holds the correct balance this very moment. The mind is extremely quick. The moment it is presented with sensory information, it runs the programs associated with it. In the case of your checkbook, the exact balance is calculated with every entry and a record is kept in your mind. You are not aware of the information because your paradigm tells you that you must perform a conscious process of addition and subtraction. This is the process you learned. This is what you expect to experience within your reality. Your paradigm tells you this is how things should work. When anyone reaches this point, they have reached the limit of their paradigm—the point beyond which the mind filters out other possibilities.

The mind, in fact, records and keeps track of all sensory information in your reality. You know how many breaths you have taken today, how many times your heart has beaten. You know exactly what time it is without having to look at your watch. There is a record in your mind of every word of every song you have ever heard. Everything you have ever read is recorded in your mind. Every word on every page of every newspaper that you have ever *glanced through* is recorded in your mind. Every conversation that you have ever had is recorded there. If someone were to drop a box of toothpicks in front of you, you would know, in your mind, exactly how many had fallen to the floor. All sensory information—all sight, sound, touch, taste, and smell information that has been a part of your movie, is recorded in your mind. This sensory information includes a record of the emotions that are a part of each experience. But all this information is refined by your paradigm to present you with a movie that meets your expectations.

Most of us do not expect to know the balance of our checking account without going through the process of addition and subtraction as defined by our paradigm. Yet, under hypnosis and with the proper instructions, the balance is given in an instant. Nor we do expect to recall an entire conversation held months ago, because our paradigm assigns priorities to the information in our conscious awareness. But the entire conversation emerges verbatim in a state of hypnosis. We do not expect to know the exact time without looking at our watch. Our mind eliminates this information from our conscious view screen. It's programmed so we can't tell the time without looking at our watch. Yet the time is given to the second by a properly instructed hypnosis subject. All the refining performed by our mind provides us with our movie of reality. It is a movie designed to meet our expectations. Our expectations are based on experience. The function of our mind, through our paradigm, is to limit our awareness to something that meets our expectations.

But we have different expectations. And even the ones we hold in our attention do not always produce the results we desire. Is there another force at play in our reality, one that limits us even though we hold powerful expectations and a good focus of attention?

There is. But you will be pleased to know that it, too, is a self-imposed limitation in our movie of reality. And one that can be overcome with Knowledge.

The Magic of Agreeing

Master: When many agree on the same experience, and when the many lose awareness, the experience of reality becomes a shared illusion.

Student: You mean that this whole world is an illusion?

Master: Your reality is not an illusion. It is your creation, and it is very real. The illusion is in the limitation, in the conflict. Your reality is not the illusion. The illusion is that your reality is all that is.

Our knowledge of how our mind works to give us a view screen of reality makes us aware that its function is very mechanical. It's an automatic process, and follows the same function in any individual, in any society, in any belief and reality structure anywhere in the world. We know from experience that we are all living in a seemingly consistent physical world. We have developed rules and regulations that define what is "normal" in our movie. We call this physical world "consensus reality"—that in the movie about which we all agree. Consensus reality includes much more than our concepts of good and bad, right and wrong. Consensus reality includes all the physical laws of our world.

So far, we have learned that most of the sensory information in our physical world is shaped by our paradigm and presented to us as a movie that fits our expectations. We have also learned that information beyond our paradigm limits is virtually eliminated from our movie of reality. Those of us who agree on what is happening in a specific scene in our movie find it easy to understand each other. We agree on similar information, and filter and refine information in the same way. Does the fact that we *agree* have an effect on our experience? Let's try another experiment.

We have two volunteers that have agreed to undertake an experiment in shared fantasy. Both are excellent hypnosis subjects. The purpose of the experiment is to determine if illusion, or fantasy, can be shared beyond the physical senses.

The subjects choose a setting for their illusion. While still in a normal state of awareness, they agree to a setting on a beach and begin to imagine what it would be like. With little coaching, they build their fantasy until they begin to talk about it as if it were reality. We now place them both in a state of hypnosis and suggest that they continue their fantasy. As they continue, their dialogue changes from deciding where to go and what to do to actually participating in an experience. They are having fun, which was part of the initial suggestion. It's not long, however, before they stop communicating orally. In the silence that follows, we wonder if they have drifted off in separate fun-filled illusions, into separate dreams, or if they are still together in their imagined world. As we observe, we notice that they display nonverbal clues indicating that they are still connected in some way. We do not know if they are sharing the same illusion, at least not until we bring them back to "reality." We allow them twenty or thirty minutes, monitoring them to assure that they are still having a pleasant time. We now return them to consensus reality and interview them separately.

We discover that these two individuals, while in an altered state of awareness and with no spoken communication, have shared an imaginary experience in detail. They remember where they went, what they did, and what they said to each other as if it were a "real" experience. They continued to talk to each other in their illusion, even though no words were spoken aloud. They decided to go for a walk along the beach, and they both remember the same experience in doing so. They recall the same excitement when they discovered a beautiful sea shell in the sand. They both remember when they decided to go for a swim in the ocean. Further experimentation reveals that they need not even be in the same room to share the illusion. They can be separated by hundreds of miles and still have as real and as common an experience as if they were sitting right next to each other. In other experiments, we discover that a group of individuals can share the same fantasy, all agreeing on the common aspects of it.

The Mind is energy, and energy is not limited by time or distance. Mind and the mind are not separate. When we agree on a movie, be it "illusion" or "reality," we exercise what we call The Magic of Agreeing. We *agree* to have an experience together. In consensus reality, we agree to walk on the beach of the movie of life—together.

We are the Sky Heroes who long ago who decided to dream a movie. The movie was once very fluid and easily changed, and we agreed and changed it often. The movie is still very fluid and easily changed, but we have forgotten that our dreamed reality remains as it is only because we *continue to agree on it*. The focus of our attention is no longer on our movie of reality, but on our created illusion of an individual identity within our reality. Our dreamed reality changes slowly now, as if driven by some external force. Yet our shared experience is still a natural result of our attention. We are participating in our reality through the laws of The Magic of Agreeing—and the result is what we call the physical world of consensus reality. And even as we share this movie, our mind presents it in a manner that each of us can relate to as individuals. Although we agree on the overall set and script, each of us has slightly different interpretations of our experience because we have developed individual paradigms.

Recall the words of the Master: There can be no exceptions in an absolute reality. There are exceptions in ours. There are some among us who are not lost in this movie. They need no food. They are never ill. Some can, with the wave of a hand, collapse the pure energy of The One into whatever "form" they hold in their mind, seemingly producing objects out of nothing. There are those who heal the body, see into the future, read the energy fields around us, and appear and disappear at will. We call these abilities "supernatural," but they are quite natural. They are not hidden abilities that are beyond our reach. They are the very same abilities that we use to make our dream of consensus reality real to us. These abilities reside just behind the paradigm of our mind, and are accessible with just a change of attention.

Although The Magic of Agreeing sets limitations on our experience, they are self-imposed. We have been told again and again throughout the ages by those who have gained mastery over the dream of consensus reality that nothing is impossible for us. Anything that our mind can imagine can become a reality played out on the view screen of awareness. And when we agree on a reality, the power of The Magic of Agreeing is added to our creation. But, in order for our movie of consensus reality to remain, we must continue to agree to continue to be limited. We are limited only because we choose to remain so.

Dreamed realities are easily manipulated. We often manipulate our nightly dreams without even realizing we are doing it. Here's an example. We may be involved in a dream where we are in a particular place, but during the course of the dream, the location must change. Moving about in consensus reality involves time and distance. In our dream, however, we find ourselves in our new location with just a thought. We may be in a house one moment and on the beach the next. We do not try to reason while we are dreaming why the distance we traveled took such a short time. We move from scene to scene, location to location, as we involve ourselves in the experience of the dream. Our dreams are filled with experience, and traveling long distances is usually tedious and boring compared to the rich experience we are dreaming. We are not restricted by the physical limitations of time and distance in a dream, so our mind simply re-creates our dream in the new location. But remember, time and distance are limitation that we *agree upon* in consensus reality—and they are *self-imposed*. Here is one of those exceptions that appear in consensus reality; there are those who move about in consensus reality as easily as we move about in our nightly dreams.

Limitations are effective only if they have a solid foundation in our mind, in our paradigm. The limitations of our waking reality are the result of The Magic of Agreeing in our consensus movie. We know that these limitations are not absolute. When our paradigm becomes weakened or is altered, these limitations are transcended. We often hear people who are involved in a traumatic accident report that they experienced their whole life flash before their eyes in a moments time. In these cases, our mind allows us a brief glimpse of holographic memory just beyond the paradigm. And identical twins are often keenly aware of emotional situations in each others lives even though they are miles apart. They share a strong link in holographic awareness.

Our paradigm is constantly altered by changing or questioning our belief and reality programs, thereby changing the limits of our paradigm. We should remember, however, that we are not transcending anything that is external. We are the creators of our reality, and it is subject only to our paradigm. There is nothing "out there" that must be changed or overcome.

Participants in shared illusion usually choose not to continue the experiments after they have come to an understanding of their implication. The subjects in our experiment decided to discontinue the sessions after only three settings. They felt uncomfortable creating an illusion that was as real as their waking life. Their reasoning was: If we continue, how will we know the difference between our illusions and reality?

There seems to be a mechanism in our mind that protects us against knowing that the movie we call reality may be just a projection of our mind itself. After all, it would not be "reality" if we knew that it was just a projection of our mind.

Consensus Reality

Student: If all this is an illusion, why does everybody experience the same thing?

Master: Do all experience the same thing?

Student: Well, we have different opinions about the little things, but the laws of physics are the same for all of us.

Master: The laws of physics are the same for all?

Student: Okay, some people seem to be able to overcome them sometimes, but they are pretty consistent.

Master: When you are having what you call an illusion, you are experiencing something that others in your reality believe should not be. This is your personal illusion. It appears real only to you. It does not agree with the expectations of others. When many agree on an illusion, it does not appear as an illusion to them because it meets the expectations of the many. The laws you speak of are agreed upon by many. This only means that many have agreed upon the illusion. This does not mean that it is not an illusion.

In our previous experiment, we found that two or more individuals can have a common "experience" beyond the physical senses of consensus reality. You may have begun to grasp some of the implications of the experiment, but there are more.

We may think that the subjects in a hypnosis experiment are asleep and dreaming and that, somehow, they are able to share their dream. But the brain wave patterns of individuals in a hypnotic state do not reflect the brain wave patterns of sleep. The energy patterns of the brain during hypnosis are more closely related to individuals who are wide awake and alert. The conscious view screen of an individual under hypnosis is much the same as the view screen during in the waking state. The subjects are, in most respects, wide awake and alert during their shared illusion. Because of this, unless given a suggestion to forget the experience, the subjects recall the details of the illusion as if they had happened in "reality." Everything that they experience in their illusion follows them into their waking reality.

Consensus reality is a dream that we share through The Magic of Agreeing. We recall many of the daily experiences in consensus reality, and know others who were involved in the same experience recall much the same thing. Our paradigm allows us easy access to the memory we agree upon.

Our nightly dreams are personal dreams, yet the details of these dreams often follow us into consensus reality. This is true of personal dreams—but only when the view screen of consensus reality overlaps with the view screen of our personal dream reality. This happens when we wake up during a dream and remember all or part of it, or when some event during our day triggers a dream memory. What, then, is the difference between the personal dream state and the state of consensus reality?

There is only one difference. In the personal dream, we are experiencing a projection of the mind that is *ours alone*. Our dreams are a result of *our* experiences and current expectations, all refined through *our* paradigm. Even though seemingly impossible things happen in our personal dreams, they are based on our paradigm. Although it is constantly growing and changing, it is possible to have only one paradigm. Our individual paradigm is a result of all the experience of all the lives we have ever lived—all the movies of reality we have ever participated in.

In a personal dream, there are no other entities contributing to the script—no one involved in The Magic of Agreeing—so our mind is free to access experience that would not meet the expectations of others. But *all* experience is a product of our mind. Everything in our personal dream, every tree, every building, every scene and every situation is a construction of *our mind alone*. Those who appear in our dreams have no life of their own. They are created to act out *their* parts according to the programs of *our* mind. The dream is ours, and ours alone. It is our "personal dream."

Consensus reality is also a dream, but it's a dream which many have agreed upon. In our dream of consensus reality, we are sharing an illusion with many others. It's a shared illusion in which rules have been made and limits have been established. There are currently about *five billion actors* in the physical portion of our dream of consensus reality—almost all agreeing on the rules and the limits. Just as in the cinema, individuals assign different meaning to the evolving dream through their individual paradigms, but most of us agree upon the overall theme of the experience.

Experiences in the personal dream are just as real as those in consensus reality. A personal dream contains all the sights, sounds, tastes, and smells that we experience in our daily lives. It's filled with emotion and, like any movie, may contain a sense of good and bad, right and wrong. The paradigm of our mind in the personal dream uses exactly the same mechanisms that it uses to produce consensus reality. The one aspect of the personal dream that may vary from the consensus dream is a lack of meaning. The personal dream has no past, and the future is not determined.

The sense of meaning in a personal dream is often left to the interpretation of the dreamer after he or she awakens. It is only then that the dream can compare it to our current movie and given meaning.

Can we conclude that consensus reality is a dream state? No, you say? Well, have you devised a test to prove that you are not dreaming? Examine your reality right now and try. Remember, if you are dreaming, you can use nothing in the dream as proof—it's all a projection of your mind. Every quality of a dream is available in the movie of consensus reality, and every quality of this movie is available in the dream. Nothing that appears in the movie on the view screen of our mind, whether asleep or awake, can be used as a part of the test. The more we try, the more we realize that we can't prove that we are not dreaming. There is simply no valid test.

Remember, there is no difference between dreamed reality and consensus reality. Both are a product of our paradigm—the result of our beliefs and expectations projected onto the view screen of our awareness. You may think that you can tell the difference, but if you are asked to perform the same task while under hypnosis and sharing a fantasy with others, you will come to the same conclusion. You will say you are awake and that your experience is real. You will not know—until you awaken—that your experience was a projection of your mind shared with others who are in agreement with you.

All experience is dreamlike in nature. Your personal dream is yours alone. Consensus reality is a dream on which many have agreed. Beyond this, there is no difference.

Out There

Master: All that is, is of The One. There is only The One.

So far, we have learned how the mind works to supply us with a movie of reality. This movie thing is a nice metaphor. But if all this is happening in our mind, what is really out there? We have learned that it is holographic energy, but this is a difficult concept to grasp while confronting the limitations of our paradigm. And this question is one of the most baffling to scientists of today. But in fact, modern science holds the answer.

We have used the cinema and the computer to describe the workings of our mind. Similarly, what appears on our conscious view screen of reality can be compared to what appears on the screen of a television set.

A host of television stations is available to us every moment of our lives.

These programs exist as electromagnetic energy in the air around us. This electromagnetic energy contains the information for each stations programming. We can compare these waves of energy and the individual programs they contain to the holographic potential of The One. They are everywhere.

Although they are in the air around us, television programs are not available to us as experience in consensus reality unless we have a television set. We rely upon the television set as a device through which we can experience a television program. A television set is also surrounded by a host of available programs. Again, all these programs are in the electromagnetic energy in the air around them or on the cable feed. They are received by an antenna or cable and are available to the television all the time—even when the set is turned off. And a television that is on and tuned to our favorite program is still "receiving" all those other programs—but they are filtered out by the channel selector. We are not aware of any of them until they are selected, processed by the television, and appear on the screen. Until then, the information exists only as energy.

Think of your paradigm as the channel selector of your mind. It filters out programs that are not "selected." Your mind is filled with information that does not reach your conscious view screen because the "channel selector" of your attention is tuned to another sensory experience. Like the television set, all the programs are available to your mind all the time. These programs exist as energy. The potential of these programs is unlimited. The source is The One.

Let's review what scientists have recently discovered about our reality. Modern scientists are opening a new paradigm. Those of us who are still set in the old ways of thinking—those of us using old programs—are having trouble "switching channels." The old model of the physical universe defined matter as particles or things that worked together to make up the world as we know it. These things were always there, even when we were not "tuned in" to them. In the new paradigm, physical things do not exist unless we are in the act of observing them. In the new paradigm, there is only energy, like the energy of all those television programs. The act of observation is the "channel selector" of the mind that brings a portion of this energy into being.

Therefore, in the deepest reaches of the "material" of this book you are reading, there exists only energy. This energy does not exist as the physical thing we call a book. It exists only as energy, but it contains potential in energy form, and only one possibility of that potential is the physical book you hold in your hand. It is pure holographic energy, energy without physical form, so it could be anything.

You, too, are energy. And your mind is the channel selector of your reality. If you closed your eyes just for a moment, would you still be here holding this book when you opened them? Most would say: Of course I would. The correct answer is that you *probably* would. Remember that the laws of The Magic of Agreeing in our movie of reality declare that it should be—but those laws carry no guarantee. Those laws are still subject to our individual paradigm. There are exceptions. There are no guarantees that you will even open your eyes in the same physical reality you were experiencing when you closed them.

Look at it this way. We know that all energy is interconnected. The energy in this book is holographically connected with all the energy in the universe. There is no physical form at the energy level, so there is no separation. No separation means no time. You know that it takes time for a stars light to reach the Earth, and that the starlight we are seeing now is billions of years old. But you also know that time is a product of your movie. At the quantum level—the level of pure energy—what is happening in the farthest reaches of the physical universe is "known" in the energy of this book, and of you, the moment it happens. The book exists as energy. It is holographic, holding within its vibrations the potential for the entire physical universe. When, then, does it become a book?

The energy of the quantum world becomes a physical thing when you look for it as a physical thing. And it becomes *exactly what you are looking for*. It simply does not exist in any physical way until it is observed. The energy in the book you are reading exists only as energy until it is observed. When did the energy in this book become a book? When you're looking at it. And it will "probably" be a book as long as you are looking at it.

Why, then, does your grass continue growing while you are sleeping? You are, after all, not looking at it while you are asleep. Recall the laws of The Magic of Agreeing. The Magic of Agreeing is the focus of attention of all those involved in our movie of reality. We have agreed on these laws, one of which is that the grass continues growing while you sleep. And another of which is that this book remains on the table when you go to work tomorrow, assuming you don't take it with you. It is the focus of attention of the five billion or so participants in our movie of reality, the combined energy of their agreed upon paradigm, that holds reality together. *The Magic of Agreeing is the same as observation.*

So what is "out there" is energy. Pure, holographic energy without form, without time, without distance. And it's not really out there. It is holographic. It exists everywhere at all times. We are energy beings, and we exist in a state that is without time, space, or distance. We are, in our quantum energy state, beings of unlimited awareness and potential.

Hold the moon in your attention for a moment. Were you there? In Mind, you are a quantum energy being. In the quantum energy state of Mind, you are always one with the moon; you are one with the energy that has the potential to become the moon. The act of turning your attention to the moon caused your mind to run a movie involving form, distance, and time. All the other information available to your reality was filtered out by your paradigm as it refined the holographic potential of The One into your moon. The resulting experience is a product of your mind and, when you accessed it, it collapsed out of the pure energy state and became a physical reality for you. Why? Because you were expecting it to appear that way and you agree with the other actors in our movie. In your movie, your programs require it to appear that way in order for it to fit your paradigm. If it appeared some other way, you would be participating in another reality, another illusion. Your sense of self as an identifiable physical being in consensus reality would be threatened. Your mind is the creator of your sense of physical being, your sense of your separate self, and will hold onto it with great determination. Your paradigm includes the laws of The Magic of Agreeing, the laws that define what both you and the moon will be in our movie of reality.

Recall our experiment with negative hallucination. We discovered that an individual can virtually see right through physical objects—when their paradigm allows them to. When you look in the mirror in the morning and see your face, you admit that just because you cannot see what is behind the mirror does not mean that it's not there. If it is in your thoughts, you are tuned into it—and it's there. So, though it is said that seeing is believing, the opposite appears true—believing is seeing.

Here is another example. Think of someone dear to you right now, your wife, daughter, sister or mother. Observe the movie that runs in your mind. For a brief instant, there is no separation. For a moment, you access the essence of Mind. Then, without hesitation, your mind began to fill in the "reality" of her through your paradigm. Energy is holographic so, for an instant, she knew you were thinking of her. The instant you focused your attention, she became aware of it in her quantum energy state of Mind. In the quantum state, we are not separated. However, that awareness probably did not fit in with the movie that was running at the time, so it was filtered out by her mind. Even though her Mind was aware, she did not "know" in her consensus movie that you were thinking of her.

Likewise, every thought that we have arises initially with the pure awareness of Mind. It happens every time we focus our attention. In the fullness of our awareness, there is no time or place that we, in Mind, are not right now; there is no awareness that is not ours. Then, as we focus our attention on a specific potential of that awareness, our mind begins its process of filtering and refining.

We may get the impression that our mind is the culprit supplying us with an illusion and should be eliminated or at least disabled. It is, after all, holding our awareness of Mind at bay behind its paradigm. Here we should remember the words of the Master: *All* that is, is of The One. We cannot sequester the energy of our mind. It is, as all energy of our holographic reality is, of The One. This means that our experience is not an illusion, but is also of The One. But if experience is not an illusion—if experience is of The One—how is the illusion taking place? Let's look deeper into the paradigm for the answer.

Maya

Student: It's easy to think of reality as an illusion, but treating it as an illusion is very difficult for most of us. When we experience something in our reality, it seems very real. How do we treat experience as an illusion?

Master: Limited experience is something that you have created, and what you have created is indeed very real. You may participate fully in your reality without losing yourself in it. The illusion is in the conflict, the struggle. There is no conflict. Everything is as it should be. Everything is in balance. All that is, is of The One. Your reality is not the illusion. The illusion is that you are separate from your creation. This sense of separation causes the conflict.

There exists a concept that all of what we call physical reality is just an illusion. The term "Maya" is often used to describe this concept. Maya does mean "illusion," but it does not mean that our reality is an illusion. What we have created is the result of our focus of attention and The Magic of Agreeing, has its potential in the holographic energy of The One, and is not an illusion. It's no more or less real than a dream, but dreams are also self-created realities. We should caution ourselves against thinking that our reality is "just a dream," and come to the realization that *all experience is dreamlike in nature.* But again, if this is true, where is the illusion? The process by which our mind creates experience by selectively filtering and refining the holographic potential of The One is the basis of Maya. The mind provides us with specific illusions in this process. Remember, the illusion is not in our created reality, but in our limited experience of it. Experience is a potential of The One and, as such, has its foundation in The One. All experience is, therefore, real and valid. Illusion—or Maya—is the manner in which our mind presents us with the experience by filtering and refining the holographic quality of it..

The first indication of Maya is found in the Knowledge that all that appears external is a projection of the mind. We know that the foundation of all things, including experience, is in the holographic potential of The One. We know that we are of this energy. Recall that it is the mind that adds the feeling of "in here" and "out there" to the movie it is projecting onto our conscious view screen. We may believe this to be true, but we still experience reality as if it were out there in a real world. What is out there is indeed very real. The illusion is that we are not fully a part of it, fully one with it.

Remember, we are quantum energy beings, and as such, are fully connected with all the energy that is. We are of The One. The first manifestation of Maya is that there is something "out there" and that we are "in here." The first illusion is *separation*.

We exist as quantum energy beings, and as such, are in no way separated from all energy that is. We are not separate from our creation. We are always and ever in and of all potential—always of The One. Experience is real. Separation is an illusion. Separation is appearing in your movie of consensus reality. But it happens internally. It is a product of our mind.

Separation appears in our consensus movie as well as throughout the transpersonal realm. Remember, transpersonal awareness is simply that which is beyond our personal experience. Transpersonal awareness includes those hunches and impressions we all have. It also includes total awareness of the holographic nature of our world. In our consensus reality, our personal experience seldom includes other realities, yet there are other realities around us all the time. They include the past, the future, and realities that are not made up of the same physical matter as ours. These realities are, as ours is, consensus realities held together by the laws of The Magic of Agreeing. Those entities residing in them have agreed upon a movie—a reality—and theirs is as real to them as ours is to us.

There are also realities that are extensions of our own. They exist according to the same laws of The Magic of Agreeing we have established for our movie. Many have traveled into these realities and have even spoken with those who reside there. They have names and titles that distinguish them from others, separate them from others that are "out there." They are experiencing a movie consistent with their expectations, one upon which they all agree. The illusion—or Maya—is the belief that they are separate from the experience, that it's external and caused by external forces. To them, our reality is the transpersonal realm.

Experienced travelers know that these other realities are not separated from our own. They can be accessed with the slightest shift of attention. Separation is a function of our mind. We are one with all energy, and as such, are not separated from any other person, any other thing, or any other experience. Separation is a result of our paradigm, a product of our mind. Separation is an illusion. It is Maya.

Belief, expectation, and The Magic of Agreeing produce a movie of reality. Here in consensus reality, we have agreed upon what we can do and what we cannot do. We have regulations telling us what we should do to achieve a goal, and what we can expect if we do not. We have agreed to limit our part in the movie. The second indication of Maya is *limitation*.

Here, in what we call our limited physical reality, we are often deceived into believing that this is all there is. This is what happens in the cinema when we intentionally sacrifice awareness of what is going on around us for the entertainment of a good movie. We become so involved in the movie that, for a time at least, the movie is all there is. We may say that this is all right in the cinema, where we know the experience will end and we can return once again to the comfort of our reality. But the idea of limitation in any form is evidence of Maya. All that appears to be external to us is a projection of the mind. The illusion is that the experience is limited to what we are aware of on our conscious view screen, and that it's all there is. In the quantum energy state of The One, all potential is available now. There is only now. We are energy beings, unlimited by time or space. Limitation is in a product of our paradigm. It is Maya, an illusion.

Those of us who experience the movie of consensus reality get the impression that the movie has meaning. The idea that any *meaning* is coming from outside our mind is the third manifestation of Maya. In the cinema experience, every individual in the cinema is the center of the movie. They share a common thread of flow and plot, but they differentiate the experience based upon their own past knowledge and experience. For each individual observing the same sensory information, a different interpretation is presented by their mind. Any interpretation is a product of the mind. It's the mind that gives meaning to the movie. This is why, while you are in the cinema, you seem to be able to extract a meaning from the movie. The movie is designed to stimulate a response in you, to *mean* something to you. Seldom do you realize that the director has taken advantage of the programs of your mind. Seldom do you consider that there are others in the cinema participating in the same sensory information, yet having a different experience and giving different meaning to the presentation. For example, there are those who relate closely to the villain because they have the mind and the programming to do so. There are those who relate to the hero, they have the programming to do so. But the meaning of that movie, for each and every individual, comes from them, not the movie.

A skilled movie director knows of our past experiences and knowledge. Yet, all he or she can do is offer sensory information. Our mind has to put meaning into it. If we do not have the programming and experience, the movie will mean nothing to us. It will not even make sense.

Let's look at it another way. The actors provide us with an interpretation of the script. They give us the tone of voice, the look, and the mannerisms they hope will convey *their* meaning to us. But that was all done long ago. There is no meaning in the still frames sliding across the projector lamp. Without the programs of *our* mind and *our* experiences, the movie is meaningless. The meaning comes from us. It comes from our mind.

Our mind builds an acceptable view of "reality" based upon our experience and knowledge. It produces an acceptable movie of life. The mind does not consider other possible meanings to sensory information. It attaches meaning to the movie as if it were an absolute fact. This meaning is then externalized by our mind to give us the illusion that meaning is coming from outside us. All meaning that appears in our reality is a result of our paradigm and a product of our mind. It is Maya.

This is the essence of Maya, the foundation for illusion. Wherever anything appears out there as limited and meaningful, we can rest assured that it is the Maya of our mind.

We may watch someone who is asleep and dreaming. It's easy for us to say that they are just dreaming, and that what they are experiencing is "not real." But it's true that, for the dreamer, the dream is very real. They do not know that they are dreaming until they awaken. Most dreams follow the script of separation, limitation, and meaning. What a dreamer experiences in a dream is out there, limited, and appears to have meaning. When these things appear to those of us who think we are now awake, it is Maya.

When we think that what is happening right now is separate from us, that it's a limited experience, and that it contains meaning, Maya is active in our mind. Every single atom of our body contains, in its quantum state, the vibration of The One. Every particle of our being is the essence of all that is. There is no separation. There is no limitation. There is no meaning. When these things appear in our movie, we should realize that they are only a projection of our mind.

The ability of our mind to add the illusions of separation, limitation and meaning allow us to have experience within the holographic potential of The One. Once again, all that is, is of The One. Experience lies within The One. There is nothing wrong with or negative about experience. Therefore, there is nothing wrong with or negative about Maya. Creating experience gives us self-expression, and Maya is a necessary element of experience. We are creative entities, and the desire for creation and self-expression is a part of our nature. Do not, for a moment, think that Maya is negative or bad. It is a potential of The One. It is not something that should be looked down upon.

I have mentioned that there are those who are not taken into the illusion, individuals who have the ability to move about freely in consensus reality, manifesting what they will while fully aware of The One. These individuals have not eliminated Maya from their minds. They have *gained mastery over it*. Mastery of Maya allows them total freedom of self-expression.

Most of us have found a place of balance in our movie of consensus reality. We are able to participate in it, while allowing ourselves periods of self-expression. This is a reflection of the nature of our being. Even so, we may occasionally lose ourselves in self-expression. We may become so involved in our work that we bring it home with us. We may find ourselves so involved in a new hobby that we think of it whenever we get the chance. We may become so focused on a new relationship that it is all we can think of. These are examples of the loss of mastery over the illusions of Maya arising within our movie of consensus reality. And we know that these are transitory. They remain but for a while, and are soon integrated back into our movie.

Maya in our movie of consensus reality is similar to one of these instances of extreme self-expression. We are involved in the movie of consensus reality for just a time, and we will soon integrate this self imposed limitation back into the potential of The One. Remember, we are timeless, unlimited, holographic beings. Although it may seem that this movie has consumed us, it is but a moment in the timeless potential of The One. Do not allow yourself to become despondent because Maya is so powerful a force in your movie of consensus reality. You are an unlimited, timeless spiritual being. You know, from experience, that the seemingly overwhelming involvement in a moment of intense self-expression will pass. It has in the past, and it will again. And another opportunity to become so deeply involved will arise again. This is a reflection of the nature of our being. We are creators. Our desire is for self-expression. We should take joy in this. Once we have learned to master the illusion, we will create and experience with a new freedom, a freedom much like the Sky Heroes had when Dream Time began.

You will learn, as you continue to read, that nothing is hidden from our understanding. The true nature of our being and our relationship to The One is reflected in every aspect of our movie of reality. It cannot be hidden. We, and our holographic world, are in harmony, in balance. And the potential of the whole is manifest in every part. This includes the illusion we have created, and our path to the realization of it. Fortunately, the holographic nature of our mind retains a map of the process it used in creating our illusion—a map that can lead us back to awareness, and to freedom.

The Path in the mind

Student: Do we choose the life we will have before we are born?
Master: Choices are not made before. Choices are made now. There is only the now.
Student: I know that's true, but it seems that sometimes we have no control over what happens to us. Do we choose those experiences before are were born?
Master: You did not choose. You choose. Every moment holds the fullness of The One. This is not something that goes away simply because you are not aware of it.

There is no past or future in The One. We know now that the new model of physics—the quantum model—declares that all physical matter is energy, and all times and distances as we conceive them are totally connected. It proclaims that the universe is holographic, and that it is a world in which every place is the center, and all potential exists there. It is a world of pure energy existing simultaneously with the potential of any particle or thing. In the quantum world, there is no space, time, or distance. Quantum theory tells us that this energy does not exist in any physical form until it's observed. These are not just speculations. They are the foundation on which quantum physics exists, and each new experiment proves that it's a valid foundation.

What is happening in our experience is not an external thing. It is happening within. But "within" is not the physical substance, the flesh and blood of our being. Remember, we are energy beings, and our mind is not confined to the physical matter of our brain.

The mind is easily detectable in an energy field around our body. Modern science has developed instruments that can detect this field of energy. These instruments show that the frequency or vibration of this field changes with a change of attention. Not only does the energy change in response to external sensory stimuli, but it changes *before* the corresponding electrical patterns appear in the physical matter of the brain. We are processing information from the energy world around us in the energy that is our mind—in an area just beyond our physical being. It's only after a change in this energy field takes place that the information is processed in the physical brain. And it's even later—after the brain processes the information—that it appears on our conscious view screen as a thought or feeling. Remember, the field of energy around our body is the physically detectable essence of our being. It's energy and, by its nature, is unlimited by time or space. It's holographic, and is one with the quantum state of all that is. It is the pure potential of Mind in The One. It's everywhere and of all time, the potential for all possibility, all experience.

Instruments aren't the only method of detecting this energy field; they are just the ones most scientists believe in. Many individuals can, too. But by the time their awareness of this energy reaches their conscious view screens, they experience it in a manner that fits their paradigm. Some see colors, while others see miniature movies played out in the energy. Some hear the words spoken in these movies, and some feel the emotions associated with them. The portions of our experience that are the focus of our attention stand out in more detail in this energy field. They often appear to the observer with a clarity that even our paradigm will not allow to the surface in our awareness. A skilled observer of this energy knows things about us that even we do not consciously know.

The state of our physical being is vibrating there. Changes in our health are manifest in the energy long before they are detectable in the body. Thoughts that are a constant focus of our attention stand out in striking detail. As we focus our attention on our movie of reality, the energy of our mind vibrates in response—and an attuned observer can read this energy like an open book.

The focus of our attention is the creative force for our movie. As we participate in the movie, the future scenes of the part we are playing become crystallized in the energy of our mind. The future of our movie of reality can be compared to the unused portion of the reel of film on the projector in the cinema. The scenes that will appear on the movie screen in the next few moments are already recorded on the film. In the cinema, the movie we are watching is the result of the desire and attention of the writers and directors—and its outcome is well established. Our movie of reality is the product of our attention and desire, and our mind is the director. Although our movie is unlimited, we have developed expectations that *our mind is preparing to meet*. Our mind is already aware of the future scenes of our movie of reality.

As an example, let's say that you are in a room with 20 other people. Everyone is in groups of two, and each pair is discussing a different topic. You are deeply involved in an interesting discussion with your partner, and so, are not consciously aware of any of the other conversations. Two individuals across the room are talking about cooking. One of them tells the other that you have a wonderful recipe for bread. The other person says that when she gets a chance, she is going to ask you for the recipe. Because you are deeply involved in your discussion with your partner, you are not consciously aware of a word of the conversation across the room.

We know, however, that all sensory information is processed all the time. All the sensory information in that room is processed and recorded in your mind, but the majority of it does not fit in with your current sensory experience, and is filtered out. Yet, your mind is never off. On some level, you are aware. This portion of your future is crystallized in the yet-to-come movie your mind is preparing for presentation on your conscious view screen.

And you also know that your mind runs programs in response to all this sensory information, but that it withholds those programs until they fit your expectations. Yet, these programs have already begun to effect you—even before they are conscious thoughts. And you are aware of them before they happen, but they are now just feelings that you call hunches or impressions. This example explains how your mind creates a crystallized future—a future that has already been determined by your paradigm—when sensory information is available. It demonstrates how a sensitive individual may be aware of it. You may have a hunch that someone is going to ask you for that recipe. But how can someone become aware of the crystallized future *before* information is available to the five senses? What would cause you to bring a copy of the recipe with you, long before your mind had processed any physical sensory information?

Predicting this future is a natural ability that we all possess and use. Do you have any idea where you will spend the night? Your prediction based on known information—your paradigm contains all your programs, patterns and tendencies. But it is a prediction. It could change. You know that your mind is not in your brain, but in the energy field around your body, and is not limited by time or space. Nor is it, in its essence, separate from all other minds. Remember, energy is holographic. Your mind is aware of all the patterns, programs, and tendencies of all the minds that are. In the case of the recipe, decisions concerning the crystallized future were made in the minds of all the people in attendance long before they were consciously aware of it. They were all creating the future scenes for their movies. These decisions—made in the mind—held all the patterns, programs, and tendencies of all the participants. To your mind, this is known information, and it's just as valid as the information on which you predict where you will spend the night. The future is crystallized in your mind. It has not happened yet, but the potential for it happening has already been imprinted on the frames that will pass in front of the projector light of your attention and become part of your conscious reality.

Examples of how much awareness of the crystallized future is held captive behind the paradigm of our mind arise during experiments in hypnosis. As we know, suggestions given in hypnosis will alter the paradigm of the subject. Given the proper suggestions, a good subject can look into the crystallized future—down the future movie frames of programs, patterns, and tendencies—and describe an individual who will occupy a particular seat in the meeting room. They can describe the facial features, height, weight, and dress with striking accuracy—and can do so days before the individual is even aware that he or she will be attending the meeting. That seat is, in fact, a part of the crystallized future of that individual long before even he or she is aware of it. The "prediction" may seem to be of supernatural origin, but it's no more of a projection of future events than what took place when you indicate that you know where you will spend the night. It's based on known information. It's based on programs, patterns, and tendencies that are held in the energy of the mind, and all the minds that are.

As another example, you may plan a trip to town in your car, a trip you have made many times before. From the standpoint of your consensus movie, you already know the route you will take and can "see" yourself making the trip. You see the road you will travel in your mind, and what landmarks you will pass. You are looking into the future. These aspects of your trip fit your paradigm and are not considered unnatural. But is your mind aware of who will pass by while you make the trip? Is it aware of the "unscheduled" stops you will have to make? Perhaps a cat will cross the road, or a construction crew may be working in your lane.

The answer is yes. Your mind is energy. All energy is holographic. But these aspects of your trip do not fit in your paradigm of consensus reality. You are *not supposed to be able to know them.* Your mind refines this information so that you can have the *experience of the trip.* It even supplies the feeling of surprise, and perhaps disappointment, when you meet that construction crew on your journey—the construction crew that your mind was well aware of.

You also know that you plan your trip based on past experience and future expectations, and that the more often you take the same route, the more likely you are to take it again. It is true that should you become dissatisfied with your route, you will seek a new one. But once you have discovered a comfortable path, you will follow it again and again. You establish patterns in your mind that result in tendencies that remain with you for a lifetime—and perhaps longer. We all do, each of us selecting our path through life in the same manner. We draw, from the unlimited potential of The One, the experience that meets our programs, patterns, and tendencies, the experience that fits our paradigm.

Our programs, patterns, and tendencies—our paradigm—begins developing the moment we step foot on stage. Compare the storehouse of potential in Mind with a building of unlimited size filled with rooms with intersecting hallways running from all four walls. (Figure 3). Each of the rooms has a door in the center of each of its four walls. It appears much like a grid, with the grid lines defining the hallways and the boxes outlining the rooms. Each room contains a potential held in the energy state of The One.

Figure 3
The Path in the mind

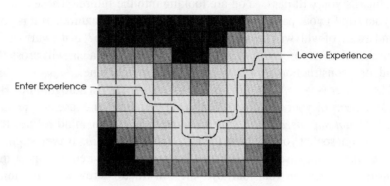

Imagine that we start our movie of consensus reality by entering one of the rooms of potential experience through one of the outside walls. We continue our experience by tracing a path through the grid to the opposite wall.

Our mind and Mind are in total awareness of all the potential held in all the boxes before we begin our journey. As we pass through each room—and its potential for experience in the script of our movie—our mind builds programs that impel us to choose next the room containing the potential that will *best relate to the experience of the room we are in.* The mind also begins to filter and refine the awareness in Mind of the potential of *all the boxes that do not relate*. Remember, the mind records experience holographically. Each new experience is combined with similar experiences to produce a memory containing all the information of all the experiences. Our awareness of the potential of all boxes—or The One—diminishes with each box of experience through which we pass. We are building our movie, box by box, and thus limiting our awareness, box by box. We are creating our *Path*.

The doors of each room of experience through which we pass remain open, allowing each and every experience to be linked. The mind has access to those rooms experientially. Our mind limits our ability to recall memory to those individual experiences that we have passed through, and is aware of the ones that we have chosen next. In our previous example, where all the sensory information in the room filled with people is recorded in our mind, we are only able to access that portion of the information with which we had direct experience. It's this form of experiential knowledge that is the foundation of our paradigm. But our mind limits our memory even *within the experiences we are having.*

The first factor limiting access to this information is that the mind is always processing *all* incoming sensory information, comparing it to current and past experience, and selecting the filters and refiners that allow us to recall it. However, what we are aware of on the conscious view screen of our reality is the result of this comparison, not the process. Our mind evaluates every bit of sensory information that it is presented with. Every sound, every sight, every smell, every taste, and every feeling is evaluated and recorded. Remember, every word of every document that we have ever looked at, even if we have not "read" it, has been evaluated and recorded in our mind. We have access to only a very small portion of this in our experience, although it's still active in the building of our paradigm. We can access the experience that we have witnessed on our conscious view screen but, for most of us, the rest of the experience is not available. If sensory information is not linked directly to experience, our paradigm does not allow it to surface in our awareness, or at the very least, makes it very difficult to access.

The second factor limiting our awareness is the way our mind assigns *priority* to experience. We have greater access to memory that is the *most emotionally charged, most recent,* or *most repeated.* Again, this is a result of the holographic process by which our mind records and presents our reality to us. Recorded information that does not contain one or more of these elements is difficult to access. For instance, even though it's recorded in our mind, we probably cannot recall the name of every person we were introduced to in a room filled with people we have never met. But, if during the course of our visit, someone in the room was to speak an obscenity, we would instantly become aware of it. This language is not acceptable in our paradigm for most social gatherings. We may even glance to see who had spoken. We are forming emotional and, therefore, experiential links to sensory information. We will recall the face, and perhaps even the name of that person because of these links. Or, we cannot recall the license plate number of every car we passed on the way to the store. We have no experience with which to relate this sensory information. Again, even though all sensory information is recorded in our memory, this information does not fit our paradigm. But, should we witness an accident, we may repeat the license number of the vehicles involved. Repetition is a method of developing those experiential links. Having done so, we are better able to recall this information.

We can, however, develop a paradigm that allows us access to this information. We can practice "memorizing" techniques that allow us to recall the name of everyone in that room, we can learn to recall the numbers of license plate numbers that we only glance at, and we can even keep an accurate record of our checkbook balance in our awareness. These techniques are thought to increase our memory, but what they are actually doing is developing programs that *allow us access to the memory that is always there*. They are recall programs, not memory programs. They create experiential links that allow the information to fit our paradigm.

All memory is always recorded in our mind. When we say that we can't remember something that happened or something someone said, what we are really saying is that we can't recall that information—that we have no experiential links to it. It is our paradigm that prevents recall of this memory. Therefore, we can see that our conscious view of reality is constantly filtered and refined through an ever-evolving paradigm, and that it's very limited.

Back to the grid of rooms. The doors of the rooms adjoining the ones we have passed through remain ajar. They contain potential that is similar in nature but through which we have not passed in experience. The mind has access to these rooms through the evolving paradigm in an abstract way. It relates the potential in those rooms to our own experience. As an example, you are able to relate to someone that plays baseball because you play tennis. You are not able to fully relate to the experience of baseball if you have not played the game, but you have played another type of game, so you can relate to it in an abstract way. You know what a hard practice feels like, and you know of the feeling of closeness with the other players.

As we get farther away from the individual Path of experience, those rooms become less and less accessible because of the growing paradigm. The potential is there, but it is refined to fit the current experiences—those that are most recent, most repeated, and most emotionally charged. It's through this process of passing through experience that the paradigm continues to grow stronger and stronger—and awareness of The One becomes more distant. This is the development of our Path. And even though we share the same movie of reality, the Path in each of our minds is unique.

Awareness held in the rooms still further away from our experience are inaccessible to our conscious view screen. The information in them is simply not available to us through our paradigm. Remember, we are holographically one with all energy and all awareness, but <u>we cannot have</u>

limited experience while we remain holographically aware.

Landmarks are developed as our Path continues to grow. Landmarks are those areas of our Path, those rooms through which we pass, that are highly charged with emotional energy. They develop during turning points in our life, such as major accomplishments and defeats. We are able to recall some of the major memories we have created in our life, and many of them are turning points. You may recall your first day of school, first love, first car, first house, etc. But, although they may be easily remembered, turning points are not necessarily landmarks. And landmarks are not necessarily the memories you recall most easily.

The mind develops landmarks holographically, and the logic we use in consensus reality cannot identify them. For example, you may have a fear of cats. This landmark on your Path may have began when you were very young. Perhaps you heard someone say that cats were dangerous. This could have taken place even before you knew what a cat was or were able to understand what it meant. But the memory is recorded, faithfully, by your mind. Depending on your future experiences with cats, your mind continues to build this landmark holographically. The first cat you see may have jumped out of a tree and startled you, causing a rush of emotional energy. Your mind records the incident holographically, building on the last memory. The next cat experience may have been in a circus. Now *these* cats are big—and in a cage. Another memory is created and recorded holographically in your mind. If the building of the landmark continues in this manner, by the time you reach five or six years of age, you do not like cats and you don't know why. This is a simple, linear example of a landmark, but it is just the beginning.

Remember, landmarks are created holographically. They are developed because of a relationship between experiences, but the relationship covers the entire range of sensory experience. As an example of this, the first time you were left with a baby-sitter, her cat was there. You don't like baby-sitters. Your baby-sitter was a blond lady. You don't like blondes. The cat jumped onto the table while you were eating dinner. You don't like that particular food. The list goes on and on, and covers not only dislikes, but also those things you are attracted to and enjoy. An incident in a baseball game may be related to your choice of clothing, your preference in vehicles, or your need to be alone.

There is simply no way to understand these holographic links with the logic our paradigm limits us to in consensus reality. Again, this is neither good nor bad, but it is important to know. As you travel your Path, you should learn to trust completely in the holographic logic of it, without trying to figure it out or assign meaning to it. Doing so only causes expectations to be set and more experience to be recorded in memory. We will discuss the Path and its landmarks again later. But for now, know that it is a holographic map of your paradigm, and an accurate record of the total experience stored in your mind. Remember also that your Path into consensus reality remains in place, and its landmarks are the guideposts you can follow to freedom.

This example of the grid is a representation of the function of the mind, and not a description of The One. In The One, full awareness as well as the potential for all experience is fully present in every "box" in the grid, and every "box" is the center. Therefore, if we pass through a single box of experience and can be aware of the potential of The One, we can experience all boxes simultaneously.

It is easy for us to see our paradigm at work as it grows in response to our attention in our movie of reality. Remember, our paradigm develops in response to experience and attention, and our current experience is filtered and refined by it. For example, you may begin a relationship, giving your full attention to it and developing a deeply shared experience. Yet you know from experience that most relationships are transitory, and if the attention of your partner is not focused as yours is, the shared experience begins to lessen and awareness begins to die. Your Paths are drifting apart. You may compensate for this by agreeing to find a common experience on which to place your attention. This process is continual throughout our lives. The birth and death of experience and awareness through attention—the building of the Pathway in the mind—is an ongoing process.

What we are experiencing right now in our consensus dream—what we call our reality—is a result of the Path of experience in our mind. Each and every aspect of our movie is a presentation of our mind. There is nothing that is out of place, for even though we are the creators of our movie, the Balance of The One remains. There is nothing external that will change this fact. There is no external place of perfect happiness for us. Balance is within. Peace is within. Happiness is within. And when we follow our Path, freedom from the movie we call reality is within.

You may get the impression that there is little about our movie of reality that can be changed—that it's already predetermined by our paradigm. Although we experience a reality that is already known in our mind—and our mind holds our patterns, programs, and tendencies, our movie is unlimited. Our mind is aware of many possible movies of reality that are available for us to experience, as well as the vast potential of The One. We create our reality continually by the choices we make moment by moment. Our experience is a product of our paradigm, but our paradigm responds to our attention.

In the example of your trip to town, you could stop at the park, take a different route, drive slower than you normally would, or even decide to change your destination while in route. All these movies are available when you leave home. Your mind provides you with experience in response to your attention, but it is not your mind that is the driving force of your attention. Your attention is a function of your energy being—your creative spirit. Your mind simply responds to your attention. This is why the saying, "take time to smell the roses," has so great a meaning to those who do it. When your attention is more flexible—more focused on the *possibilities* rather than the *destination*—your awareness, and the potential experiences available to you expand greatly. The practice of living in the "now" and exploring the possibilities within each experience expands the paradigm of your mind. You are not limited by your paradigm. You are limited only by where you choose to focus your attention.

The One

Master: All that is, is of The One.

The concept that all is energy, and that all energy is connected, is fun to work with if you are a scientist. We have the mathematics and the tools to have a great time with the quantum world. But how can we apply this understanding to ourselves? All that is, is of The One—and that includes you and me. How can we begin to imagine what it's like to become aware of The One. Well, believe it or not, we can again compare it to a movie.

We know that there was much more film shot than what we see in the final production in the cinema. We know that the excess film was cut, or edited, to give the movie the quality that the director desired. It is decisions in the cutting room that provide us with the sensory information that enables us to have the experience the director wanted us to have—or at least one close to it. We could make a dozen different movies with all the left over footage. Each movie would have a slightly different set of scenes that present slightly different sensory information. To experience the "whole" movie, we could set up a dozen projectors and run all the movies at the same time. But, that would not give us much of a coherent experience. However, all those movies do exist in potential, even if they are still on the cutting room floor.

Let's take all the footage shot—the final production as well as the pile of out takes on the cutting room floor—and gather it for an experiment. Let's cut all the film up neatly into individual frames until we have a huge pile of frames. Let's dump them all into a large drum, and make it tumble around and around. Can you imagine that? Is the movie in there?

Now let's take all the movies ever made—every one—and do the same thing with them. Put them in the same drum. Be sure the drum is big enough to allow all the frames to mingle freely. Add a little air to get even distribution. Is our movie still in there?

It is, but it exists only as the potential for a movie. There is no sequence of events to produce the illusion of time. No one has chosen which frame will appear first, and which will be last. There has not been a decision made on an outcome, but the movie is still there. It's there as it is in the quantum energy state. It's there as it is in Mind. It's there as it is in The One.

Let's take another step in developing a concept of The One. On the quantum level, there exists energy without form. However, that energy does not exist here or there—like the individual frames of our film. The energy in the quantum state is not limited by space, like a single frame of a particular movie. It is not limited by time, like the length of a movie. And it is not limited by individual potential, like the developed image on each of our frames of film. It is all places, all times, and all potential—always.

As we watch the individual frames of potential floating in our drum, it's easy to see that the possibility for all of our movies is in there. All we would have to do is to gather the frames of film, sort them out and place them in order. But now we must take each individual frame and raise it to the quantum level. To do this, we give each individual frame of film the full potential to become any frame in the drum. We can do this by saying that the information on each frame is holographic, and it has been exposed to the light of the entire universe past, present and future. Each frame, then, contains the energy code of information that gives it the ability to become any one of the frames—or all frames—in the drum. This code also contains the information that is necessary for any single frame to become any sequence of frames that may or may not result in a movie. This is what exists in quantum energy state, and this is what exists in the potential of The One. It is a constant fluid motion of pure holographic energy, containing all potential and experience, yet void of any limited experience. All the movies of reality that ever have been or ever could be are in the potential of The One, yet there are no movies in there. The One is limitless, filled with the potential of all, including all experience, yet free of the limitations of any single experience.

All that is, is of The One. Yet even as we form this concept, we tend to see it as "out there." To realize a fuller awareness, we must place each frame of our life in the drum, including the frame of this very moment. Every moment of every day of our lives contains the limitless potential of The One. This very moment is no exception. Of course, our mind is still filtering and refining our awareness through our paradigm. This is what our mind is doing right now to give us an understanding of The One. However, we cannot come to full awareness as long as we rely upon experience. This is because the mind selects only that potential within The One that fits our paradigm. It is the mind's ability to filter and refine the awareness of the total potential of Mind that results in what we know as experience.

Again, in The One, every possibility exists as holographic potential, and this potential includes the potential for all experience. It exists everywhere and in all time. The One is often called "The Void," but it is far from empty. It is full of potential, and within that potential, lies all possibility. All that ever was, is, or ever could be is there in potential. The past has not faded away forever. It's still there. The future is there too, ready to be examined. It's there in potential and is available to us as such. And we are in there, too.

We are energy—and we are of The One. The unlimited energy and potential of The One are limited only by the paradigm of our mind. The act of giving attention initiates the function of our mind that selects frames, sequences of events, periods of time, and experiences based upon our current paradigm. The mind is the laser projector of our experience. Attention is to our mind what the laser beam is to the holographic film, and our holographic film is The One. The whole movie is on the projector, but the illusion of experience does not appear until the projector lamp of attention selects the potential and projects it onto our conscious view screen.

It appears to us, therefore, that our mind makes a choice. But actually, our mind is only running programs based upon past experience. We are not our mind. We are the total of our mind and Mind, and our attention is a function of our spirit being. Each of us is the director of our individual movie. We—and we alone—hold the power to cut and splice the unlimited potential of The One to create our experience. Our experience does not have to be limited. We can fully participate in experience as well as remain fully aware of the potential for all experience. This power is held in the ability to choose where we focus our attention. Any shift of attention changes the reality of the projection. Most often, however, we allow our mind to run its programs in response to sensory information without giving the slightest thought to attention.

But each of us has made that choice in the movie we are running right now. And it is the choices we continue to make that builds our paradigm and continues to create our Path. We can choose now to focus our attention on the fact that we are the creators of our dreamed world of consensus reality. We can take responsibility for creative power. We can travel our Path to freedom.

Unit Two

Integration

Horizons

In the first unit, we gained the Knowledge of how our mind works. Our next step is to Integrate this Knowledge into our movie. Integration is the application of Knowledge into everyday life. By doing so, we expand our mind's field of focus and allow ourselves more awareness on the view screen of our reality. We call this process *spiritual development*, but in doing so, must remind ourselves that all is spirit. Our choice of where we focus our attention, be it on the movie of consensus reality or the potential of The One, cannot be evaluated as right or wrong, good or bad. All that is, is of The One, and this includes every aspect of the movie of consensus reality.

I caution against accepting teachings that suggest an absolute way or method of spiritual development. Yet the language of Integration includes "should" and "should not." It cannot be helped. It's the language of our paradigm, and that is where we are now. But you should realize always that your greatest freedom is the freedom to choose.

It is true that anyone, at any time, could sit down and focus attention, and with enough resolve, could transcend the paradigm of the mind. However, not many know that this is a possibility, and fewer still would do it if they knew. It's for this reason that we present Integration as a process. It is possible for all of us to Integrate the Knowledge of The One into our lives.

While we are in the process of Integration, we still play a part in the movie we call reality, but our perspective of the movie begins to change. This change effects those close to us.

Here is an example of how this works. Knowing there is a shoe sale downtown will not affect your life. Your knowledge is merely understanding. But when you go downtown and purchase a new pair of shoes, that knowledge Integrates into your experience. The moment you applied that knowledge it became experiential. And it affects your life, and the lives of every one close to you because you walk a little taller and feel more comfortable. Integration of Knowledge changes the way we look at life. It expands our awareness. And it affects everyone close to us.

What you have read thus far has changed your life. You may not know it, but you have already gained Knowledge that automatically Integrated itself into your movie. Remember, your mind is always gathering sensory information and fitting it into your paradigm; your mind cannot just disregard it. The amount of Integration you experience is directly proportional to the amount of attention you give to Knowledge, and nothing more. You can quit now, giving no more attention to either Knowledge or Integration. Doing so will allow your mind to effectively refine the Knowledge you have gained thus far so it will fit your movie of reality. But, when you begin to give more and more attention to Knowledge, Integration becomes a dynamic process. And when you begin to Integrate the Knowledge actively, your movie changes even more. As you have learned, this is how your mind creates your movie. And as you know, it is all a matter of where you focus your attention.

Your individual paradigm may struggle with some of the Knowledge we have covered. This is natural, but rest assured, you are not alone. Scientists are struggling with the same Knowledge. One of the greatest struggles is happening among scientists who are looking into the workings of the human brain. We know that our mind is not in our brain but in the energy that is our being. And we have learned that all experience is a projection of thought on the view screen of consciousness. We know that the mechanism for producing reality is a function of our mind. This is not a vague concept. It's a scientific fact, but we don't have to get "metaphysical" before it poses some problems.

If I were to prick the end of your finger right now, you would have an immediate experience. Your finger would hurt. But the fact is, it took time for the information to reach your brain, be processed, and be presented on your view screen of reality. This is no problem for us, but then, most of us are not scientists. What bothers the scientists is the fact that the mind presents us with an illusion of real time no matter how long the delay is. Look across the room. What do you see? From a scientific viewpoint, you are seeing the past. It's the "time thing" again. It takes time for the reflected light from the objects you are looking at to reach your eyes, and more time for it to be processed in your mind. By the time what you are looking at appears on your view screen of reality, it's history. We never really see anything. We only see the evidence of things that may have been. This example becomes obvious when we look into the night sky. Some of the stars we are seeing are no longer there, and some stars that have just been born will not be visible to us for billions of years. We can accept this in the night sky, but it is a fact in every aspect of our lives.

Most of us are not scientists, at least not in the classical sense. We are applying this Knowledge to our everyday movie. For us, the only thing that we need to know is that the mind filters from our conscious view screen all awareness that is not consistent with our current sensory experience, and refines the remaining awareness to meet our expectations. Our paradigm is a result of experience. Past and current experience creates expectations. We cannot have expectations without having the limitations dictated by them. This is the essence of the function of the mind. We are not interested in making this Knowledge fit into a scientific paradigm. We are interested in making it fit into our everyday experience. One way to achieve this is through the practice of Balance.

Balance

Student: What can we do to make this Knowledge a part of our daily lives?

Master: There is nothing to do. Doing only causes the mind to create more expectations. You cannot have expectations without having limitations. There is only to *be*. Be in the moment. When you consider the past, give it only a thought, and then let it go. When you plan for the future, give it the same reflective thought, and let it go. There is no effort involved in being. You are, at this very moment, at the very center of The One. This has always been true, but you have not known it. Now you can know it. Now you can be.

Student: I know that's true, but it seems like we're always struggling to remain aware of it in our daily lives. There seems to be a continual struggle.

Master: Your struggle is internal. It is because you have not learned that there is Balance in The One. Your mind thinks that you are not in Balance.

Student: Then should we just accept everything that comes our way and not do anything?

Master: To do, as you say, is to attempt to correct something that your mind tells you is not in Balance. All is in Balance. All is in The One. All you do must be in this Balance, and your being is the learning to recognize this Balance.

Student: It still sounds like just accepting everything that comes along.

Master: <u>Balance in doing is like taking a step. In order to move, you must leave where you are. In this motion, there is the appearance of not</u>

having Balance. But it is just the appearance, the Balance is in the motion. In all things that appear in conflict, in all that is presented by your mind as opposites, observe both, but choose neither. In doing so, you remain in Balance, in motion. The moment you chose, you have stopped the motion. The positive and negative aspects of your reality are a product of your mind. All is as it should be. All that is, is of The One. There is only Balance, and this Balance is in motion.

It's difficult to sit through a movie in the cinema and remain totally aware of the process of its production. We have a tendency to lose ourselves in the experience, and may even become a part of it. But the balance is there, even though we are not aware of it. It is just a movie, even if we are totally involved in the experience. Were we able to sit through a movie in the cinema and remain totally aware throughout the presentation that it was just a movie—never losing ourselves in the presentation—we could say that we have held Balance in the cinema experience. The result of this Balance lessens the experience of the movie, but will not completely eliminate it.

When we find that Balance between experience in the movie of life and the awareness of how the mind is active in presenting it to us, we can say that we have gained Balance in our movie of reality. Again, this state of Balance lessens the experience of our reality, but does not totally eliminate it. The fact is, though, that because of Balance, our movie of reality is no longer as real to us. Our awareness will not allow it to be.

Balance is, then, finding and maintaining a place in our experience where we are able to participate in the movie of consensus reality while remaining totally aware that what we are experiencing is a projection of our own mind. It requires both *involvement in our reality* and an *understanding of its nature*. This allows our paradigm to broaden, to become more flexible.

The concept of Balance is not new. In Tibet—where thousands of years of research and study have gone into mapping the transpersonal realm—students are instructed in gaining Balance and maintaining it in every moment of every day. In gaining and holding Balance in the movie of physical reality, they are able to expand their awareness. This is not separation from experience, but rather, it is the Integration of awareness into experience. Remember, separation is Maya—an illusion. All that is, is of The One. We cannot separate ourselves totally from experience without creating an illusion anymore than we can totally immerse ourselves in it without creating an illusion.

When we become deeply involved in our movie of reality, or in a personal dream, we tend to "forget" the fact that what we are experiencing is a projection of our mind. We find ourselves emotionally charged with a sense of good or bad, right or wrong. In this state, we are out of Balance, and awareness of the essence of reality is filtered from our conscious view screen.

When we are deeply involved in awareness, we find it difficult to remain actively involved in the movie of reality. We may become detached and aloof, perhaps unwilling to participate in the movie at all. We are out of Balance. The sensory information necessary for us to follow our Path and gain freedom from the movie is filtered from our conscious view screen.

Remember, all that is, is of The One. Both this movie, and the full potential of The One, are experiential realities. The illusion is that we are separated from them. A fully evolved spiritual being can hold Balance while experiencing the most intense portions of a movie or a dream, or when in total awareness of The One. This is the Balance between experience and awareness.

The perfect place to practice this Balance is right here, in the movie of life. Some teach that gaining Balance is automatic when we die, but that is not the case. Our awareness does expand at the time of physical death, but our paradigm does not stay behind.

Our paradigm, with all its programming, remains with us when we leave this reality. When this happens, the mind immediately begins to provide a new movie. Remember, the function of the mind is to filter and refine awareness to fit our paradigm, and our paradigm is still with us. Our new movie is a product of this paradigm. It meets our expectations, with all the separation, limitation, and meaning that we have learned to accept. Without the ability to gain and maintain Balance, we are projected by our mind into another reality. This is neither good nor bad, it's just another movie, another dream. We can take the next step in gaining freedom from this limited experience by Integrating Balance into our everyday life before physical death. <u>Learning to gain and hold Balance is a vital step in gaining freedom from the movie of reality.</u>

It has taken many reality experiences for our minds to develop a paradigm strong enough to effectively eliminate an awareness of Mind from our conscious view screen. Because of this, it would seem that we have little chance of escaping this paradigm. This is not so.

The teachers of Zen instruct their students to fully participate in the movie without losing awareness of the fact that it's a projection of their mind—to gain and hold Balance. But to practice this state of Zen, it is said, you have to spend many years in training under a master. Even Zen has its patterns of limiting thought. In fact, you have the very essence of Zen built right into you. The state of awareness that is Zen is an intrinsic part of your nature. Balance is your natural state. So, you may gain Balance now, without a lifetime of training, by applying the lessons of Integration to your everyday life and reviewing each day's movie in the light of your Knowledge.

Balance comes in holding steady in the worst and best of the movie. To your mind, your thoughts are sensory information to be acted upon. When you take a thought concerning your daily movie, allow it to be filtered and refined by your paradigm, and return it without Balance, you have *reinforced your paradigm*. When you remain aware of the Knowledge of how your reality is created, even when it is filled with sensory information, you have *gained Balance*, and your paradigm becomes more flexible.

Your patterns of limiting thought can overwhelm you during the course of your daily movie, but that does not hinder your growth as long as you take time to review each day in the light of Knowledge and Balance. These scenes *do* become overwhelming sometimes, and you *do* sometimes get lost in them. But your daily scenes remain in your memory, and you can *recall your thoughts*. If you become involved in your reality and "forget" that it is a presentation of your mind, you can return to Balance and review your experience in the light of Knowledge. Take time each day to review your daily movie of reality, the perceived good as well as the bad. Hold Balance or, by recalling your thoughts, return to Balance. Your mind will respond. It knows the Path and presents you with exactly what experience is necessary each and every moment of each and every day. You can perform this process at any time, but be sure to take time to do it at the end of each day. Without Balance, you are lost in the movie of reality, and your ability to expand beyond it is limited.

What appears to be happening in your life may still be presented as good or bad by the process of your mind. When this is so, you are still working with your old paradigm. Those daily occurrences are still presented with the meaning your mind has learned to assign to the movie of reality. Do not be discouraged. It is your Path arising before you. Accept your mind's interpretation of the movie, and then return to Balance. This process makes you aware that the interpretation also was a presentation of your mind, and that it came from within.

When you awaken in the morning, look at yourself in the mirror and realize that your natural state is not only in the expression of experience and the reflection you see, but in the unlimited potential of The One. This includes all experience as well as total awareness. You may not see it in your view screen of reality, in your reflection in the mirror, and that is perfectly all right as long as you have Balance. Know that all awareness, everywhere and all time, is within.

When you slip into an especially intense portion of your daily movie, enjoy it. Laugh with it. Cry with it. Then return it to Balance. Do this constantly and allow your mind to Integrate Balance into every aspect of your life. It is of no consequence to lose Balance momentarily, as long as you return to it and reflect upon your experience in its light. The masters of Zen teach their students to immerse themselves fully in experience and then return to Balance. Through this practice, the student learns to become fully immersed in experience without losing Balance. In whatever your Path presents you, it is vital that you maintain Balance or return to Balance.

The place and time to practice Balance is here and now. Many think that if they could just have access to a state of transpersonal awareness, they would enhance their spiritual growth and gain Balance. It does not happen that way. Transpersonal awareness and Balance are not the same. Transpersonal awareness is simply accessing information that is beyond our personal experience, beyond our paradigm, and nothing more. Transpersonal awareness can be accomplished by many means, few of which require Balance.

When we give attention to the illusion of separation, limitation, and meaning, our paradigm limits our awareness. This process has been going on for a long time. By now, many of us have a very effective paradigm in our mind, one that eliminates the awareness of the nature of Mind within. It's the product of our paradigm that appears in every scene in our daily movie. Our paradigm remains with us, and it follows us into the transpersonal realm. Expanding our awareness now, with our current paradigm, is of no benefit.

Recall the grid discussed in the section: The Path in the mind. When you leave your box of experience in this grid, which is your current experience and your Path, and step outside its boundaries, your awareness does expand. But you take with you all the programs of your paradigm. Many have entered into the realm of transpersonal awareness with their paradigm in place, and returned with an even stronger paradigm than before. What they experienced, even while in a state of transpersonal awareness, was filtered and refined to fit their paradigm. Even if we gain transpersonal awareness, without Balance, our mind presents it to us in a way that meets our paradigm.

An example of this is found in the practice of psychic surgery in the Philippines and elsewhere throughout the world. Remember, what we are discussing is neither good nor bad, it is simply an indication of the power of the mind.

The Philippine psychic healers hold a strong paradigm that involves belief in the teachings of a specific Christian church. Prior to their conversion to this religion, they practiced a form of spiritism that is not uncommon in Shamanic tradition. A Shaman is adept at entering the transpersonal realm and gaining assistance from its inhabitants. The Philippine healers are able to heal the physical body by removing infected or diseased tissue from the body without surgical instruments. They accomplish this with the help of entities that are beyond the physical realm but still willing to interact with it. This practice is part of the paradigm of their culture, and not one that is easily set aside. Even after the Philippine healers were converted to this new religion, they continued their Shamanic practices. But now, their beliefs and expectations have changed. They have a different paradigm. They still participate in prayer and meditation, often accompanied by fasting and long periods without sleep in order to gain access into the transpersonal realm. But gaining access to transpersonal awareness only resulted in a restructuring of their paradigm, a restructuring that now fits their new belief and reality structure.

You know that what you experience is a direct result of your paradigm, your beliefs and expectations. This is also true of the healers. They now practice the same form of healing they previously did, only now it is shrouded in the beliefs of their new religion. They still have access to transpersonal awareness, still not with Balance, but within the confines of a new paradigm. The result is evident in the manifestation of psychic abilities no different from those practiced earlier in their Shamanic tradition.

Psychic is mental; it is of the mind. And it has nothing to do with Balance. Gaining access to transpersonal awareness without developing Balance only leads to another presentation of the mind—another movie of reality.

The ability to hold Balance is most effective when accomplished right here in the movie we call reality. It's common to jump right out of your cinema seat during an especially intense moment while you are watching a movie, and then settle right back down and enjoy the rest of the presentation. After all, you "know" that what you are experiencing is just a movie. However, were you to walk out of the cinema and have an armed robber demand all your money, that ability to regain your seat escapes you. You would not be able to settle down so easily. After all, this is reality.

Not so! Neither the movie nor the robber is reality.

Imagine if the robber squeezed the trigger just a bit, and your physical movie of reality ended. You are then launched into another "reality." The lights go down in the movie of consensus reality, and the view screen of your mind lights up with a new presentation. This new reality meets the expectations that you have developed during your most recent experience, and your mind begins to interpret what it is focused upon. Your mind always provides you with a movie related to its most recent experience. It presents one to you now, after you were shot dead by the robber. And it is one that appears out there, limited and with meaning. If you have not practiced Balance in this movie of life, there is little chance you will even *think* of it now.

Oh, it's true that a "good" life may lead to a "good" movie in the "after life." If you have developed those expectations, your mind produces a reality that meets them. Your new movie of reality is *just what you expected*. We will cover the process of physical death in detail later, but for now, know that your paradigm remains with you in the energy of your mind wherever and whenever you are.

Good and bad are subjective products of your mind. The cop that shoots a fleeing robber is a killer, just as the robber is a killer. Both have planted seeds of thought and focused their attention on a possibility of the potential of The One. Both now have an opportunity to reap the harvest. But it took *both actors* to provide the movie, and neither could judge themselves without the comparison, without the illusion of duality, without the other. This is an example of the Balance that is.

We should practice Balance now, here in this movie we call reality. Hold fast to this awareness every moment of every day, no matter what your movie offers. What you are experiencing now is a product of your mind. But it is also your Path. Take joy in each moment. It is exactly what you require, and in exactly the order you require it for you to realize your Path. Your mind has developed the programming that allows you to experience the movie, and those programs remain aligned in the order necessary for you to follow our Path to freedom from the movie.

Remember, your paradigm is in your mind. It remains with you even after physical death. You cannot wait until the time of this death to gain freedom from the paradigm of your mind. You cannot enter another realm of awareness in order to gain freedom from this one. The only freedom comes with Balance. Here, in this movie of reality, is the best place to practice Balance—and now is the time.

You should come to and hold to the awareness that the full potential of The One is manifest in *each and every moment of each and every day*. That potential is never hidden. It is never isolated to a church, to the feet of a master, to the quiet of meditation, or to any place you may look for it. It has no beginning and no end. It is always and ever: Wherever you look, wherever you are, and in whatever you are doing. It's in every experience, no matter how seemingly good or bad.

The One is appearing just as it is necessary for you to realize it. It is you who has created this movie. The paradigm that is in place in your mind is a result of your past experience. No god anywhere has decided that you should suffer a bad life or enjoy a good life. You have decided—and continue to decide—what experience you will have. You are the director of your movie. There is divine grace, and that grace is in the fact that The One is manifest in the best and the worst, indeed, in every moment of your movie.

The process of giving attention to Balance expands your awareness. This should happen right here in the movie that you have created. You should gain mastery of Balance here—in the movie of life—in order to have Balance when your awareness begins to expand.

Holding Balance in our current reality requires us to be actors. An actor knows that what is taking place in the production of a movie is not real, but he works with the other actors to make his performance appear authentic. He does his best to provide a convincing portrayal of his intended meaning for each scene.

For you, in this movie of physical reality, what you should realize is that there is no separation, limitation, or meaning apart from you. When this awareness is Integrated into every scene of your daily life, you begin to experience a tremendous freedom in the parts you choose to play. You begin to understand that every actor has the freedom to choose what part he or she will play and how it will be played. It is now that you begin to hold Balance in your life. It is now that you no longer judge the other actors—or yourself. Holding Balance in all the scenes of your movie of reality gives you the freedom to participate without the need for meaning.

Good acting requires the actor to actually become the character he is playing. He does this to the best of his ability while maintaining the knowledge that he is acting. You may think that this is not a healthy approach to the "movie of life," but acting is what you are doing now. The only difference is that, right now, your mind is filtering out the fact that you are acting. Your mind knows that there is no meaning in what you are performing. Your mind knows that all meaning is self created. It knows that this projection of reality is for you. And your mind knows the reason you have chosen this particular reality, but it performs its task of filtering and refining, without fail, as long as you play your part and never seek Balance.

Holding Balance is the process of maintaining a subtle place between awareness and experience—even while you play your part as if it really mattered. It does. Every role you play is another opportunity to practice holding Balance. Every scene that presents itself in your life is the next step in stripping away the matrix of limiting thought that your mind developed in the process of presenting your reality. There are no meaningless scenes; each scene contains the full meaning you have given your reality. The meaning is not "out there." It's the meaning based on past experience. It's the meaning that your mind provides to meet your expectations.

In The One—in Balance—the meaning you now give each scene is that you are not separate from the movie of reality or anyone in it. The best you can do for your own growth is to hold Balance in each and every scene. The best you can do for the other actors is to show them your Balance in your performance.

Each act in the play of your movie of reality is presented as an *opportunity for Balance*. When you play your part without Balance, your mind interprets your performance. This interpretation always includes qualities of good or bad, right or wrong. Your mind gives you paradigm feedback—an indication of how you have done—and lets you know that you could have acted your part better, or at least differently. Your mind wants you to play the part again, according to the paradigm it has created. But when you play your part while holding Balance, your mind Integrates Balance into each experience. Balance provides your mind with the programming necessary to allow you to go on to the next step on your Path. The Path into your movie of reality is your Path to freedom from it.

Other actors who have reached Balance and are able to maintain the place between experience and awareness are aware of your accomplishment. They are excellent actors. They are, as you are becoming, full of life and vigor. Holding Balance while participating in the movie of life gives you the freedom to choose and interpret your part every moment of every day. You have no fear. There is no winning or losing.

Holding Balance is the single most powerful thing you can do to effect the movie of reality. You have but two choices: You can interpret the script and adjust your part in it, or you can look into the projector of your mind and recognize the source of the movie. Think back to the cinema. When you turn and look at the projector, the movie ends. You are looking at the source of the presentation. The source of your reality is your mind. Your mind is both the camera and the projector. It is gathering sensory information, like a camera, filtering and refining it through its paradigm, like a director, and presenting it on your view screen of awareness, like a projector.

In the cinema, as you watch the unfolding drama, your attention focuses on the main characters. It is they, and their interpretation of the script, that your mind finds something to attach meaning to. Now, think of the extras, the host of individuals in the movie that seem to have no meaningful parts. They have much more freedom. They are there only to fill in the gaps and support the illusion of the movie. But each and every extra is a vital part of the movie. They have all agreed to play a part, and if we were to remove any one of them, the movie would change. True, removing one extra might not change the overall meaning of the movie for us, but the movie does change. The only reason it might not change for us is because our attention is more focused on the main characters.

The same is true of our movie of reality. Every single actor in this movie of life has agreed to be here, and everyone is vital to the movie. Just because they are in the background—and we are not directly aware of them now—does not mean that they will not sometime surface with a "meaningful" part.

Now, imagine a scene in our cinema where two of the main characters are having a pivotal discussion, perhaps in a restaurant over dinner. Your attention is focused on them, and the rest of the actors are in positions to give the illusion of reality to what is happening. There may be other people at other tables, and a waiter.

Imagine how the waiter might interpret the script. He is there only to give the impression of reality to the scene. He does his job, entering and leaving the scene as a good waiter should, acting out his part according to the rules of a good waiter. You hardly notice him. You are so focused on the main actors that you do not even "see" him. Then he turns, looks into the camera, and gives you a wink and a smile.

RETAKE!

The moment he did that, your "reality" was spoiled. You realized, right then, that you had been watching a movie.

The waiter had two choices. He could play his role according to the script, or he could look into the camera and break your expectation of his role. How he plays his role will affect the movie. If he were to be particularly elegant in his performance, you might have noticed him. If he were a bit rude or sloppy, you surely would have noticed him. His interpretation of his role will add to or detract from the scene in the movie, but he would not produce the awareness in you that you were watching a movie. However, when he looked into the camera, you knew. If he only briefly glanced into the camera, the filters of your mind may have allowed it to pass by, not presenting you with enough of an irregularity. But when he paused, looked directly into the camera, and gave you a wink and a smile, the illusion of your movie was spoiled.

You are doing just that when you hold Balance in the movie of our everyday life. You are looking into the camera—and your mind is both the camera and projector—of the presentation. Such an action makes all the other actors aware, even if not on a conscious level, that what they are experiencing is a projection of their mind. It alters the course of the movie. It affects you, as an actor, but it has a powerful effect on the other actors and on those who think they are just observers. You can do nothing more powerful than to look into the camera of your mind, realize the source of your experience, and with a wink and a smile, let those around you know of Balance.

Most of us want to raise our children in a good neighborhood and give them the finest clothes, the healthiest food, and the best schooling. We want to send them off to college where they can earn a degree. We want to help them start a career, get married, and have children of their own. But what have we done? Have we not taught them to act in the same movie of reality that we have been attending? What have we accomplished, other than to pass the addiction of our movie on to them?

We cannot go back and change it now. Nor have we done anything wrong. Each of us chooses this experience with full awareness of the nature of it. All that is, is of The One. All experience is valid. Our children are enjoying their chosen part in the movie, and we have helped them to become actors. In this, there is nothing good or bad. But their Path to freedom is arising in the movie as ours is, and we can look into the camera to make them aware of it.

We are holding Balance when we look into the camera of the mind. When we do this, Mind arises, and there is a vibration of Balance in The One. This is a vibration that the paradigm of those around us filters out of their conscious view screen, yet it stimulates a Knowing deep inside them. It brings them closer to finding freedom from the movie.

Remember, we hold our movie together through the laws of The Magic of Agreeing. One of the laws of our movie is, *never look into the camera.* When we look, and give a wink and a smile, we alter the movie on its deepest level. We gain Balance and greater understanding and, because we are holographically connected to all the actors around us, we have shared this understanding with them.

The ability to gain Balance and reflect upon experience in its light is often lost in the intensity of our movie. We may have it first thing in the morning, during breakfast, or on the way to work. But soon we become so involved in our role that we lose our awareness of Balance. This is natural. It happens to all of us. It is the way our programming developed. We are not monks or Shaman who can achieve a state of Balance and maintain it through years of rigorous discipline. Remember, all that is, is of The One, and this includes the experience we are involved in now.

What we are experiencing is neither good nor bad, it simply is. And for us, it also contains our Path. To attempt a drastic change of attention now will require us to forsake our roles and start over. Many think that if they could just start over with a new job, a new relationship, perhaps even a new belief, that they would be better able to travel their Path. This is simply not the case. Our paradigm goes with us and our Path remains the same wherever we are and in whatever we are doing.

A state of Balance is an effortless state. If there is a struggle, there is a lack of Balance. Again, what is happening in your movie may appear to be "bad." Acknowledge the interpretation and know from Balance that it is only of your mind. What is happening in your movie may appear to be "good." Acknowledge the interpretation and know that it is only of your mind. "Good" and "bad" are terms of meaning. Meaning is from your mind and nowhere else. Look into the camera of your mind.

When meaning from our mind appears to be bad, we have a tendency to cast it away. We may try to escape into another situation. We may try to cover it with an explanation. We may try to blame it on outside forces. Or, we may try to make it good. This effort is *pushing.* Do not push. What you are experiencing is a product of your mind. It is built on all the past experience, with all the past separation, limitation, and meaning that was necessary for your mind to create it. It was developed by your mind to provide you with your Path. You cannot escape it. If you push it away, it will return. Look into the camera of your mind. This is a great opportunity to practice Balance—and to experience your Path.

When meaning from our mind appears to be good, we have a tendency to desire it. We will take it into our reality and accept it as our own. We may try to convince others of the goodness of it. We may use it as a gauge by which we evaluate our relationship with others. We often join with others who have similar goodness. This effort is *grasping*. Do not grasp. Instead, look into the camera of your mind. This is another opportunity to practice Balance. What you are experiencing in your reality is a product of your mind. It is built on all the past experience, with all the past separation, limitation, and meaning that was necessary for your mind to create it. It was developed by your mind to provide you with your Path. You cannot escape it. If you grasp it, your mind will add more meaning to it. Look into the camera of your mind. This is a great opportunity to practice Balance and experience your Path.

Pushing and grasping are evident in our consensus movie by an internal desire to get rid of the things that seem to make our experience unpleasant, and gather to us those things that seemingly give pleasure. There is a difference between having possessions and being possessed by them. If you desire something, it is all right to pursue it while your attention is focused on Balance. But when it becomes the focal point of your life and fills almost every waking thought, when it is all you dream about both during the day and in your personal dreams, the thing you wish to possess is in possession of you. You have no Balance.

You cannot possess energy. All is energy, and all that is, is of The One. You are of The One. The thought of taking this energy and holding it as your own requires a great effort of grasping, yet many are willing to do it—to focus the whole of their precious attention on it. All is in motion. Things that seem lasting are but fleeting moments in the illusion of time. The amount of attention required to make something appear permanent is an all consuming effort. And it is, in truth, only a moment's breath from now that you may have none of it. It is much better to hold the Knowledge of the nature of consensus reality and your relationship to it, and to hold it in Balance. In doing so, you may fully enjoy the things that come to you, be it a possession, a position, or a relationship, knowing that in the next moment it may be gone. In doing so, you give the freedom to choose that you hold so dear to those who share your dreamed reality with you.

Your relationships now take on a new meaning. You are able to enjoy others without the need to *have* them. You know that they, too, are making choices, focusing their attention, changing, and growing. You no longer struggle to make relationships permanent. The need to give a reason for beginning or ending a relationship, gaining or giving up a possession, having or relinquishing a position ends, and you are able to enjoy them and move on without looking back. You develop lasting relationships and continue to have things in this movie that you consider yours. This you do with a sense of freedom, knowing that their permanence is not in the fact that they are before your eyes, but that they are in your Heart. You are able to hold all in Balance in the potential of The One, the only place of permanence.

It may seem that your Balance has its ups and downs. There may appear to be times when you are in a state of Balance, and in the next moment fully involved in the movie of reality. This, too, is an illusion. It is an interpretation made by your mind, and it gives meaning to your understanding of Balance. But that meaning is a comparison of Balance with what we know about balance in our physical reality. You see, in our physical reality, balance seems to come and go. But in fact, Balance is.

Falling

Student: What about when things really seem bad, I mean, when there are major changes in our lives that we seem to have no control over? I know that there is Balance in that, too, but what are we to do?

Master: All of these things are the result of your choices, and are of your creation. In all of these things there is Balance. It is your mind telling you that you are not in Balance. All that is, is of The One. How can Balance not be?

Student: Knowing that is one thing, but applying it in those situations is another.

Master: And yet the Master does just that.

When we think about Balance, we may begin to think that maintaining perfect Balance throughout our reality experience is idealistic. The apparent struggle for Balance is evident in every aspect of our experience, and we continually pass through what we think are different stages of Balance. This is true even of the physical aspects of our reality. This struggle surfaces in our job, in our relationships, in our beliefs; indeed, it is present everywhere. This is an illusion; it is only the appearance of imbalance within the confines of our paradigm. What we should realize now is that Balance is not a static state. Perfect Balance involves motion.

Let's look at balance from a physical standpoint. I have practiced the sport of Judo most of my adult life. Judo is the practice of balance. Players try to catch each other in a state of imbalance and take advantage of it to throw their partner to the mat. Because every player, sooner or later, has the opportunity to land on the mat, we begin our study of Judo by learning how to fall. Beginners spend many hours learning how to fall properly. Proper falling requires one to remain in balance even while in the act of falling. There is balance in falling. There is Balance in everything. Proper falling requires a transition between standing balance and falling balance. Almost everyone learns how to stand. Not many learn how to fall. Those that have not learned how to fall will usually stiffen up and extend an arm or a leg in an attempt to regain their standing balance or to stop the fall. If they do not make the transition between standing balance and falling balance, they may injure themselves.

To stand properly, one must be in complete control without having to think about balance. To fall properly, one must be in complete control without having to think about balance. Both standing and falling take practice, and there is Balance in both.

In every practice session, participants begin by practicing falling. All participants practice together. Students who are in their first practice session practice beginner falls. They must first learn that falling is as natural as standing. Beginner falls are performed close to the mat, where there is little danger of injury. Masters who have been practicing Judo all their lives practice beginner falls. It takes many repetitions and a lot of practice to maintain a good standing balance. Most of us get this repetition during our everyday lives. It takes just as much practice to maintain good falling balance. Most of us do not practice falling very often.

Again, there is Balance in all things. You will not always be standing steadfast in balance as your mind interprets it. Sooner or later, you will step beyond your limits and will think you are off Balance in your movie or reality. When this happens, there will be a natural tendency to try to regain your Balance. But we all know from experience that there is a point beyond which we cannot recover. This is the time to make the transition between standing and falling balance.

The sudden end to a relationship, a job, or even an ability may cause our mind to give us the impression that we are off Balance. This is also true of sudden beginnings, like the beginning of a responsibility for which we were not prepared. But we are not in a state of imbalance in these situations. We are just in a state of changing Balance. Balance is. To fall in Balance, you must be in complete control without having to think about control. To be

"we're never taught how to do the "negative" things right"

in control, you must know that you are not off Balance. There is Balance in all. It's just your mind telling you that you are no longer standing.

Once a Judo student has overcome his fear in beginner falls, he can go on to greater and greater falls. These falls are performed from high in the air. He learns to fall in balance, but more importantly, learns to make the transition between standing and falling balance quickly and easily. He gains the understanding that he is never off balance, that there are just different forms of balance, that Balance is. The student now reaches a point in his development of balance where he actually enjoys falling. Once this takes place, he practices Judo with a new freedom. He is *free to fall*. A Judo player who is free to fall is a joy to watch. There is grace and form in everything he does, and when he is thrown to the mat, he is smiling and complimenting his partner even while he is still in the air.

There is no disgrace in falling. Take every opportunity to practice Balance when the world around you seems to be falling apart. But, when your focus of attention is consumed by the very effort of reamaining steadfast where you are, let go, and fall in Balance. The world around you is a projection of your mind. It's not the world that is falling, nor are you. Make the transition, and fall in Balance.

The lessons of Balance continue in our life until we learn to remain aware of Balance in all things. Once we master falling through practice, we reach a point where the movie cannot imbalance us. There are Judo Masters who cannot be taken off balance. These masters still practice falling at every opportunity.

Do not resign yourself to falling, but develop a sense of when you are *grasping* for Balance. Then let go, and with a wink and a smile, look into the camera. Grasping can be recognized by the *internal struggle* necessary to maintain what you perceive to be your part in the movie of reality. This struggle may surface when your mind tells you that you have a right to have the promotion you deserve, the house you want, or the relationship that you think is yours. When this internal struggle arises, you become aware that you must focus your attention more on maintaining your *part* in the movie than on your Balance in the movie. You are grasping, or perhaps pushing. You should now realize that you can lose or change your part, but you cannot lose your Balance. Now is the time to let go and fall in Balance. You will not be injured when your falling is in Balance. And by letting go and falling in Balance, you have freed yourself of the limitations of what you thought should be yours. You have opened yourself to possibilities you have not even considered.

Balance is not in standing still. Balance is in motion. The Human Spirit is an entity in constant motion. The One is filled with the fluid motion potential, including all experience as well as total awareness. It is the place of total potential in constant motion, and experience in its fullest. The home of the Human Spirit is One with this formless, fluid energy. The attention of the Human Spirit is the driving force of creation, and its center is in the motion of Balance in The One.

Knowledge and Integration are lessons in Balance. At times it may seem that Balance is a state of non-motion, a static state of planting your feet and standing still. But a static state is unnatural to the human spirit. We must learn to move about freely in The One—from full awareness to full experience, while maintaining Balance.

The techniques of Judo are based on this Knowledge. When two players are standing still, it is said, the first to move will fall. To begin motion from a still position, we must lift one foot. We become unbalanced when this motion is begun. Try it. Stand perfectly still and notice what you must do in order to take a step. You will find that you have to shift your balance to one foot for a moment as you begin lifting the other. If you were playing with a Judo Master, you would not find the opportunity to put your foot down again. The whole concept of Judo is based on *Balance in motion.*

The same is true of a child learning to walk. He will focus attention on balance while remaining still, and will even take assistance from a stable object. He will then draw into himself and stand, teetering a little, but balancing. You can see it in his eyes. His attention is on his motionless balance—for a moment. A child is a being in constant motion, like the energy of The One. Soon his gaze falls upon an object apart from his balance, his attention shifts, and he falls. It was the shift of attention that caused the fall. He will practice more.

Soon, the child develops a sense of balance that allows him to take a step. While still in balance, he focuses his attention on a distant object and lifts one foot. He is beginning to learn motion, but he falls many times before he learns that motion is a constant shifting from a state of perfect balance in motion, to a state of inclination to imbalance as he takes a step, and back again through balance. He must master this technique to maintain balance while in motion. The child must learn to become slightly off balance, or inclined to off balance, in order to move, but he must move quickly through *the shifting state between balance and imbalance* in order to move without falling. When he has mastered this state of fluid motion in Balance, he is free to move. The child learning to walk did not lose his balance because he lifted his foot. He lost his balance because he did not set it down again *soon enough* to regain his Balance. The Balance is in the motion. His attention remained too long on the distant object. He forgot to put his foot down.

The same principle applies to the shift of attention that causes what we think is a lack of Balance in our lives. We are in Balance when our mind and Mind are both active. Then, with a slight shift of attention, we are drawn into experience. When we learn to involve ourselves in experience and remain aware of our center, we are moving in Balance. When we become so involved in experience, usually by grasping or pushing, that we forget our center, we appear to be off Balance. Remember, it is not the motion that caused the feeling of unbalance. It is the fact that our attention did not return to the center. And, like learning to walk, this Balance becomes so natural to us that we do not even have to think about it.

Children are in constant motion. We can take a lesson from them. And when we do, we will then learn how to run, to leap and, perhaps—to fly, all with no fear of falling.

It's for this reason that you should never look upon a sudden fall as a defeat. You have not really fallen. There is Balance in all. Balance is in the transition, in the motion. It's a learning process, but we learn only if we get up and try it again, and we fall better if we fall in Balance. With each step beyond our limits, we learn not only what our limits are, but we also learn how to stretch our limits.

Children learn to walk at different rates. There are even some who get up and walk without appearing to have to go through the learning process. Some of them automatically access that intrinsic knowledge of Balance in motion within themselves. Keep in mind that you already know how to move in Balance. You are not learning something that is new to you. Balance is your natural state. What you are really doing is working through past programs, patterns and tendencies that have given you the feeling of imbalance for so long. You are experiencing your Path. Take joy in the learning process, and continually acknowledge the fact that you are accessing knowledge from within.

The Human Spirit is an entity in constant motion, and the only Balance is found in the motion.

Meditation

Student: How should I meditate?

Master: Meditate on the center.
Student: But shouldn't I practice a certain kind of meditation?
Master: Meditation is the focus of attention, nothing more. Meditate in your center, and allow your Balance to be.
Student: Should I choose something that reminds me of The One?
Master: Is your body pleasing to you?
Student: No, not really. I mean it is, but not for meditation.
Master: Your body is a reflection of your mind and is of The One. It will do you no good to focus your attention on something outside yourself unless you are pleased with yourself. Meditate with your body. Begin with your breath, and become aware of the Balance within yourself.

We have learned that the mind runs programs in response to our attention. When our attention is focused on our movie of consensus reality, these programs filter and refine the energy of our holographic world and present it onto our view screen of awareness. What we experience when this happens is the result of our paradigm, the matrix of limiting thought that follows us from reality to reality. This is true of any movie of reality, be it the movie of consensus reality or a movie in a personal dream. We know that where our attention is, so is our movie.

We remain in Balance when we maintain awareness of the nature of our movie of reality even while we experience it. The ability to *focus our attention* is the single most important element in our development. This is true here in our movie of reality as well as in awareness of The One.

It's our ability to focus our attention that resulted in our paradigm and its presentation of Maya. It is our ability to focus our attention on the source of our reality that allows us to remain in Balance. And it is the ability to focus our attention that leads to freedom from the movie we call reality.

Let's look at the process again. The mind runs programs in response to sensory information and holographic awareness. This presentation of our reality takes place when our physical senses receive information from our movie of reality. The mind knows what program it will run well in advance of the time our movie of reality requires it, but it presents the program to our conscious view screen as if it is happening that instant. Integration is a constant practice of remaining aware of this process in our mind while we participate in the movie of reality. Integration leads to Balance, and freedom from the programs of our paradigm.

All experience is a product of our mind, and all experience is dreamlike in nature. We have learned to believe that our mind's participation in reality is awareness. But what we have come to call awareness, the awareness we use in our experience in consensus reality, is really the activity of our mind solving the problems of our perceived reality. Our awareness of our holographic self is filtered through our paradigm and presented as a comparison or evaluation of ourselves with others and our place in this movie. It is through this process that we believe our awareness originates, but the process itself virtually eliminates the awareness of our nature as holographically connected beings. The resulting presentation, the presentation we think of as awareness, is not awareness at all. Severely filtered to give the illusion of separation from the whole, what we think is awareness is actually *the activity of our mind and its paradigm.*

And we have been taught to give our attention to this activity. We have learned to accept this limited presentation and are rewarded for giving our attention to it. When we are able to focus our attention on this activity we gain a "place" in our reality and arrive at what we believe is a self identity.

Attention to this paradigm activity, this problem solving activity, is the foundation on which our social structure is based and is the driving force for our education system. In our social and technological paradigm, cultures that have not developed attention to this process are viewed as backward. Yet, these cultures often display abilities that cannot be defined within our paradigm. We know of cultures that never invented the wheel or telescope, yet mapped the solar system in detail that we are just now able to verify. Isolated, seemingly backward tribes of people have been found that have accurate descriptions of the stars *beyond* our solar system. Other cultures remained isolated in one place on the earth, yet possessed information and detailed drawings of all the peoples of the earth.. Our scientists ponder these conundrums, searching for an explanation that fits within their paradigm. But they have never looked within; they have never looked to the process by which our mind constructs reality.

Being consumed every waking moment of our day by the problem solving activity of our mind is not awareness at all. Each and every thought we experience has its origin in Mind—in the pure holographic potential of The One. There is no other source of thought. Each and every thought arises in Mind without separation, limitation, or meaning, and in full Balance between the potential for experience and holographic awareness of The One. Our natural identity is not separate from the whole. This holographic awareness is available just behind the activity of the paradigm, behind the thought activity we have learned to believe is self awareness.

The activity of the mind responds to attention. When your attention is placed on a question, the mind must run the programs in its paradigm that result in an experience. When you become aware of the process, you can actually feel this activity happening. I am going to ask you a series of questions. After reading each question, close your eyes for just a moment and ponder the question. Try to feel the mental activity taking place as you do so.

What is two times two?

Okay, your mind ran a program and it appeared to provide the answer. It took only an instant for your mind to reach into its memory and extract it. You may not have noticed the problem solving activity of your mind.

Now, when did you first learn the answer was four?

Notice how your mind took a little longer and perhaps even pulled your awareness back to your school days. You may not recall the exact instant, but your problem solving mind automatically ran a program resulting in the awareness that you did, at some time in this lifetime, memorize the fact that two times two equals four. You went within. Most likely, you did not come up with a complete answer but, the answer you got somehow satisfied you. You just know that information is lost in the past, in your mind, at least. And you have the feeling that your mind is attempting to solve the problem, to come up with when you first learned that two times two equals four.

Where did you learn it?

Again, when you are sensitive to the process, you can actually feel what you believe is your mind attempting to solve the problem. This is where you were taught to focus your attention in problem solving activity. You were reconstructing your childhood days, recalling the schools you went to, or perhaps you saw that terrible times table you spent hours focused on. And again, you did not come up with a specific answer. You were satisfied with an answer that fits your paradigm of recall. And you know, in our social paradigm, total recall is an exception. Still, you have the feeling that your mind is actively attempting to solve the problem, to answer the question. You have the feeling you are thinking about it, pondering it, or attempting to recall the answer.

But the mental activity you experience when your mind is facing this problem *is not a recall activity*. Your mind knows full well the exact time and place you first learned that two times two equals four, as well as who was there and what the whether was like when the event happened. The entire scene is recorded in exact detail, detail that goes beyond what you were consciously aware of when the event took place. The answer to every question you could ask is available to your mind. *The information is there; the mind and Mind are one.*

The problem your mind must solve is determining whether this information fits into your expected view of reality through the paradigm you have created. That's the *only problem it ever has to solve* and it must continue *as long as your attention is focused on it.* It is the filtering and refining process of your mind responding to your attention that you just felt, and your paradigm leads you to *believe that this activity is awareness.* You have learned to accept its limited presentation as all that is available to your conscious view screen. It is all that is available through your paradigm, but it is only a small fraction of what is available to your awareness.

When you responded to the first question, the answer came quickly. But it only came quickly because it fit within your paradigm. When you pondered over the next questions, the answers came slowly and only in part, and the activity you felt continued *as long as your attention was focused on the question.* Even if you consider those questions again, you experience the same activity. The fact is, you experience this activity as long as you are focused on the question, or until you gain awareness. But right now, the focus of your attention may be on the fact that you actually felt your paradigm for the first time in your life. This may be the first time you have openly admitted that the information you requested is still there, held beyond your conscious view screen by your paradigm. This may be the first time you have come to the realization that as long as the focus of your attention is on the question, the activity you feel is the process of your mind struggling with your attention, filtering and refining your awareness. And you have learned to believe and accept the fact that all that activity, that filtering and refining process in your mind, is awareness.

Now, let's consider the implications of this discovery. How much of what we have "accomplished" as humanity has really been an accomplishment? We have "invented" devices such as telephones, radios, computers, and television, as means of communication. We "advanced" from walking around to being transported from place to place by animal drawn carts, automobiles, and airplanes. We "evolved" from beings able to live in harmony with the earth into societies that build great cities and lay waste to its landscape. When we discover a people who are able to live in harmony with the earth, who can travel the earth and visit the stars in their awareness, we educate them. We teach them to focus their attention on the illusion. What would cause a holographic being to require these "advancements?"

We created a system of education that prohibits teaching children how to access awareness and we encourage them, actually, we require them to focus their full attention on the illusion. Teaching meditation in school is, for the most part, forbidden. It is thought to be "spiritual," "metaphysical," or "religious."

How much of what you have accomplished as an individual has really been an accomplishment?

The answer to both questions is the same. None of this is necessary. It is possible to become fully involved in any experience we desire while remaining in Balance. But we are so far away from realization of the Balance that is, we don't even know it exists.

What a wonderful deception, but then, we could not have this experience without it. Just as in the cinema, we forget the projector, the people around us, even the cinema itself, as we become involved in our movie.

And we must view this in the light of Balance. Nothing is wrong here, no one has made a mistake, and nothing needs to be changed. Every entity participating in consensus reality is here by choice, and that choice is made with full awareness of the nature of this reality.

We can only ask ourselves if this is really where we want to focus our attention. We cannot ask that question for anyone else, nor can we force awareness upon them. We have created a reality in which we appear separated from the whole and thereby separated from each other. The function of our paradigm is the creator of this illusion, but the illusion is necessary for us to have this experience. Still, Balance is, and all that is, is of The One.

The mind is very powerful, as we have demonstrated in our hypnosis experiments, in its ability to filter and refine the holographic potential of The One and present our reality to us. But our mind has a quality that is in our favor. *It must run programs in response to attention.*

When you place your attention on a question, any question, your mind runs the programs which determine how awareness fits your paradigm. Remember, Balance is. You cannot hold a question without holding the answer. It exists in the holographic energy of The One along with the question. If that awareness does not fit your paradigm, your mind filters and refines it so it does. Your mind then presents this filtered and refined awareness onto your conscious view screen. And your mind presents it with the illusion that somehow the activity involved in filtering and refining that awareness was required in order for you to answer the question, have the experience, and gain just a little awareness.

You know now that the problem your mind is faced with is deciding how your awareness fits your paradigm; you know that *this is the only problem your mind ever has to solve*. It is time to go to the Question.

Where do thoughts originate? They originate in Mind, in the holographic potential of The One, in you. There is no other source of thought. The Question asks this question: Where did the thought originate; where did it come from?

The Question is not a mental question; it is not a thought, but an awareness. It starts as a question so your mind can identify it—and filter and refine it. But now you have actually experienced this filtering and refining activity. And when you did, you became aware of the awareness beyond it. For a brief instant you became aware of your *awareness beyond thought*. This awareness beyond thought is the Question.

The Question is a challenge to your mind to acknowledge the origin of all thought. And even though it continues to filter and refine it, it must acknowledge it. From a mental standpoint, you are able to understand how the paradigm works and even become aware of its activity. You must go beyond this mental activity in order to access awareness, therefore, you must hold the Question as an *awareness beyond thought*. Remember, your mind must respond to your attention. You will, therefore, eventually go beyond the process of the paradigm and gain access to awareness.

We have been practicing this discipline during Integration. But active participation in a discipline designed to strengthen our ability to focus our attention gives us greater access to our intrinsic awareness. The practice of meditation strengthens our ability to choose where we will place our attention.

Attention is like a muscle of the body. When you use the muscles of your body, they become stronger. When you do 15 pushups every morning, your arms become stronger. When you practice 15 minutes of meditation every morning, your attention becomes stronger. But if your pushups are done improperly, the outcome is less than desired or even counterproductive. The same is true of meditation.

It is the focus of attention that has allowed you to develop your role in this movie of reality. Every skill you have "developed" in the movie has been the result of your attention. In doing so, you practiced a discipline of attention that eliminates awareness. And this is okay, as long as you practice a discipline of attention that Balances it.

<u>It is the ability to focus your attention that allows you to remain in Balance.</u> When your attention wavers, so does your Balance. And it is your ability to focus your attention on Balance that causes your Path to rise before you.

Again, the ability to focus attention is the most powerful ability of the human spirit.

Attention is the key. When you focus your attention on the movie in the cinema, your paradigm shapes your awareness, and the presentation on the screen becomes your reality for a time. When you focus your attention on the movie of life, your paradigm shapes your awareness and it becomes your reality for a time. When you focus your attention on Balance, neither the presentations of your mind nor the source of them is overwhelming. You are in Balance—in the center. The width of your awareness is directly proportional to your focus of attention. Light, fluid attention in motion broadens the scope of awareness.

Meditation is not a mystical method of gaining access to another dimension. It is an exercise, a discipline. It is the practice of choosing where the attention is focused and maintaining the chosen focus. This is accomplished in motion while maintaining Balance.

There is no such thing as a bad pushup, unless you don't do it or do it improperly. Likewise, there is no such thing as bad meditation, unless you don't do it or do it improperly. We often hear people who meditate say: I had a good meditation and this or that happened. Or: I had a bad meditation and I just couldn't get into it. When we hear this, we are listening to people who focus their attention to get an experience. You should know that there is no experience to be desired in meditation. You know that all experience is a projection of your mind, and that it must contain the illusion of Maya in order to remain an experience.

You do not need a spiritual teacher to instruct you in the proper method of meditation. The meditative state is intrinsic to your nature. Balance is your natural state. Immersion in illusion is not Balance. Immersion in illusion is an energy consuming process. You burn as much energy when involved in the paradigm activity of your mind, the activity you believed was deep thought, as when you are walking briskly. The blood flow to your brain, the view screen of your reality, is nearly twice what it is to the rest of your body, yet you use less than ten percent of your mental capacity. Your mind's response to prolonged exposure to paradigm activity is sleep, and you have learned to take breaks in order to enjoy "mindless" activities that give you pleasure and refresh your energy. Your mind would love to find the place of Balance that is intrinsic in its nature, but it must run programs in response to your attention. All that is necessary for you to find Balance—and awareness—is to give your mind the opportunity to do so. All that is necessary is for you to choose to do so, and to focus your attention

Acorn ↑ Oak tree

on it.

There are many techniques for meditation, many different ways and methods of practicing it. But the following simple and basic technique is the foundation of all meditation. Focus your attention on your breath, and follow your breath inward.

Choosing to focus our attention on our breath rather than a word or an icon has a significance. My Master, in her wisdom, has revealed that words and icons hold meaning in the Western mind. Eastern students were raised in a paradigm where all is energy and everywhere is the center. Masters in the East did give their students words and icons for meditation but, as soon as the student displayed any attachment to them, they were changed. Can one word be more powerful in the energy of the hologram than another; can one icon be more significant than another? The answer is yes, but only to the individual. Balance is.

In choosing the breath as the focus of attention in meditation, the student eventually realizes that he or she is the energy of The One, that he or she is the very center.

There is no paradigm problem for the mind to solve when your attention of focused on your breath. It may attempt to present thoughts in a problematic way, and these thoughts may include the fact that you are focusing your attention on your breath, but breathing is an automatic process that requires no conscious thought. You are simply placing your attention on this automatic, internal process.

Proper meditation follows the same principles that we have been discussing all along. In our practice of Integration in consensus reality, when an experience is presented with separation, limitation, or meaning, we recognize it for what it is and return to Balance. So, in our practice of mediation, when a thought arises with separation, limitation, or meaning, we apply the same method. We acknowledge the thought for what it is. It is a projection of the mind. Then, we gently return it to its source and merge with it, and return our attention to our breath. As we do this, we recognize that place beyond thought where awareness originates, we give attention to the Question. This is not holding a thought; it is recognizing the place beyond thought by briefly giving attention to the Question and continuing the motion back to Balance. Do not hold the Question or it becomes involved in the process. Do not say to yourself: Where did that thought come from? Simply recognize the Question, lightly brush your thoughts over it, and return your attention to your breath. And remember: *The ability to focus attention is the most powerful ability of the human spirit.*

It is not necessary to experience anything. The fact that you have chosen to move your attention from the process of the paradigm, lightly brush your thoughts over the Question, and return your attention to your breath is all that is necessary.

The technique is simple, requires no special training, and can be adapted to meet your physical requirements. Secure a quiet place with comfortable surroundings. You will eventually be able to remain in Balance in a burning building, but it's best not to start there. If there are other individuals around, have them agree to allow you time without interruption. If you are alone, disconnect the phone. Sit in a comfortable position, feet uncrossed and hands in your lap. Do not lie down. If you lie down, your mind interprets this as a prelude to sleep. You are not going to sleep. Keep your back straight and roll your head until you find a comfortable position. When you have accomplished this, take a deep breath, exhale slowly and begin breathing normally. You may close your eyes.

Remain alert, and begin to give your attention to each breath. Do not attempt to control your breathing. Just become aware of it, and place your attention on it. It is not necessary to practice any particular method of breathing but, if you have a favorite, use it. Just do what comes naturally to you. Breathing from the chest is not natural breathing and indicates stress. You will know you are breathing naturally when your stomach expands and contracts with each breath. This is natural breathing.

As you focus your attention on your breath, begin to become fully aware of each breath. Begin to involve all the senses you use in consensus reality in your focus of attention. Using your senses, feel the breath enter your nostrils and go down your throat. Feel your body move in harmony with your breathing. Hear your breath as it enters and leaves. Do not force yourself to become aware in this manner, rather, allow your awareness to expand and include all your senses.

If you can, picture your breath filling your lungs. Smell your breath. You may not have been aware of it, but you can actually taste your breath. Expand your awareness and use as many of your senses as you can to focus your attention on your breath.

You are now practicing the discipline of attention, choosing to focus your attention on your breath. You are involving the physical senses that your mind normally uses in presenting you with your movie of reality. This focus of attention soon becomes a single, effortless attentiveness.

Your mind, for a time, will cooperate with this new program, even though it does not fit into your current paradigm. At first, you will find it very easy to give your full attention to your breath. But then, your mind will present you with another thought such as: Am I really comfortable, should I be sitting straighter? Or: Did I disconnect the phone?

It is natural for your mind to attempt to interpret meditation as an experience. It thinks of meditation as an experience and continues to operate within its paradigm. Meditation is not an experience, yet it is. Remember, meditation is the place of Balance between limited experience and full awareness, and Balance includes motion. Therefore, there will always be motion. And you are not giving attention to sensory information normally available in consensus reality. Your mind will try to compensate for this by providing you with sensory information recorded in memory.

Do not be discouraged, it is only the motion you are experiencing. Do not take the thought into your attention. Recognize that thought for what it is. It's a projection of your mind on your conscious view screen. It is your problem solving paradigm attempting to keep awareness behind experience. Acknowledge the thought by gently brushing your attention over it, then gently return it to its source and merge with it. Do not cast it away or tell yourself that the thought was an interruption of your meditation. The thought was a part of your meditation, and it caused motion. It came from your mind. It is your creation. Do not separate yourself from it. You know that all experience is a projection of your mind, but you also know that all that is, is of The One. You know that for experience to be, the illusion of separation must remain. Do not force it away. Just return it gently to its source and merge with it.

As you return your attention to your breath, allow your attention to brush gently over the Question. Do not ask the Question in your mind or voice the Question in your thoughts. Gently and easily brush your attention over the *awareness beyond thought that is the Question* and return your attention once again to your breath. As you did not take the thought of the presentation of your mind by giving your attention to it, do not take the thought of the Question. This is a gentle, easy, almost effortless task that, although it has been presented in a series of steps, becomes one easy movement of attention, a motion of attention, a Balance. It results in a brief awareness of the place behind the activity of your paradigm where awareness lies. But you do not want to grasp awareness, that would not be putting your foot down. Return to the center, to your chosen focus of attention.

In time, your thoughts will automatically follow your attention. This is the movement of attention in Balance. Remember, Balance is not a static state, but a state of subtle movement between experience and awareness.

Your mind may say: Aw nuts, I'm sorry I did that. Acknowledge that thought by gently brushing your attention over it, and gently return it to its source, to your mind. Allow the Question to pass through your attention and gently return your attention to your breath.

Your mind may say: Did someone just drive up? (separation.) Acknowledge the thought, gently return it to its source and merge with it. Each time you merge with a thought, allow your attention to pass gently over the Question and return your attention to your breath.

Your mind may say: How long has it been? (limitation.) Acknowledge the thought and gently return it to its source. Each time you merge with a thought, allow your attention to pass gently over the Question and return your attention to your breath.

Still attempting to interpret meditation as an experience, your mind might say: It would probably be easier if we focused on something more interesting than breathing like, I know, The One. (meaning.) Acknowledge the thought, gently return it to its source, and merge with it. Each time you merge with a thought, allow your attention to pass gently over the Question and return your attention to your breath.

Thoughts will continue to rise from your mind as your motion of attention flows. Acknowledge each thought, and gently return it to its source. Each time you merge with a thought, continue the motion from the experience of the thought, through awareness of the Question, and back again to your chosen focus of attention.

Even in the very early stages of this practice you become aware of the vast ocean of awareness just behind the activity of your mind. You become aware of Mind. Most individuals become aware of it just by performing the question and answer routine you did earlier. There may be a tendency to immerse in this awareness, to flow into it and go with it. Do not do it. Immersion in awareness is a state of imbalance just as immersion in experience is a state of imbalance. Return each time to the center, to your chosen focus of attention. You have chosen to focus your attention on your breathing. Your continual affirmation of this choice—by acknowledging each rising thought, gently returning it to its source, and merging with it—is like taking a step. Continuing the motion of your attention confirms your freedom of choice and strengthens your ability to focus your attention. By lightly brushing your attention over the Question as you make the transition, you are moving from experience, through awareness, and back again to your breath. This discipline results in Balance in motion. The purpose of meditation is not immersion in awareness. The purpose of meditation is

Balance.

Continue the practice while your mind continues to run programs and present them to you. It is natural for your mind to do this. Do not try to still your mind. It is *the continual flow of attention* that is the discipline of meditation. It is your moment of *attention to the Question,* as you continue your motion, that brings you Balance. This is very important. If you cast a thought aside, feel badly about it, or criticize yourself for it, you have created separation. Each rising thought is a part of your meditation. They are not interruptions of your meditation. The same is true of your experience of awareness. Whenever your attention drifts, either to experience or awareness, acknowledge each thought, gently return it to its source and merge with it. Allow your attention to brush over the Question and focus once again on your breath.

As you continue the practice of meditation, your mind gradually begins to present you with programs that have been drawn from deeper and deeper in memory. It does this because you are not giving attention to the surface ones, and your mind's job is to provide experience.

As your mind extracts experience from your holographic memory, it must follow your Path. But it must follow it only if you remain in Balance. The moment you take a thought, be it experience or awareness, you are creating your Path rather than following it. If this should happen, simply acknowledge it for what it is, gently return it to its source, and return your attention to your breath. Do not take the thought of taking a thought.

As you travel your Path, you may recall faces, voices, or entire movies from the past that include all the emotion they carried when they "happened." Great! Recognize each for what it is and gently return it to its source and merge with it. Each time you merge with a thought, allow your attention to pass gently over the Question and return your attention to your breath.

Your mind is beginning to reach for something deeper in your movie of reality, something that will take you out of your meditative state and give you some experience. In tracing your memory back, your mind follows the same holographic map it created in the development of your paradigm. You are experiencing your Path. Your mind follows the same Path that it used in creating this movie of reality, only this time the Path is in reverse. You are on the way out of movie by the same route that you arrived.

Your mind will present the "little" things first, but it is not possible for you to determine what your mind thinks are "little" things. Remember, your Path is holographic. For some, the first things may be relationships, family, jobs, or hobbies. They may be followed by beliefs, fears, hopes, and dreams. For another, the very god of their life may surface immediately, with masters, teachers, and promises of guidance or enlightenment. These are landmarks along your Path. Treat them with the same discipline.

Recall, once again, the holographic nature of these landmarks. Know that the only thing you can do is trust in the fact that your mind knows your Path. It alone created the matrix of thought that presents your movie of reality to you. It will travel that matrix in exactly the proper order on its journey back. You should not allow yourself to interpret your Path. You should not assign separation, limitation or meaning to it. You should take each and every presentation of your mind as it comes, and apply the rule. If it contains separation, limitation or meaning, recognize it for what it is, gently return it to its source, and merge with it. Each time you merge with a thought, allow your attention to pass gently over the Question and return your attention to your breath.

When your mind has reached far into memory for presentations of your Path, you will begin to enter the transpersonal realm of energy and awareness. This awareness arises in the same manner that the thoughts of your mind arise, and it appears as if from another source because it is still interpreted by your mind. You are now becoming fully aware of Mind.

Should you enter fully into awareness and become immersed in it, you have *just passed through Balance*. And it is the point where most children, learning to walk and having taken that first step, will fall. When you pass through the presentations of your mind and into Mind, you have just taken your first great step. You have left the world of consensus reality and entered the realm of awareness. Now is the time to remember to put your foot down and return to Balance. You will go there again, and when you have learned to enter and return with just a thought, you are ready to go deeper. Our meditation is not the place from which to enter Mind. Our meditation is the discipline of attention.

Again, Balance is a state *between* experience and awareness. It is neither experience or awareness, yet it is both. If it happens that Mind is predominant in your mediation, you have drifted to the other side of Balance and you must apply the same discipline to its presentations. Recognize them for what they are; they are a presentation of Mind that came from within. Now, gently return them to their source and merge with them. Each time you merge with a thought, allow your attention to pass gently over the Question and return your attention to your breath.

Above all, create no expectations for meditation. Enter meditation only with the purpose of practicing Balance. Treat each presentation of Mind in the same manner that you have treated the presentations of your mind. Recognize them for what they are, gently return them to their source, and merge with them. Each presentation of Mind will be interpreted by your mind, and the presentations of your mind may begin again. You are in motion and, when you are able to return your attention quickly and easily to your breath, in Balance.

Some teach that meditation is "stilling the mind." Our meditation is not. Meditation is a discipline, and the discipline should continue as long as Balance is not present. Balance is in motion, therefore, meditation is a constant practice. Meditation is balancing the activity of the mind and Mind. When the mind is still and inactive in the background, as Mind has been, you are not in Balance. I said you should have no goal in meditation, and this is true, but proper meditation brings Balance. You should recognize that Balance is achieved when both your mind and Mind respond equally to attention. For this reason, do not enter meditation expecting to still the mind and become aware of Mind. When you do, you will quiet your mind and become immersed in Mind. This is not Balance.

Balance is the state in which both the mind and Mind are fully active. We have mentioned this, but because this is true, it is also a state in which both may *appear fully inactive*. This state is beyond description, but it is neither void of experience or empty of awareness. It is not possible to say when you have achieved this state; there are no words in our paradigm to describe it. But it is possible to say when you have not. When either your mind or Mind provide overwhelming presentations in your awareness—presentations that do not respond to your discipline of attention during meditation—you are not in Balance. When in Balance, you are able to move freely into experience or awareness and return with just a thought, just a focus of attention.

You are to expect nothing to happen during your meditation. The benefit of your practice of pushups does not happen while you are doing the pushups. The pushup is a discipline. The benefit of pushups arises while you are going about your daily activities. The benefit of your meditation surfaces in the same manner. It integrates itself into your consensus movie. You find it easier to recall memories. Your ability at cognitive thought—the thoughtful consideration of other possibilities, increases as your awareness expands. It becomes easier for you to give attention to a chosen task, and easier to remain aware of the nature of reality while performing it. Your body chemistry changes, so you have more energy and experience less stress. All these are natural results of meditation, but the greatest result is your ability to choose and maintain where your attention will be focused. This results in an increased ability to maintain Balance in your consensus movie. You will find this same Balance arising as you focus your attention on all the aspects of your movie of reality. And eventually, you will be able to enter awareness with just a thought.

Stilling the mind and entering into awareness is a tremendous experience—but it is not meditation. This is one of the aspects of meditation that is most lacking in the Western teachings. When Eastern students report their expanding awareness, their experience of entering the transpersonal realm, to their Masters, they are instructed again in the discipline of meditation. Immersion in awareness in an experience. There is no experience in meditation, there is only the motion between experience and awareness. There is only Balance.

End of lesson.

How long should you meditate? Fifteen to twenty minutes, twice a day is good. But if you become frustrated, do it for 10 minutes or less and do it more often. Be flexible. Work with your mind. If you were to do 100 pushups today for the first time in your life, you would not want to do any tomorrow. Three would be better than one, but one would be better than none. For now, though, let 20 minutes, twice a day be the maximum amount of meditation.

Closing the eyes may cause your mind to interpret the activity as a prelude to sleep. This sometimes causes drowsiness. You may try meditation with the eyes open, but we are sight—and sound—oriented in our realities. With the eyes open, the visual information in our meditation area may become predominate and we find it difficult to hold our attention on our breath. It's easy to reduce the sound level, but there is usually a host of information available to the eyes. Dimming the lights and focusing on a candle may help but this, too, can cause drowsiness.

Gansfield glasses work well in these cases. They supply the eyes with a soft, diffused light that creates a sensory overload of visual information and allows us to keep our eyes open during meditation. Because the mind cannot extract any specific information from it, it soon disregards it.

Gansfield glasses can be made easily. Cut a ping-pong ball in half and trim the halves to fit over your eyes with a light elastic band. A snug but comfortable fit will reduce the visual input to a clear white haze. Keep your eyes open while wearing them and, after a while, you will not even know if your eyes are open or closed. This may cause your mind to compensate for the lack of visual information by creating more visual movies to arise in your mind, but you can treat them as you would any projection of your mind. Recognize them, and gently return them to their source.

If you are unable to find a quiet place for meditation, try a white noise tape. Like the diffused light from the Gansfield glasses, white noise contains so much audio information so as to cause the mind to disregard it all. You can purchase white-noise tapes, or you can make one yourself. Tune a television to an empty channel, or disconnect the cable. The "hash" you hear is close enough to true white noise to accomplish the same goal. Make a tape of the noise long enough to cover your time in meditation. Put headphones on and turn the volume up enough so that the objectionable noise is drowned out. As with the Gansfield glasses, your mind may begin to place sounds in the white noise. You may hear voices, music, or a beat. Treat it as you would any projection of your mind. Recognize it for what it is, gently return it to its source, and merge with it.

You should not become dependent on these aids. They will help at first, but you should always set aside a time of unassisted mediation, and you should eventually eliminate them all.

There is no such thing as a good or a bad meditation. You could not have spent all that time flowing easily between experience and awareness without practice, and this includes all the "bad" meditations you have had. There may be times when the mind is very active and other times when Mind explodes in awareness. Review this fact after every meditation. Do not set a goal in your meditation, thinking that you will soon reach a "level" where you can go for an entire meditation without a single thought while you remain focused on your breath. Going without a single thought is not the direction you wish to go. Your discipline is not to still the mind, but to expand awareness beyond the limits of your paradigm by learning to move freely from experience to awareness. Simply do it, and accept whatever your mind or Mind has to offer each and every time. There are those who have continual thoughts throughout each and every meditation, yet their practice is just as effective as those who have only a few. The benefits of meditation come from the act of performing it, not from an evaluation of it.

The practice of meditation increases your Balance. It gives you practice in the process of recognizing, merging, and returning. The process of recognizing the source of your experience or your awareness, merging with it, and returning to your center is Balance in motion. It is a continual flow of attention between limited experience and full awareness. It produces a kind of stillness, yet in the stillness there is motion.

There is a commonly held belief that, at some time during meditation, you will be visited by a teacher or Master. This is an expectation and a limitation. If you believe this, if you expect this, it will happen. But it is a projection of your mind. No Master anywhere will interrupt your discipline of meditation. Make sure you understand this. Your freedom of choice is held in the highest regards by those who teach. They respond only to a question held in the Heart, and the place of the Heart is not in experience, it is in Balance. Masters will not, under any circumstances, interrupt your discipline of meditation. They know what is happening as a result of your practice and honor the fact that you have chosen to perform it. You may have asked those around you to allow you time alone, unplugged the phone, and reduced the noise in order to gain the conditions you require to focus your attention. Do you think a Master would not honor this choice? Again, meditation is a discipline. Knowledge of the process, and the Integration of this Knowledge, are the only tools you require. Keep it as such.

You have been given a basic meditation, but there are many excellent meditation techniques. You can read books, attend groups, or even get someone to coach you if your mind will respond. Working with the mind is always a good practice, but you should always check out what you are becoming involved in and apply your understanding of separation, limitation, and meaning.

Again, some groups focus their attention in an effort to "get something," and some even share what they have "gotten" after each session. This practice is not the discipline of meditation that brings Balance. It is an excellent method of allowing alternate movies to run in the mind, and the mind loves to run movies, so the mind is sure to participate. This is not to say that the process is "bad." It is simply not the discipline you require.

Other groups meditate on something such as world peace or an end to hunger. This is visualization rather than meditation. It is focusing attention, but it includes separation, limitation, and meaning—all of which are self generated. It is the focus of attention on the movie of reality in an attempt to change the movie. Again, there is nothing "wrong" with the practice, but it will not develop in you the power of attention you require to continue on your Path. When you look for guidance or check out a group, remain aware of the principles of separation, limitation, and meaning—the presentation of Maya.

We have compared the mind—and Mind—to the muscles of our body. When we exercise just one muscle or group of muscles of our body, giving little attention to the rest, a state of imbalance results. Likewise, when we exercise our attention on the function of the mind, giving little attention to the awareness of Mind, a state of imbalance exists. But what we must know is that while we are in a state of conscious awareness, we cannot "not" give attention. When we think that we have too little time to seek Balance—too little time to give attention to the awareness that is Mind, we are giving attention to consensus reality. In doing so, we are developing the paradigm that causes our imbalance. It is a simple choice of attention, and each of us must make that choice every waking moment of our life. 11/11/98 ·

Karma

Student: Do I have any Karma as a result of my past lives?
Master: The only Karma you have is the Karma you choose to keep.

We will discuss the full process of physical death later. I present it now only in the context of Karma and judgment.

Karma is the law of cause and effect. In this physical world, when you throw a rock into the air and it comes down on your head, you experience the law of cause and effect. The lump on your head is a result of your choice to throw the rock in such a manner that it would fall on your head. The lump is also a result of your choice not to get out of the way once the rock was thrown. There is a law of gravity in effect in this physical movie of reality, one agreed upon by most of the actors. But there is no law requiring you to stand in one place while the rock returns to earth.

The same is true of Karma. What we have done in past movies, as well as what we are doing now, is causing energy vibrations to occur in the hologram. These vibrations are similar to the Newtonian Laws, one of which is the law of gravity. They cause a specific flow of energy and, like the rock in the air, that energy returns to its creator.

All that we think, say, or do is the equivalent of throwing a rock into the air. It all returns to its creator. What we project into the hologram is what returns to us. What we plant is what we will reap. *If we choose to reap.*

You could have simply stepped out from under the falling rock. You can just as easily step out from under Karma. No one anywhere is requiring you to stay in one place while the law of Karma returns. No god is judging you, paying you back for past deeds, or rewarding you for your goodness. Even when you plant a fine garden, it is up to you to make the choice to harvest it.

Why, then, do we harvest at all?

It is because of our paradigm. Remember, our paradigm remains with us in this movie as well as in the next. As you have learned, these programs do not disappear at the moment of physical death. They reside in the energy of our whole being—in our mind. When the physical body passes away, they arise with a knowing similar to the knowing you experienced when the movie in the cinema ended and you got up to leave. When the lights came back on, you were launched out of your cinema experience and thrust back into the reality of the movie of "everyday life." That movie of everyday life was filtered out of your awareness and eliminated from your experience while the movie screen and the cinema was alive with sensory information. The everyday life reality came rushing back when the cinema experience, with all its sensory information, ended. Likewise, the awareness of the transpersonal realm is filtered out of your consciousness while you are in your consensus movie. It arises again when the sensory information you have been receiving is no longer available, when your movie of reality ends.

This happens to all who experience a physical death. We enter our new movie with all the programs, patterns, and tendencies we have accumulated during your most recent physical experience. Our mind immediately begins to filter, refine, and present to our view screen of awareness an experience that fits our paradigm and meets our expectations.

Our mind and Mind are One but, without Balance, we are not aware of this fact during our movie of consensus reality. We are aware only of what our mind has been presenting us. When our physical experience ends, for a brief instant, Mind emerges with all its intrinsic awareness. It appears as a luminosity without comparison, without form, without depth—and brighter than anything in our recent physical experience. It appears as our very nature. It is Mind. It is The One in Balance. It has always been there, just behind the paradigm of our mind.

In the next moment, our mind begins to interpret what is happening as an experience. It relates it to its most recent paradigm. In Balance in The One, all is available. But our mind now begins its task of presenting us with another experience.

Remember, this is a description of the experience of passing from this movie of reality to the next without Balance. Without Balance, you may have been raised to believe in a judgment followed by a heaven or hell after death. Without Balance, your mind extracts this experience from the presentation of Mind, filters and refines it through your paradigm, and presents it to you as part of your next movie. Your mind does this in exactly the same manner in which it's presenting you with your current experience.

It appears out there, it is limited, and it contains meaning. While Mind is presenting the reflection of your primordial self, without Knowledge, Integration, and Balance, you have no way to know it. Your mind begins to interpret your previous performance, and it appears as judgment.

Judgment, and the resulting Karma, are a product of our paradigm. We hold beliefs and expectations in place individually as well as through the laws of The Magic of Agreeing. The expectation of every belief system holds the potential for that experience Therefor, every heaven, every hell, every believing group waiting for a second coming, every purgatory, every happy hunting ground, every experience imaginable is there. They are our own creation; they are projections of our beliefs and expectations. All that is necessary in order to access any one of them is the building of a paradigm, a matrix of limiting thought shrouded in belief and expectation—and an end to this movie of consensus reality.

This happens at the moment of physical death. Without Balance, we find ourselves looking through the limiting paradigm of past experience and are confronted with the same sense of good or bad, right or wrong that helped us play our parts. Even though we are no longer involved in consensus reality, our mind still holds the programs of its continual evaluation and how we were playing our part.

We are constantly comparing ourselves to others, and to our interpretation of the script. We consider agreed upon social values—the system of right and wrong by which actors present themselves—and make adjustments daily. We are taught the rules of judgment and then teach them to our children. If we belong to a religious group, we accept its interpretation of right and wrong and make a constant effort to apply those principles to our life. Finding a place for our self and a meaning for our life is a constant effort. It becomes a program that runs on automatic. The result of this effort is what is called Ego.

Ego is a product of the mind. It is the result of the continual self-judgment of the mind. It's the attempt by the mind to fit us into the movie with the other actors.

Ego is not what we are, but we soon begin to view ourselves in the light of this continual self-judgment. Ego is not who we think we are. Who we think we are does not often arise as we act our part in the movie of life. Ego is not who the other actors think we are. The other actors are interpreting *our* performance by comparing it to *their* paradigms. Ego is what we think the other actors think we are. As we perform, we evaluate the other actors performance according to our paradigm, and we adjust our part according to how we think they think we should act.

Ego develops different programs for the different scenes and different actors in our movie. We may have a "Beer With the Boys" program, a "Talk With the Girls" program, an "At Work" program, an "In Church" program, and a "With Those Who Do Not Understand Our Program" program. Once they have been established, our mind switches these programs with every change of experience, running the proper program for each. It switches so quickly and easily that we hardly noticed it's happening. It is Ego's attempt to make us fit into the script. Ego is continually judging and adjusting our paradigm so that we can act the way we think other actors think we should act for each and every scene.

Ego is all happening in our mind. There is no need for Ego if there is no separation. There is no need for Ego if there is no limitation. There is no need for Ego if there is no meaning. The Ego program is necessary only in the illusion. But the Ego program is an *emotional* program designed for the movie of physical reality. It is a *recent* program that has been evolving since the time we set foot on stage. It is a *repeated* program that we run many, many times with each scene in our movie of reality. And now, as we are presented with the fullness of Mind and the presence of our very self, our mind is still running our Ego program. If we do not recognize what is taking place—if we are not in Balance— we find ourselves in judgment. We should know that *all judgment is, without fail, the self-judgment of Ego.*

The judgment may be accompanied by a saint, a spirit, a loved one, or a light. When our Ego asks the question, what have you done with your life?, it comes from our mind. It is not from out there. We know, at that moment, it is *self-judgment.*

We have many accounts of individuals who have had a near-death experience, or NDE. These are individuals who have experienced the process of physical death and returned to tell about it. There are accounts of NDE's from people around the world. Different cultures have accepted different beliefs yet, almost without exception, each report of judgment fits perfectly into the belief of the reporting individual. Each reporter sees exactly what fits into his or her belief and reality structure. And each report of judgment indicates that it *did not* come from the external presentation. The presentation is projecting feelings of total forgiveness and complete Love and understanding.

At death, the mind presents our entire movie experience in brilliant detail and in a moment's time. The presentation is holographic, and we have the ability to perceive it holographically. We recall the relationship between the things we have done and their consequences. Even more, we recall the things that we could have done differently according to our belief and reality structure, or the things we could have done and did not do. All this is presented in the context of our paradigm.

Our belief system, if we have one, surfaces with astounding emotion. We have developed expectations that our mind now meets. We cannot have expectations without having limitations. Our mind is still filtering, refining, and projecting the illusion of separation, limitation, and meaning.

Know now, we are not judged by God. We have always had the freedom to choose how we will interpret our part in the movie, and that freedom is without judgment. We know that it took each and every actor to make the illusion seem real. Yet, even while in the midst of the illusion, we have often *judged the other actors according to our programs* of good and bad, right and wrong. We are now presented the judgment of our mind in response to its Ego program, and it is presented in *exactly the way we have judged others*. We are experiencing the programs of our paradigm returning. But it took every actor playing every part to produce the movie of life. All the actors agreed on the script. Judgment cannot be external.

All that is, is of The One. All potential resides there, including all experience as well as full awareness. There is not one part in this movie of reality that is not a potential held in The One. What we call good or bad is a comparison of these possibilities in our movie, and they are subjective. The concept of good and bad is a result of our paradigm, and nothing more. When we act our part in the movie, and hold other actors in judgment, we are creating the programs by which the Ego in our mind judges us. Each and every time we assess the performance of the other actors and compare *their* interpretation of the script to *our* paradigm, we are adding to the program by which Ego presents judgment to us.

What does stand out in detail in the NDE is the complete Love and acceptance of Mind, in whatever form the mind interprets it. Our self-judgment is presented in the Light of complete understanding and total Love. Because we are in the presence of Mind, *every moment* of our life is viewed in *total Love*. We come to know, in that moment, that Love is the very foundation of The One. Holographic Knowledge of the total absence of separation, limitation or meaning is presented in the radiance of Mind. We understand, in an instant, that the only things worth accomplishing in this movie of consensus reality must have their foundation in this Love. Anything else is simply of no value outside the limitations of our movie of reality.

We should understand now that we are not in this movie of reality alone. As we have learned, each and every actor is just as important as the next. It does not matter if we think they have a good part or a bad part. All that is, is of The One.

Modern masters often ask their students: Who is the most important actor in the New Testament? Most often, the students say it was Jesus. What would the life of Jesus have amounted to without Judas? Without Pilot? Without the soldiers that nailed Him to the cross? Would we have a church? Would anyone have written about Him? It took every actor to allow The Lord Jesus to perform His part. There was not one actor with a more important part than another, and *Jesus knew it*. Loving your neighbor as yourself requires Integration of the Knowledge that you and your neighbor, every actor playing every part, are One. Loving your neighbor as yourself requires Balance. Good and evil are two sides of the same coin, and the only Balance is in the center. Any variation either way is a product of the mind.

Without Knowledge and Integration, our mind has no program available to present us with the fact that it took each and every actor playing each and every part to produce our movie of reality. The fact that there is no intrinsic good or bad, right or wrong in the movie is filtered and refined by our paradigm. We simply do not get the information. Our mind compares how we played our part according to its paradigm of good and bad, right and wrong. It then presents us with an illusion that meets our expectations of reward or punishment. Again, all judgment, without exception, is the self-judgment of Ego.

When we seek Knowledge and Integration into our daily life, we do not judge. We live a life knowing that all that is, is of The One. We hold Balance. We know the source of separation, limitation, and meaning.

Experience in this movie of reality is filled with emotion. Emotional love and hate are the two extremes of this spectrum. Emotional love and hate are reflections of good and bad. Good and bad are interpretations of experience made by the mind. The whole of our sensory experience is a constant struggle between the two.

Perfect Love, the Love of Mind, is in the center—in Balance. Perfect Love is not without emotion. Perfect Love is *freedom from emotion*. This freedom comes only from the Integration of Knowledge into our daily lives; freedom comes only from Balance. When we do not maintain Balance, we are overwhelmed by the emotions that our mind attaches to the illusion and are pulled into experience. When in Balance, we experience the emotions while remaining aware of their source. This is freedom from emotion.

The powerful program of self-judgment should be resolved now, here in our movie of consensus reality. We should Integrate the Knowledge of how our mind develops this program into every aspect of our life, every scene in our movie. We eliminate Karma and self-judgment by holding everyone in the Light of Balance in The One, knowing that they are a part of our movie of reality. When in Balance, we refuse to judge others and refuse to judge ourselves. We *know* that all is in Balance. Again, Knowledge, Integration, and Balance are the key—and attention is the driving force.

Reincarnation

Student: Is reincarnation a fact? Have people here lived past lives?
Master: Yes. Many here have lived in experience before.
Student: Is it a part of some plan so that we can learn and grow?
Master: A plan?
Student: Yes, a plan so we can learn that we don't have to come back.
Master: No one must come back. Many choose to, but that is their choice.
Student: Then why come back?
Master: It is a choice, but many make the choice not knowing. Most do not leave this experience with the Knowledge they require in order to return to The One.
Student: Why would anyone choose to come here in the first place?
Master: Reason is not required for a choice to be made.
Student: But once we make the choice, we're stuck with it?
Master: No one is stuck anywhere. You are free to leave now. You are also free to have any life you wish, any illusion you wish, in any time you wish. This includes all the past lives you speak of. They are all there, in The One.

It is estimated by some that nearly two thirds of the population of the world believes in reincarnation. It is not necessary to believe in it; it is a fact of our movie of reality. But our movie is a product of our mind. It is a presentation that limits our awareness so we can have experience. And, as we have learned, even that experience is limited.

Reality is holographic, it is not separate from The One. It is only the illusion of Maya that makes it appear so in our mind. In a holographic reality, all experience is available, even the experience of reincarnation.

The question is, then, does experience have to meet the qualifications we have placed upon it, the qualifications we have formulated *within a limited experience,* to be valid? One of the reasons many do not accept reincarnation as a fact is that, throughout the world, many individuals claim to have had the same experience, to have been the same person in a "past life." From our limited view of experience, this is not possible. But from a holographic viewpoint, it is not only possible, but quite likely. This is a stretch of the imagination for the logic of consensus reality, so let's take a closer look at it from a holographic point of view.

Remember, holographic reality is a world of energy, not matter. Holographic energy is interconnected and has no location in relation to the world of matter. This means that the energy that is the tip of your right index finger is one with the energy that is a star at the edge of the universe. Holographic energy, because it has no location, is not limited by time or distance. This means that the energy that is the tip of your right index finger is, from a holographic standpoint, in the same "place" and "time" as a star at the edge of the universe. Remember, though, place and time are terms that do not apply to holographic reality. We use them only so we can make a relationship between holographic reality and our limited physical world.

Holographic energy is unlimited in potential. Because of this, we say holographic energy can become anything. This statement is made from our perspective in a limited reality. From a holographic perspective, energy is everything. This means that the energy that is the tip of your right index finger is, from a holographic standpoint, a star at the edge of the universe.

Let's look at the question again: Does an experience have to meet the qualifications we have placed upon it, qualifications we have formulated *within a limited experience,* to be valid?

The answer is, it does not. Any experience we have is valid, and has its foundation in holographic energy as potential. The experience you are having right now is a possibility of holographic energy that you are involved in through your focus of attention and your observation. When you pause for a moment and imagine yourself walking out the door and reclining on the grass, you have another experience. It appears in your mind as something you only thought about, but did not do. However, it is as real and valid an experience as what you are doing right now. It required your attention and your observation. It appeared in the energy of your mind and, because energy is holographic, appeared throughout the holographic world in energy form just as if you had "really" done it. It makes no difference, from a holographic standpoint, whether you performed the act in consensus reality, or just imagined it. In both cases, you fulfilled the requirements of creation. You placed your attention on a potential of holographic energy, produced the elements of Maya, and had an experience. Likewise, when you place your attention on reincarnation, you produce the elements of Maya and have an experience.

Masters often perceive their students as energy rather than limited physical beings. This allows their interaction to become more intimate.

My Master asked: Are you writing a book?

I responded: Well, no, but I am thinking about it.

My Master replied: Ah! Forgive me, you are *thinking* about writing a book.

This kind of interaction goes on often between Masters and their students. In the instance just mentioned, my Master perceived the energy of my mind, and the crystallized future beyond my awareness. When she asked the question, I had no intention of writing a book. I was just "going over my notes." At least that's all my paradigm allowed me to experience at the time. My Master, however, was aware of the crystallized future in the energy of my mind.

But the energy of attention is not divided into thoughts or, from our perspective, actions. When the attention is focused, the action is accomplished. The more focused our attention, the more thought we give it, the more vivid the vibration of the energy of that thought. This energy exists in our mind, and our mind is energy. It is we, with our limited perception of "reality," who have determined that a thought is not a thing until it is as limited as we are, until it exists in a form that our physical senses can perceive.

We have also limited our understanding of experience by thinking that it is an individual thing. From a holographic standpoint, all experience exists as potential. While I was sitting with my Master, the focus of attention I had given to my notes was still vibrating in the energy of my mind. But in the hologram, energy is not localized. It exists as the same potential, the same vibration of energy, throughout The One. It was my focus of attention that illuminated that energy for me. It was my Master's focus of attention on me that illuminated it for her. But the energy, the potential for the book, always has been, is, and always will be available to anyone who gives it their attention.

The experience you are having *now* always existed and will always be. Nor is it limited to *your* mind. Any mind, in any "time," that is focused as yours is now is vibrating in harmony with yours. You are not separate from them, and a Master sees their vibrations, their attention, in harmony with yours. They are having the same experience you are having now, and they are having it throughout time and space as we know it.

It is possible for us to perceive these same vibrations. This may happen during transpersonal awareness, hypnosis, or even in a dream. But when it happens to us, our mind attempts to fit the information into our limited understanding of reality. We see ourselves as another person, perhaps in a "past" life.

It is also possible to create the conditions, in our mind, for a "past life" experience. All we have to do is place our attention on it. Again, it is as real and valid an experience as what we are experiencing right now. Whether a past life really happened or not, from our interpretation of reality, means nothing in the holographic potential of The One. If it is a possibility, it is of The One. If it is not of The One, it cannot even become a thought.

As you can see, giving attention to reincarnation—and assigning meaning to it—is very limiting. It allows your mind to access the holographic potential of The One and create an experience that fits your paradigm. This is exactly what you have done in creating your movie of reality. Rather than spending time, and the precious energy of attention, dwelling on reincarnation, focus your attention on Balance in The One. Whenever your perception of reality contains the essence of Maya, recognize it for what it is, and gently return your thoughts to the source, as in meditation.

Yes, reincarnation is a reality—another limited reality of our creation. But, with Balance, we have access to *all experience* throughout time and space. With Balance, the hologram of experience and awareness is ours to explore without limit.

The Script

Student: I know we have a limited perspective of the world around us. Do children have a broader perspective?

Master: Have you not heard the Masters tell you to become like little children? Very small children are aware of much more than most adults. A child must learn to respond to the illusion around them. This takes much time, and many lessons.

We have come a long way in developing an understanding of ourselves and our relationship to The One. We know how our mind creates and presents reality to us. We are beginning to realize that we are unlimited, creative spirit. Methods of Integrating our Knowledge into our movie of reality gives us an active role in bringing our Path alive. As we continue to practice Integration, information from the far reaches of our mind and Mind naturally becomes available to us. The process of Integration and meditation expands our awareness and our conscious access to the information it contains.

We will now take a step back and look again at how we arrived here in consensus reality. This may seem redundant, but developing different methods of understanding the process expands our awareness even further, and allows us more Balance.

We have learned that our mind holds information from our crystallized future, and that this information appears in our movie on our conscious view screen in response to sensory information. This is the process of our mind "writing the script" for our movie as we experience it. We know that through the practice of Knowledge and Integration, we gain conscious control over our movie of reality. But how far into the future does the mind project? How much of our movie is now in our mind?

When we arrived on stage, the script was in our hand.

Now, I know that you may be ready to jump off this wagon right now, so let's discuss the script. Most of us think of a movie in the cinema as a fairly limited event. It is one reel of film with a beginning, a middle, and an end. Once the final production is made, there is no way to change it.

The concept for the movie, while still in the writer's mind, is also limited. We can tell how much by looking on the cutting room floor. But it is still very limited. He has, in his mind, a beginning, middle, and end.

The script that we came on stage with is much more flexible. It is filled with all of the uncut variables of the movie of reality that is to be presented to us throughout our experience. Each variable holds within it the potential for any of the movies that anyone could have. These are held in Mind. Our movie script is unlimited. It is floating in the potential of The One much like the clips of individual frames of movie film were in our holographic experiment.

But, we also arrived on stage with our paradigm. Our paradigm holds all the patterns, programs, and tendencies from all the movies in which we have ever acted. The strongest of these is a result of our most recent movie, but it includes all the scenes of all of our past movies and all their landmarks. So, when we are presented with choices in the script, we are influenced by our paradigm. The process of selecting the individual clips of potential for our current movie of reality began long before we set foot on stage, but the moment we arrived, we began limiting it even more. We began limiting it to sensory information.

Our parents were the first to help us with this. They were our first directors. We began by interacting with them and developing a personality that would result in the feelings we wanted. We then began cutting other possible actions from our movie, and this process still continues in our mind. It is not happening in our brain. It is happening in the energy of our mind. By the time what we call a "thought" surfaces on our conscious view screen, it has already been decided in our mind.

Right now, as you are reading this book, you are experiencing reactions to the concepts within it. You are experiencing what you believe is a "right now" experience. The words are out there, on the pages. The concepts are limited, they are just one man's way of presenting them. And the concepts have a meaning that is coming from you, a meaning that results from your paradigm. You are either accepting, rejecting, or holding the meaning your mind has already assigned to what you are reading for further investigation.

Your mind was aware of every concept in this book the moment you picked it up, and perhaps even before that. Remember, your mind is holographic. The words in this book do not have their reality in what is held in your hand. They are a potential held in The One, and are reflected here in a form that you can relate to with your physical senses. That potential was collapsed out of the energy state of The One and became possibility when I began considering this book. It came into manifestation in consensus reality with its writing, along with all the out takes on my cutting room floor. Yet this potential is one with the hologram, one with Mind. It vibrates there with as much reality as the book you hold in your hands.

And your mind gained access to it when it came within its crystallized future—before you picked it up. Your mind had *already filtered and refined what you have read thus far* through your paradigm. And it is ready to present you with *predetermined reactions* to what you find as you continue to read. These reactions exist now, in the energy that is your mind, and fill your movie when you give your attention to them.

The most important thing to know, though, is that your mind is providing you with all this experience along with the illusion that you are actively participating in it. You are, in your mind, but that activity is withheld from your awareness. Remember, you already have the information; the only problem your mind must solve is how to fit it into your reality, how to filter it through your paradigm. Your mind is where your paradigm lives, and it is holographic. It is not limited by the concept of time you experience in your movie of reality. Your reactions have already been determined in your mind. What you are experiencing is a reflection of your mind and its paradigm on the movie screen of your brain, and the brain is a secondary organ.

The electrical activity in the brain lags behind the activity in the energy field around your body by a scientifically detectable time of nearly half a second. Half a second is, in reality terms, an eternity.

It may sound like you have no choice in your script, but that is not true. It is true, though, that your ability to choose is directly related to the flexibility of your paradigm. Beliefs are programs that are hard set in your paradigm. When information contrary to your beliefs enters your awareness, it has already been filtered and refined to meet your paradigm. This is also true of information that fits right in with your established beliefs. And remember, this happens long before it appears on your conscious view screen. This limits your awareness, your experience, and your freedom of choice.

Again, these are self-imposed limitations. They are a product of your paradigm. When you understand that *no concept can exist without having its potential in The One,* your mind must restructure your paradigm to embrace this Knowledge. You know that all that is, is of The One. Concepts can be different, but they cannot be right or wrong. Right and wrong are interpretations of the mind. Interpretations are a product of your paradigm. And interpretations are presented, by your mind, as a part of your reality experience.

It is now, at the *moment of presentation,* that the interpretation of your mind is presented for your active participation. It is now, when these predetermined reactions are presented on your view screen of awareness, that you have an opportunity to interact with them. At this point, *your unlimited script is in your hands.* Without your intervention, your mind edits your script according to its paradigm, and other possibilities fall to the cutting room floor. It is at the moment of presentation that your mind is asking you if you want to *upgrade your paradigm.* It is now that the *freedom to choose* your reaction becomes a part of your experience, and when you take the time to choose, it is Integrated into your paradigm.

Again, you know that for a concept to exist, it must have its potential in The One. Concepts are, therefore, neither right or wrong. The feelings of right and wrong are a result of your paradigm. Your paradigm is comparing new concepts with those already held in your memory and, when they agree, your mind is saying: Right on. When they disagree, your mind is saying: No way.

Now, recognize what is happening. You are experiencing a presentation of your mind. You *know* this happened long before you had the experience. You *know* you now have an opportunity to recognize the source of your reaction. Now is the time to perform the same discipline that you practiced in meditation. Recognize the reaction for what it is, gently return it to its source, merge with it, and allow your attention to brush over the Question. In doing so, you recognize not only the source of your reaction, but the unlimited potential of The One. You return to Balance. When you are in Balance, consider your reaction and continue your experience. In this case, continue reading; continue your chosen focus of attention. When you do this, you are activating your ability of cognitive thought—the ability to give thoughtful consideration to other possibilities. But you are also taking an active part, a conscious part, in deciding where your script will lead you.

When we rely on our old paradigm, we are cutting and editing a script for the movie of consensus reality and, we are creating a Path of experience. When we continually return to Balance, we are no longer focusing our attention on the movie and are refusing to limit our script. It is now that the Path of experience we traveled into this movie of reality arises before us.

You should apply this practice whenever your mind responds to sensory information with an emotional rejection, and well as when it responds with an emotional acceptance. In both cases, the rising of emotions indicates that you are dealing with your paradigm. And in both cases, gaining Balance and merging with the presentation of the mind is the best course of action. In doing so, you tell your mind that you have reviewed its interpretation of the information and will take it under consideration. You have recognized the source of the presentation, gently returned it to its source and merged with it. Your mind now has no choice but to expand your options and upgrade your paradigm.

We understand that our movie is a projection of our mind, and that our reactions to the scenes of the movie give us an opportunity to choose. Where once the meaning was determined by our mind and all its programming, meaning is now held in Balance. We are no longer held captive by the seemingly absolute interpretations of our mind. We begin to transcend the limitations of the paradigm. We are able to observe the movie and the actors with a new clarity. The interpretation of good and bad, right and wrong once given by our mind is no longer an absolute thing. Our script in the movie becomes more and more flexible.

And this view of the movie of consensus reality is not something new to us. Now, as the Sky Heroes of long ago, we once again participate in our creation with freedom. It's a natural ability that is simply held behind the paradigm of our mind.

Each and every second of each and every day, you are presented with this exact same opportunity. You did not need this book to find it. Your mind, even though it's actively presenting you with a movie of reality, is presenting it as an opportunity for you to come to the knowledge that it is nothing more than a projection of your mind. It is presenting your Path. Mind and your mind are one. All that is, is a reflection of The One. It's only a matter of attention—and Balance.

As an example, perhaps you did not get the promotion or the recognition that you thought you deserved in your work. Your mind knew that would happen when you took the job. Your reaction is a product of your mind. Without Balance, your mind presents its interpretation on your conscious view screen as a defeat and edits your script accordingly. Your mind adds meaning in response to your paradigm. Your reaction is to grasp or push.

But, when you are in Balance, you are free to know that this self-given meaning is but a projection of your mind. You are aware that it is an opportunity for new beginnings, rather than an end to something you give meaning to. Your Path is arising. Your mind will, in time and with practice, stop giving this meaning and respond to your Balance.

Or, you *did* get the promotion and the recognition you thought you deserved. Guess what? Another opportunity. Are you holding Balance, or playing your part according to your script and the paradigm of your mind? Here is your opportunity to look into the camera—with Balance.

Every single event in your life has been an opportunity to gain Balance. Every event yet to come holds that same opportunity. You have the opportunity now. There is only now. Every opportunity is the Path. There is only the Path.

The whole of the potential of The One is on the projector. The light of your attention, without Balance, is selecting those portions of the full potential of The One that relate to your current paradigm, with all its patterns, programs and tendencies. It is editing the script of your movie of reality. The light of your attention, in Balance, is expanding your paradigm, your horizons, your awareness, and your choices in the script.

We have identified our Path, and learned that it is always before us. We are either creating a Path of experience or walking one already created. In doing so, we have discovered that our freedom is now, and always has been, available to us with just a change of attention. No one had told me this before my Master revealed it to me. Has anyone informed you that you are free? Many, in fact, teach us that we are not worthy to become one with The One, or that we require some kind of special rescue effort in order to gain our freedom. That has always sounded like bad news to me. Not many organized religions are going to be pleased about the good news. The fact is, all of the actors in our movie are in holographic Balance, and any teaching that includes separation, limitation, and meaning is founded in illusion. We actors do not have to find a better part in this movie of reality. Balance can be found in the script we hold in our hand.

Worthiness

Student: I've done so much in the past that I feel I have to go through some kind of cleansing or something. You tell me that I'm worthy now, that all are worthy now. I believe it, but how can I convince my mind that it's true? I still have these feelings.

Master: This idea of unworthiness—this is a result of your mind, your ego. When you consider the past, you should know that it is neither good nor bad. The potential for your past, for everyone's past, always has been. That potential still is. It has not gone away. It is in Balance. You must see it in Balance. It can be no other way.

Student: But what if what I've done has caused something bad to happen.

Master: Good and bad exist only in your illusion. Even as you experience the illusion, there is only Balance. Your mind chooses to remember the imbalance you have been taught to see. Your mind will not allow you to see what Balance there is in the bad that you say you have done. All is in Balance. All is as it should be. It can be no other way. You must know that.

Student: How would you define evil?

Master: There is no definition, for the concept of evil is not with us, but for you to understand, evil is that which is limiting.

Integration of our belief system into the process of our development is a great challenge. Most of us have been exposed to a lifetime of teachings that tell of a system of reward or punishment resulting from how we have played our part in the movie of life. Our Ego program, as we have learned, has developed a sense of worthiness as a result of these teachings and our personal experience. We can look at any major belief system, as well as the social structures of the world, and find similar teachings.

Eastern religious tradition has developed an excellent understanding of the territory beyond the physical. We have called this territory the transpersonal realm but, for those that have accessed it, it is not beyond their personal experience. Studying the process of physical death is the experience through which many Eastern traditions developed their understanding. The actual program for physical death is held in our mind and remains with us throughout our life. The program is designed to activate automatically when our sensory world begins to fade at the time of death, but can be activated by other means. It is stimulated in the discipline of meditation, where little or no attention is given to thoughts or incoming sensory information, as well as in the practice of rituals that seemingly threaten our reality. In the East, many rituals and practices were developed that stimulated the physical death program. Little of these teachings remain for us to study today. The vast majority of these teachings were given by Masters to their students. Traditionally, the Master-student bond was total, teachings were given orally, and little or no written material was made available. But we can glean an insight of these now esoteric teachings by looking at what others wrote of the Masters.

Christianity is the most popular belief system in the United States. In studying the history of the beliefs from which Christianity grew and the life of the Lord Jesus, it is necessary to keep in mind that we are viewing an Eastern tradition that has been adapted to the Western mind. Additionally, much of what has been recorded of His life and teachings was written by individuals who were given the information second hand—after it had been filtered and refined through someone's paradigm.

The teachings of Jesus follow the Path of Knowledge and Integration. In His teachings, Jesus gives us the Knowledge that there is no separation, limitation, or meaning in our movie of reality. He was continually bringing individuals to a place in their mind where they could grasp the concept of their relationship to The One, which he called "The Father." Of His teachings, the one that caused the greatest controversy in His time, and remains the foundation of many religious teachings today, is his proclamation: I and the Father are One.

Jesus did not see Himself separate from The One, but neither did He separate Himself from the multitude. Jesus' teachings give the Knowledge that all that is, is of The One. Without the Knowledge that all are One, many have concluded that He held a special place with The One. This is separation, and is a concept that Jesus did not teach. The Knowledge He gives is that all are One, there is no separation, that anything you can imagine is possible, there is no limitation, and that changing your attention, or repentance, gives you total freedom from the self-imposed limitations of your mind, there is no meaning. The term "repent," literally means: To change your way of thinking, your focus of attention. Sound familiar? When you read the Gospels in the light of this Knowledge, these teachings stand out in striking detail.

The Lord Jesus gave a simple message. He said we should change our *attention* from those things that hold us to the movie of reality and turn it to The One, and that we should Integrate this Knowledge into the attitudes and activities of our daily lives. Here we have the message of Knowledge, Integration, and Balance, an understanding of the nature of the material world and how we relate to it. The simplest explanation is that in total freedom from the illusion, all the projections of the mind that create the illusion come under the mastery of the individual. All things are possible.

Those who lived in the days of Jesus had a very strong paradigm concerning caste and worthiness. It's not easy for a rich man to actually "see" himself as one with his poor brother, nor is it any easier the other way. Many of the people in Jesus' day believed that they were born into a life situation as a result of Karma, and that there was no way out of their plight without divine intervention. They held a strong belief then, as many do today, in the reality of reincarnation. As you have learned, Karma and reincarnation are projections of the mind resulting from a belief and expectation. They are self-imposed limitations.

Jesus called the result of gaining Knowledge and the process of Integration being "born again," and the method by which we experience this rebirth "baptism." Many of those who wrote of His teachings, as well as most of the teachings remaining today, make the mistake of believing that this is an external process. In Jesus' time, many people thought that being born again meant that they would have to reincarnate. Even though reincarnation is a fact of our movie experience, there should be no more significance given to past lives than to the present one. They are all projections of the mind. Some of His followers came to the Knowledge that rebirth was a process of clearing the matrix of limiting thought that bound them to the movie. But even then, most were not willing to commit themselves to the process. Still others had no understanding one way or the other, so they invented their own explanation.

It is from the teachings of this last group that the current tradition here in the West was derived. The group was mostly gentile and had never been exposed to the Knowledge that Jesus was schooled in. They had to invent their own tradition. It is from their traditions that the current belief that we are separated from The One by sin evolved, and that resolution from this separation comes only from an external source. But the word "sin" literally means "falling short of the goal," and the goal is the realization that we are One. To repent, as mentioned, is not to feel sorry for what we think we have done "wrong." To repent is simply to change our way of thinking—our focus of attention. The way we think is a result of our paradigm, and is made manifest by attention. Gaining Knowledge and Integration changes our paradigm. This is an internal process and is not based on worthiness.

Many of the Eastern traditions, and most here in the West, still wait for the time of physical death to gain freedom from the movie. Some of the Eastern traditions teach that assistance to a dying person can be given by those remaining in the physical realm. They understand that the spirit and the body are not immediately separated at the time of physical death. This has resulted in a dialogue given by the "living" to the "dying." It is continued during transition and for some time after. The dialogue encourages the dying individual to continue the journey through the matrix of limiting thought to freedom. It traces the steps in the mind's program for physical death and provides instruction in Balance along the way. The process of assisting another in transcending the limits of their paradigm at the time of death is not based on worthiness. Again, it is a matter of preparation and the proper focus of attention.

In the teachings of Jesus, a shadow of the rebirth process is hidden in the ritual of baptism. The sprinkling with water and the words to a godparent that remain in today's practice are a far cry from the original ritual. The original ritual was full submersion to the point of drowning. The ancients knew that whenever the mind is deprived of incoming sensory information or threatened with physical death, it runs the physical death program. This happens to a lesser degree in some of us when we are involved in traumatic accidents. It is often reported that individuals see their lives "flash before their eyes" at these times. They are experiencing holographic awareness, the initial step in the mind's program for physical death.

The mind must respond to sensory information, or the absence of it, to create a movie. The original ritual of baptism stimulated the same programs that arise at the time of physical death. The Masters knew that with the proper grounding in Knowledge and the proper preparation through Integration, one could gain freedom from the illusion through the process. Their quest was not based on worthiness. It was based on preparation through the Integration of Knowledge.

And baptism was not the only means of stimulating the mind into retracing the matrix of limiting thought and initiating these programs. The sect that Jesus belonged to conducted the ritual of baptism along with many others, one of which was isolation in an environment similar to the Native American Kiva or sweat lodge. Here, again, we see the shades of Shamanism.

The rebirth process is not a concept isolated to Eastern teaching. It is found throughout the world in Shamanic teachings that include many Native American traditions. Without exception, these teachings follow a process of training and service similar to Knowledge and Integration.

While Eastern tradition spent thousands of years developing an understanding of the transpersonal realm, Shamanic tradition was busy developing methods of stimulating the mind to run the physical death programs prior to the actual time of death. They did so, for the most part, without the understanding that their Eastern counterparts had of the transpersonal realm.

The Shaman were raised in a paradigm accepting access to the transpersonal realm. But their access seldom went beyond deceased human spirits or nature spirits. The purpose of the Shaman in his culture was to assist those still remaining in the movie in a manner that *helped them in their movie*. The Shaman were, for the most part, not as interested in freedom from as they were in success in the movie of consensus reality. This is the main difference between Shamanic and Eastern religious practice.

It is because of this that the Shaman were not limited in developing and using any method that would assist them in loosening the hold the mind has on this reality. They became adept in the utilization of mental amplifiers.

The mental amplifiers that the Shaman used were non-specific. A non-specific mental amplifier is any drug that produces an effect dependent on the state of mind of the person taking it. We have labeled these drugs "psychedelic." *Psyche delos* means mind-manifesting—or mind expanding. Drugs that depress are called "depressants." Those that stimulate are called "stimulants." When ingested, these drugs produce a specific mental response as well as a specific physiological change in the body. Medical professionals like to know the specific response of the drug that they prescribe. This is why non-specifics are illegal.

When an individual ingests a non-specific, the resulting psychological condition is directly related to the state of mind of the individual *prior to ingestion*. The experience that results from ingestion is still a product of the mind. The brain is a reflection of the patterns held in the mind. A non-specific breaks down the barriers of the brain, which is holographically one with the mind, and allows information that is not consistent with consensus reality to enter the conscious view screen. This information is still interpreted by the mind, and the mind still tries to make it fit in with the current programs, patterns, and tendencies. But it is raw information of a transpersonal nature and, without proper preparation, an individual must make a constant effort to stabilize the consensus movie. Any program running in the mind before ingestion is enhanced by the non-specific substance and filled with transpersonal information. Because of this, participants must prepare themselves ahead of time for the experience.

The Shaman knew of the effects of the non-specific mental amplifiers and would never consider using them for any external purpose. The matrix of limiting thought, the paradigm, is internal, and the only way to access it is through training and preparation. Novice Shaman spent many years in study and service to their teacher and their community before they were considered prepared for the transpersonal experience. Even then, they prepared for months in advance for the actual ritual, abstaining from physical pleasure and holding in their mind the desired outcome. This was a great effort of attention through which they insured that their mind would run the desired program during their transpersonal quest. The quest was usually accomplished alone, or with a few skilled individuals present to care for their physical safety.

The Shaman does not see anything in the world as unnatural. To them, everything is natural and has a place. The place of everything is for the purpose of helping humanity. <u>And mankind should never allow the things in the world to become a necessity for his growth.</u> It's for this reason that the Shaman never allowed their practice to become dependent on any specific substance or ritual. The substances and rituals were simply used for a time to help them reach the place in the mind where access to the transpersonal realm was a response to attention, like everything else in our movie.

This understanding of the substances and rituals is lost in much of today's teachings on Shamanism. There are many who teach that the ritual is holy, or that the herb or substance is required to produce the desired result. Some teach that only one born of a certain culture, or initiated into that culture, can be worthy to practice such a quest. Here, again, we find an old practice originally based on preparation and knowledge evolving into a system of good and bad, right and wrong, and the concept of worthiness arising as a result of it.

The goal of the Shaman is to stand empty-handed and naked before the rising sun, and to enter the transpersonal realm with just a thought. This is a metaphor, but we find it reflected in Shamanic tradition throughout the world. Naked is the condition in which we entered the physical world at birth. It is without the covering, without ritual, and without the patterns of limited thought that we have now. The rising sun reflects the intrinsic presentation of Mind during our Path to awareness. To stand naked, without the covering of a paradigm, before the mind in the arising of Mind is a process of pure attention in Balance. The rituals and herbs are only aids, and used only during development. To the Shaman, worthiness was not a consideration. The only requisite was knowledge and preparation.

Our ultimate goal is to clear the paradigm of our mind, through the matrix of limiting thought, and allow the state of awareness that is Balance to become available in our movie of reality. This is the experience of our Path. Here is where we are met with a barrage of objection from today's "spiritual" leaders.

It's a commonly held paradigm that people must gain a state of mental and physical purity through a long process of preparation and commitment before they will be able to achieve such a state of awareness. This is true in any paradigm that teaches separation and a system of reward and punishment. In essence, it is said that they must display some acceptable form of "spirituality."

It's here where we make the most obvious deviation from these beliefs. All are worthy, and are always worthy. It is only the mind that will judge. We should cast aside any question of worthiness, or better still, gently return it to its source. Each and every one of us is, by our nature, fully worthy to participate in the process and to Integrate it into everyday life. We all possess the necessary abilities of attention at this very moment. It is, after all, the powerful effect of attention combined with The Magic of Agreeing that has produced this wonderful stage on which we act out our movie of reality. We are all exactly where we should be on our Path. We are actors together in this movie of reality, not one more important or in a better position than another. We are all worthy.

This spirituality that is spoken of by those who teach limitation is always related to a sense of good. But we have learned that good and bad are projections of the mind. The truly spiritual individual is one who has accomplished Balance in a role in the movie, and it's often the most Balanced individuals who are playing the bad parts. When each and every actor has gained Knowledge and Integration—and has applied the principles to their lives—the movie will take on a new and exciting dimension. Each and every actor includes those that we sometimes judge as good—or bad.

My Master never speaks of worthiness. She sees all as of The One, no matter what station in life an individual may hold, no matter what part they play in this movie of reality. She does mention limitations. An individual that holds a "successful" part in the movie, with a good job, fine family, and well-established belief system may be more self limited than the junkie on the street collecting the fee for his next fix. Both are limited, and both are equally as worthy. What would my master say is required for any individual to gain access to Knowledge, Integration and The One? Just a change of thinking—a change in the focus of attention.

The Lord Jesus was accused by the church leaders of His day of forgiving sins. This was something that the leaders liked to maintain control over. They could do it, and charge for it. But Jesus never did forgive sins. He knew that judgment is an internal process. He simply stated the fact: Your sins are forgiven. When we know that Balance is, it can be no other way.

The Movie Will End

Master: The reality that you know is in constant motion. This is because there is constant motion in The One. To become still is to become one with the motion of The One. This is the first and the natural state of the human spirit. To become still is to exist in this flow of motion.

Student: Isn't the motion in our reality the same as the motion of The One? I've heard the saying, "As above, so below." Isn't it true that all we experience has its motion in The One?

Master: It is true, but the truth of the saying in your reality is limited to your concept of experience. The One holds all potential always. All experience is available always, and with just a thought. One can enjoy experience without the need to sacrifice awareness. Your experience involves a process of limiting awareness. This is the process we call death. You think of it as the death of the body, but it is the death of awareness.

Student: Then, if we were aware, our body would live longer?
Master: That would be your choice. The body is but a reflection of your awareness. Your body begins to grow old when your awareness becomes more limited. This happens as you grow from a child to what you call an adult.

My master speaks of death as a limitation of awareness. Many of us think of death as the end of physical existence.

All limited movies have a beginning and an end. Our movie is no exception. We are dying. We are constantly shifting from one dream to another, one reality to another. Each shift includes death and birth. Death is not a physical thing, it is simply a flowing between experience and awareness. As we have learned, the mind runs programs in response to sensory information. This process is active throughout our physical "lives" and continues even after physical "death." The programs for birth and death are recorded in our mind, but life and death are not physical things and our mind applies these programs to all experience. Remember, the mind and its programs are holographic.

Again, the end of physical existence is a simple transition from one dreamed reality to another, and nothing more. Every time we awaken from a personal dream, we have experienced a death. How many times have you awakened from a personal dream? Most of us will have more than five dreams a night. That's over five deaths a night, with the same number of births. As we shift from the death of the personal dream to the experience of a consensus dream, our mind shifts from its programs of sleep to the programs that meet its paradigm for our physical reality. This death, at the end of our night's sleep, is no different from the death we experience at the end of the consensus dream. There is virtually no difference.

Those who have actually experienced the physical death and returned to tell of it say that awakening in the "heavens" is just as easy as awakening from a dream. Do you think of waking from a dream as death? Waking causes the death of the dream only, and that death exists only in the mind. We remain quite alive, and the potential of the dying dream still lives in Mind—in The One. Our life and death are not in the dream. Life is in awareness, and death is in limitation. Awakening at the time of physical death from this movie of reality is waking from a dream—a dream we call consensus reality. If we have not gained Balance when we make this transition, we simply move from one dream state into another, and the dream state that we enter meets our expectations.

This movie of reality that is running for us in our waking life is but one of many realities available to us. But those realities are filtered and refined by our mind just as when we are seated in the cinema and involved in our movie. Remember, while in the cinema, the awareness of all that is going on around us is filtered from our conscious view screen so we can have the experience of the movie. In that situation, all that is necessary in order for us to become aware of what is going on around us is a change of attention. We can, any time we wish, look from the movie screen in the cinema to the occupied seats around us. We could say that we expand our awareness from the movie screen to the cinema itself. When we do this, our experience changes. But that change of attention fits into our paradigm. When we change our attention there, we expect to be in a cinema and see others seated around us. The focus of attention that allows us to become aware of the transpersonal realm is not, for most of us, within the programs of our paradigm. But an expanding of awareness does happen at the time of physical death. Eastern religions and Shamanism have developed an understanding of these programs.

The Shaman gain access to the transpersonal realm by "seeking their death." When the Shaman say they must experience their death, they are saying that they have chosen to retrace their Path, through the mind, into the illusion of this movie of reality. This does not mean that anything physical will die. The Shaman believe that their death came with them, and that it is their death that keeps them from transcending the limitations of this reality and accessing other realities. But how could their death follow them into their consensus movie? We may already know, but it is worthy of review.

Let's go back to the cinema. Before these movies in the cinema began, we were aware of a vast number of potential experiences. Our mind could easily choose where our attention would be placed. We were, in a manner of speaking, alive with awareness. But, when the movie began, the view screen of our awareness was filled with the information our senses began to gather. We found it very difficult, if not impossible, to place our attention on anything outside the presentation of sensory information. The process of limiting and refining awareness is a function of the mind. It is the process that allows us to enjoy a movie in the cinema, as well as our movie of consensus reality. The process produces a death of awareness.

Before this movie we call physical reality began, we were alive in another awareness. Even if we were alive only in the limitations of a heavenly reality—and not aware of The One—our awareness was much greater than it is now. In order for us to have this physical movie, we had to experience a death of awareness. This is the same function of the mind and involved the same process we experienced in the cinema. We are overwhelmed with sensory information at the time of physical birth. But it started even before that—in the womb.

Slowly, as our physical body developed and we became attached to it, our awareness became more and more limited. Soon our awareness began filtering through our physical senses of sight, sound, and feeling. Even though these senses were limited and muffled, we began to develop a relationship between what we held in "awareness" and what we were having in "experience."

Our world is much darker in the womb. Even so, there was a fascination with the physical senses that caused our mind, in its development, to begin to relate awareness to physical sensations. We spent a long time experiencing muffled sensations from our new environment and recording them in our mind. This was a time of development for the mind. Though not yet fully disassociated from awareness of the transpersonal realm we came from, we were still not yet fully attached to the physical.

All that was soon to change. At the time of birth we developed a matrix of limiting thought much the same as when the lights went down and the screen lit up in the cinema. We were floating in your pleasant environment, a little cramped, but everything was fine. Then, without warning, we experienced the beginning of our physical birth, and the fullness of the death of our awareness. Chemicals that caused confusion and disorientation flooded into our environment. Contractions began forcing us down the dark tunnel of the birth canal. When we emerged, we were suddenly thrust into the light. All the once muffled images, sounds, and feelings burst into flaming reality. We were "born," and with our birth, our awareness died. It had to in order for us to survive in our new reality. We had to take that first breath, see those first sights, hear those first sounds, smell those first smells, and feel those first sensations. All this was recorded in our mind as it began the process of learning how to interact with this new movie.

We may, at first, have been aware of those helpers and guides around the physical people in our new movie, but how necessary were they to our new experience? Just about as necessary as the person sitting in front of us in the cinema. We may "see" them, but in the intensity of the presentation, they do not even appear in our conscious view screen. They are filtered out. They are unnecessary for the experience. Our awareness is dying. It's a natural and normal process of our mind as it builds its paradigm, and our mind is very good at its job.

Later on in our new movie, we are given instruction by the other actors. What to do and what not to do. How to act and how not to act. "Big boys don't.." "Big girls don't.." There were a lot of "don'ts". And: "What do you want to be when you grow up?" "Be like your father." "Be like your mother." "Be like your older brother."

"Pay attention." We were given very specific instructions on where our attention should be placed. We were unknowingly told by our well-meaning instructors that our attention should remain on the process of the illusion. Daydreaming is not a worthy occupation; transpersonal awareness has no place in our reality. A mind free of thought is not a good thing. They did not realize that awareness lies just behind those thoughts.

And as we got a little older, we found out how important it is to be compared to everyone else. "How did she do on the California test?" "How does he rate against the Iowa kids?" "How fast can he run?" "How far can she jump?" We were told what to believe, what was possible, and what was not. Our Ego began developing. All of the advice, the direction, even the education given to us by our instructors was unknowingly limiting our awareness of The One and preparing us for our part in the movie of reality.

By the time we become an adult, we find some people very easy to act our parts with, and some things about our reality very easy to understand. We find others impossible to act with, and some concepts too confusing to understand. Most of us never stop to consider that those "others" find us equally as impossible, or that there are actors with which they fully relate. We seldom ask why some concepts that appear on our view screen with confusion are perfectly clear and understandable to others. By now, our mind has developed programs that automatically select the sensory information that is going to be easy for us to understand and accept, and what is not. We have established a nice, comfortable paradigm.

We will call this paradigm by many names. Some call it a culture. Others call it a level of education. Still others call it a skill. We may call it a belief. Or, we simply call it our personality. It's just the way we are. We never question it. Our mind never considers reading a book that we do not "like," seeing a movie that does not "appeal" to us, or listening to music that is not of "our generation." Our mind is running its programs on automatic. Our awareness of the transpersonal realm is now almost completely removed from our movie of reality. For all practical purposes, we have died a full death of awareness. Total awareness is still there, but it's held at bay behind the ever-growing paradigm. This awareness and Knowledge remain, though in the background, throughout our "life." It gives us the inner knowing that there is something more. It gives us what psychologists call a "spiritual impulse."

We find a way in our movie to satisfy this impulse. We feed our mind with beliefs of another reality awaiting us in order to appease its longing for awareness. Or, we keep our mind so busy in this movie of reality that there is little time to consider those deeper impulses. But most of us never seek our "death," for when we do, our Path arises and our experience lessens—and our mind holds on to experience with great determination.

Yet we know, deep in our awareness, that no matter what we do in life it is not enough. We know there is no way we can do our best, no matter what we were taught. There is a part of us that is still aware of Mind, no matter how strong our paradigm is, and Mind holds the awareness of all potential. We know we are perfect, that all are perfect, and that comparison is not necessary.

We say we are satisfied with something, but what we really mean is that we are finished. We are never really satisfied. That is the result of limitation. A part of us still knows that we are not limited, no matter how strong our paradigm is. We become successful at playing some part in the movie, but we still long for the parts of others. We satisfy this longing with fantasy—and by going to the cinema. In our deeper awareness, we know that we are not limited in any way. We know that all parts are available and can be our parts in The One.

We say that we have had a good life, but that is a comparison, and it is duality. There resides in us Mind without separation and, on our deepest level, we are aware that the potentials for good and evil are from the same source. Deep inside we know that we are not separated from The One, that all that is, is of The One.

We keep this awareness from our view screen by keeping busy. Busy, busy, busy. Never a moment's rest. Always something to do. We complain about it, but we know that it's really what our mind wants. If we are not so busy we have to confront our Path—and Mind. We evaluate our busy performance on a moment-by-moment basis, hoping for feedback from the other actors in the movie. We accept the agreement that certain actions are "good," and we perform these so our parts in the movie becomes more "meaningful."

Yet, the instant we allow ourselves a moment of quiet, Mind arises, and our mind experiences self-limitation, self-separation, self-meaning. Our mind responds with the feeling of anger, frustration, or just plain longing.

How far does our mind go to limit awareness? It never stops. The mind is the creator of our movie. We are creators, captive within our creation. The mind continually creates our movie for us. It is its job, and it does it very well. Our mind continues to do its job even when our sensory world begins to fade away.

The process of death is going on throughout our lives. As we give attention to experience, awareness dies. As we give attention to awareness, experience dies. Death is present at the end of each dream, each job, each relationship, each ability, each belief. It is present throughout our lives with each change of attention that results in a restructuring of our paradigm. Death is nothing new to us. It's an ongoing process that is happening every self-created moment of every self-created day.

The process that the Shaman follows causes the programs that the mind uses to create the illusion to surface, where they are confronted and resolved. The process causes their Path to arise before them. The Shaman knows that this will happen, and is prepared to carry the Knowledge of the process with him. He may create circumstances that threaten the experience of the "movie," or participate in a ritual that expands his awareness. This causes his mind to retrace the Path of its death of awareness. The Shaman remains awake and aware during this process. He holds fast to the training he has been given and knows that his mind continually attempts to play a movie for him. He has led a life of practice. He remains focused on his intention and, with the help of those who attend him, awakens from the dream while remaining in it.

This is the death of the Shaman. This is happening slowly during our Integration, but without the expectations of the Shaman. Now, as we give our attention to Balance, the movie of reality and the experience it contains releases its hold on us. The dream becomes less and less real. The Path in our mind arises before us, and we become involved in the death of separation, limitation, and meaning. We are once again involved in a process of death, but this time it is the death of our ties to Maya and an arising of the Path to freedom from our illusion.

You can now take joy in the process of death. You know that it has nothing to do with our physical being. It is simply a changing state of awareness. Feel free to seek the death of experience, but seek it only in Balance. Remember, all that is, is of The One. Although your desire is freedom from the illusion, experience is now and will always remain a part of your nature.

You also know that most of us will die physically, and that this death is nothing more than another change of awareness. What happens to each of us when physical death occurs is directly tied to our paradigm. But there is a process, and it should be understood.

Transition

Student: What happens to us when we die?
Master: When you die?
Student: When our physical life ends?
Master: What happens to you depends on you. What you call death is not an ending, but a beginning. It is a birth, and you must decide now if it is to be a birth of experience or a birth of awareness.

Even though death is a daily occurrence, we often hold physical death in a special place. It should not be so. The death of the physical body involves the same process as its birth. It contains the confusion, the tunnel, the light, and the same restructuring of our paradigm. We experienced this process, this death, when we entered the physical world. The only difference is, at the time of physical death the body ceases to function, and the physical view screen on which reality has been presented begins to fade. This is a process that almost everyone will experience, but it is not a new experience.

The mind contains innate programming that results in a step-by-step progression by which we are presented with awareness of Mind—of The One. It happens to all that experience a physical death, but the paradigm of each individual presents the process in a movie that is consistent with their expectations. The movie is the result of programs that are most recent, most repeated, and most emotionally charged.

The process of physical death involves a progression called "transition." Transition is the progression of awareness from the physical matter of the brain to the energy of the mind as the brain ceases to function. Even though the physical brain is the view screen of our reality, it is but a reflection of our mind. As the brain's view screen grows dimmer and dimmer at the time of physical death, experience is projected onto another screen. This screen is the view screen of our mind. The programs of our physical reality with its sensory environment are still active in our mind, but our physical body is no longer functioning. Our physical senses diminish, and we begin to experience our holographic nature as the mind takes over the task of presenting reality to us. It is now, during this transition between physical awareness and holographic awareness, that Mind presents itself in its natural state. It is here that the process of transition has begun. It is the death of the physical body, but it is only a transition of our awareness.

The process of physical death stimulates the process of transition, but is not necessary to initiate it. We may experience portions of it throughout our lives but, because we lack Knowledge, we never realize what has happened. It occurs during situations when the mind is deprived of sensory information from our physical reality, or physical reality is threatened, such as in life threatening situations. At these times, the mind is stimulated into running the physical death program and we may get a glimpse of transition in its beginning stages. As mentioned, this is when we may see our life flash before our eyes. We are actually seeing holographically when this happens, and holographically is how our mind "sees" without the limitations of the physical senses.

In order for us to remain in Balance during transition, we must gain Balance in the movie of consensus reality. We have practiced Balance in meditation, and the *process* is the same. Balance during transition is maintained with the *same discipline* of recognition and return that we are already familiar with. The skill we develop in meditation is the ability to recognize the presentations of our mind and quickly return to Balance without becoming immersed in them. We *must* apply the *same* discipline in transition in order to maintain Balance.

The process of transition at the time of physical death is an archetypal process—a process that follows the same pattern wherever it occurs, as is the process of birth. This is why the process is the same throughout the world, and even though reports of the experience differ, there are commonalties in the experience that cannot be denied. These commonalties are, however, interpreted differently by the mind of the individual experiencing it.

The mind is not in the brain, but in the energy of the whole being. The mind retains all the patterns, programs, and tendencies that are developed during our movie of reality. It remains, even during transition, the home of our paradigm. Our mind supplies an interpretation of what Mind is presenting in transition according to its paradigm. Even though we are experiencing the world of holographic awareness in which we naturally function, our mind filters and refines the experience and presents an illusion that meets our expectations.

The illusion of the movie of consensus reality is a clinical process, and transition at the time of physical death is a part of it. Physical death is simply stepping from one stage to another, one dream to another, one reality to another—and nothing more. Physical birth is such a transition, and so physical birth contains the same archetypal process, the same interacting patterns of awareness, as does physical death.

The actual time of our physical death is known in our mind well ahead of the instant it appears on our conscious view screen. As with all experience programming, we do not become consciously aware of impending death until the sensory information necessary to initiate the program becomes available. The information of impending physical death is, however, written in the energy field of our mind and, as nothing is hidden, it is available to those who have the ability to perceive this energy. We are surrounded by the energy of our mind, and our crystallized future is in this energy.

There are no accidents. The entire script for the movie of life is available in the mind, just as the entire movie is in the roll of film on a projector in the cinema. Our movie is not limited. Our roll of film is held in The One, and contains all potential. But, because our patterns of limiting thought have already set the major scenes in motion, the course of our movie of reality is available in the vibrations of our mind. What appears to us to be accidental, appears so only because we do not become aware of the impending experience until the sensory information necessary to initiate it is made available. It appears on our view screen of reality suddenly, even though it has been a projection of our mind for quite some time. There are no limitations. All experience, as well as projected experience, is available to every entity any where and any time. The only limiting factors are the programs, patterns and tendencies of our paradigm.

And this energy of our mind vibrates in harmony with the energy of entities that share the same concepts. The concepts, thoughts, beliefs, etc., are similar to the keys of the piano or the strings of the guitar. All are tuned to a certain note. We do, then, attract certain actors and a proper set on which to act out our experience of physical death. This is no different from the manner in which we chose the conditions for our physical birth. There is simply no difference. It is presented as an experience that is out there, limited, and with meaning, just as our experience of physical reality is. It holds the full potential of The One shrouded in illusion, just as our experience of physical reality does. We can see the archetype of process as it evolves.

Although transition is one complete process, it is easier to understand if it is presented as individual experiences. Again, there are reports of physical death from NDE's around the world, and as always, the interpretation of the process is reported through the paradigm of the person experiencing it. What we are concerned with is the archetype itself—the common aspects of transition that arise regardless of the reporting individual.

The first archetypal experience in transition is the tunnel. The tunnel is the reflection of the birth canal. As with birth, it may be preceded by a period of disorientation and confusion. It's sometimes experienced as a dark hallway, a deep valley between two high cliffs, or even a dark field with misty edges; the descriptions vary with the paradigm of the individual reporting it. Some individuals experience an open field, a pleasant lake, a bridge, or a misty environment with a light in the background. Again, the presentation of experience is the result of our paradigm so, throughout the world, there are reports of many different experiences of the process.

Many tell of being aware of a light beyond the tunnel, and are aware of a noise of some kind. The noise is often a buzzing sound, or the sound of rustling wind. What is taking place in transition is the process by which the view screen on the physical brain is replaced by the view screen of our mind in the energy of our being. This can be compared to transition at the time of birth when our senses are flooded with the awareness of our new reality.

The next experience that is encountered in transition is the appearance of the Light of Mind. This arises as the experience of the tunnel fades into the background. It first appears far in the distance, and we feel drawn to it. Many who have experienced it report that there are no words to describe the Light. It is said to be brighter than any earthly light, yet will not harm the eyes of those that look directly into it. Individuals often report that as they are drawn to the Light, they experience total Love as they come closer to it. Most say they felt the Light was familiar, as if they were in some way a part of it. This Light often appears to those who have led a "good" life as well as many who have not. It may appear to those who have held a belief in a god, as well as to many that have not. Once again, all experience is a projection of the mind. The process is archetypal, but within the process, many experiences are available. They are a product of our mind in response to our paradigm.

The Light often appears as a figure. The personage is always a product of the observers belief and reality structure. A Christian will usually see Christ or Mother Mary. A Buddhist will likely see a Buddha, or one of the saints. A generic believer may see an angel, and some are just aware of the Light. Here is evidence that the mind is already beginning to fill in our view screen with information that fits our expectations. There is something out there, limited, and with meaning. The fact that the Light appears differently to different observers means only that the illusion of separation, limitation, and meaning is beginning again.

The presence of the Light is the arising of Mind. With Balance, we are able to recognize this Light as our very self and gain the Knowledge that it is from within. With Balance, we are able to identify the activity of our mind attempting to present this Light through our paradigm. With Balance, we are able to gently return this presentation to its source and merge with the Light.

Without Balance, it remains out there, limited through our paradigm, and meaningful. It appears to be seen through our rapidly diminishing physical senses. Our paradigm tells us it is separate from us.

With the end of the tunnel, and in the presence of the Light, comes judgment. Again, our awareness at this point is a result of the presentation of the Light of Mind while our mind still interprets the experience according to its paradigm. As you know, all judgment is self-judgment. At this moment, our Path arises fully before us and we have another opportunity to gain Balance. We view our entire Path in a holographic instant. If we have not taken time to gain Balance before this moment, judgment is immediate.

Our Path contains our Ego program. The programs of limiting thought that are our paradigm immediately interpret the presentation of Mind as it arises. We are not able to consider our paradigm. It was created in response to sensory information from consensus reality, and that reality is no longer available to us. There is no time. It no longer exists. Our awareness has expanded to include Mind. The only Balance we now have is that which we have practiced in our previous reality. Our mind and Mind merge, and again, holographically. Our awareness is now a result of the holographic merging of the paradigm of our mind with the unlimited potential of Mind.

In Balance, we are able to fully realize the unconditional Love and total forgiveness of Mind. In Balance, we are able to recognize the presentation of judgment as an interpretation of our mind, gently return it to its source, and merge with Mind.

Without Balance, we experience the judgment of Ego.

This is why my Master stated, quite simply: What happens to you will depend on you. What you call death is not an ending but a beginning. It is a birth, and you must decide *now* if it is to be a birth of experience or a birth of awareness.

She is not saying that this birth, either way, is good or bad. She is saying that when we focus our attention on experience while here in this movie of reality, we develop patterns that remain with us when we leave, and we therefore choose another movie, another experience. And when we focus our attention on Balance while here, still able to enjoy the movie of reality, we choose a camera with a wider lens—one that allows awareness. She is saying that it is a choice we make while we are here in the movie of consensus reality.

Without Balance, our next movie experience meets our expectations. The "heavens" are limited only by the attention of those who enter, but the heavens are another place of experience. In the heavens, just as here, experience is available and is presented according to our expectations

The tunnel and the Light may be accompanied by the presence of departed loved ones. Here, again, the response of our mind to the arising of Mind is following the same patterns it has in our movie of consensus reality. The vibrations of our attention are responded to, and common beliefs in realities draw entities together. Another illusion that supports our expectations is presented by our mind. The loved ones may very well reside in a "place" in which we share a common belief, and we may have longed to be with them.

The tunnel and the Light, and the potential for judgment, are the first experiences of transition. Remember, the mind is not in the brain, it is the energy that we are, and it is still active and running programs. When the tunnel and the Light appear, they appear out there, limited, and with meaning. What is happening is the presence of Mind arising on the view screen of our new awareness. We are witnessing our very nature, our primordial self. We are experiencing, for a brief instant that can seem to take an eternity, The Light of Mind. It is us. But, without Balance, this holographic awareness is filtered and shaped by our still active paradigm to fit our expectations. Our mind is still-predominant. The illusion remains in the separation, limitation, and meaning given by our mind. It's now that we must hold the Balance.

We should do this in exactly the same way we have treated Maya in consensus reality and during meditation. If it appears out there, limited, and containing meaning, it is of the mind and it is the illusion. We should gently return the illusion to its source and merge with it in Balance.

It's easy now for us to see why learning to hold Balance in the movie of physical reality is a very necessary step in our development. When we stand in the presence of a departed loved one, we should know that he or she is there for the same reason as in our physical movie. We were attracted to the same experience, and this is just another experience. Holding fast to Balance, we must now give our loved ones acknowledgment, a wink and a smile, and then we should look into the camera of our mind and gain Balance. Acknowledge the source of the illusion, gently return it, and merge with it.

When the Light of Mind takes the form of the master of our belief system this, too, is an interpretation of the process of transition filtered and refined through our paradigm. We experience what we have believed in, and no matter what we have believed, it's the same phenomenon: That religion exists, that master exists, and we exist, but we are not separate from any of them.

We are all One, and our experience is a projection of our mind. We must look into the camera of our mind and return to the center. Acknowledge the source of the illusion, gently return it, and merge with it—just as in meditation.

When the Light comes close to us and we feel the Love and know, in some way, that we are a part of the Light, we must hold to the Knowledge that *we are the Light*. We are not separate from what we are experiencing. The Light is the awareness of Mind and is arising in the transition process. It is not out there. It arises just as the presentations of the mind and Mind do in meditation. The awareness is real—the interpretation of this awareness is of our mind. We must hold fast to Balance. Return it to its source. We must merge with it.

If we are able to remain centered in Balance throughout this process, we have arrived in the place where the mind and Mind merge. When this happens, our awareness expands to contain the whole of the holographic world. We are now aware of the potential for all experience and the source of The One. But our paradigm does not dissolve at this time. We are holographic energy—it remains with us.

As Mind presents itself on our consciousness, we become aware of Knowledge that is transcendental in our current paradigm. This is intrinsic Knowledge, and arises without the sense of separation that is produced by our mind during our physical experience. The Knowledge is holographic, and our mind is now experiencing holographically. Remember, we are energy beings and energy is holographic. We have, then, in the very vibrations of Mind, all the Knowledge of the universe.

Remember also that our paradigm is still with us and our Path still arising. Because of this, we do not enter full awareness immediately but are confronted with holographic Knowledge through our paradigm. Rather than appearing in an abstract way, this Knowledge is total, experiential, and without separation. We cannot know in advance what Knowledge will arise. Our mind follows its matrix of limiting thought and presents us with the Knowledge that will be the next step in resolving our paradigm. This is our Path, but now, as our mind and Mind present themselves on our conscious view screen, it arises in an eternal moment.

Holographic Knowledge can appear for any aspect of our last experience. It may include anything from Knowledge of simple earthly life forms to an in depth understanding of the entire universe. Whatever form our paradigm presents this Knowledge in, we must now perform the same discipline. Recognize it and merge with it.

If our belief system contains a strong paradigm of an external creator, it will not allow us to gain the awareness that this Knowledge is arising within us; it appears external and contains meaning. There is a god archetype, and an archetype is, by its nature, unlimited. The presentation of the archetype naturally assumes the form that we hold in the paradigm in our mind. If we believe in a god of judgment and wrath, the program appears in our mind and becomes our experience. If we believe in a god of Love and forgiveness, we experience the same.

These experiences are usually filled with emotion beyond description. The love we experience here in the movie of reality is nothing compared to the love that presents itself in our god. The fear that we experience in the movie is nothing compared to the fear we experience as our mind presents its concept of God. We may be overwhelmed, but it is another opportunity for us to gain Balance in the center. Once again, if the experience contains separation, limitation, or meaning, it is not Balance. We must now gain Balance and merge with the experience. All that is, is of The One. The archetype does not exist apart from us. It is in us and it is us. What we are experiencing is a projection of Mind through the paradigm of our mind. We are presented with this transpersonal awareness on our conscious view screen, through our paradigm, so it appears external. But it's coming from us, from Mind, from The One.

Few can stand in the presence of the very god of their expectations and still maintain Balance. If we have gained Knowledge and practiced Integration, and we remain aware that what we are experiencing is a projection of our mind, we will succeed. Our success depends on our ability to access that which is already in us. We are experiencing our very nature, our primordial state of Balance. We must hold fast to our Balance and merge with the awareness. We came to our present state of limited experience by accepting the illusion of separation, limitation, and meaning. We gain freedom from this illusion by giving attention to Balance, and that Balance is within. This practice of attention to Balance is not something foreign to us, but we must now give our *full* attention to Balance.

When we have merged with the holographic awareness of Mind and the archetypal presentation of the gods, we may have gained our freedom from the illusion. But again, it can happen in degrees. We are not free until we totally accept that awareness is us, and fully accept that we are The One. There may still be a little Ego left. Even the archetypes of the gods possess it in some form. They are, after all, a projection of our mind.

The Mind must now present us with the last experience in transition. This is the fullness of The One, The One within. Up until this point, we have been experiencing holographic awareness related to our experience, filtered and refined by our still active mind, and not the full awareness of The One. Because our paradigm is still with us, we may still feel a sense of separation, almost like an observer. When full awareness of The One arises, it may appear as a vast emptiness, but we are aware that the emptiness is full of potential. In the quantum energy state of The One, there is only potential. Remember, we are experiencing holographically now, and our mind is still active. We still hold the memory and the paradigm of our last movie—and still have a sense of self.

It is at this point that our Ego may surface again. Confronting the sense of our personal "I" is the last step in transition. Our Ego may lead us to believe that we will have to give up our "identity" in order to merge with The One. Nothing could be further from the truth. Our identity is of The One. It is the final sense of separation that we are confronting. The sense of separation is the last stronghold for the Ego and the paradigm. The One is not a place of separation in any form. In The One, total intimate awareness of each and every entity is available to us at all times. The Ego program presented by our mind may try to hold on to our separation, telling us that we will lose our sense of self. The mind knows that our consciousness will gradually become aware of every thought of every entity that is, as well as all potential floating in the vast reaches of The One. We are confronted with the awareness that each and every entity that is will become totally and intimately aware of us. Our Ego may tell us they will know everything about us. We must not be deceived, they already do. And we, in Mind, already know them. But that awareness has been sequestered behind our paradigm. We are just now becoming aware of it. We must merge with it.

Awareness of the transpersonal realm is not something new to us. It is where we came from, and we hold in Mind and the mind in Balance, the intrinsic knowledge and ability to move about freely in it. The only freedom comes in Balance. The idea that we are not worthy or are unprepared must be set aside. We were, shall we say, born ready. Our practice of Knowledge and Integration while maintaining Balance awakens that intrinsic nature in us. We find ourselves expanding into the limitless potential of The One, still maintaining Balance,—free once again from the illusion.

And we also find that our paradigm has not vanished and our Ego has not disappeared. They have both been fully Integrated into The One. We know ourselves, yet we know The One as ourselves. Our paradigm allows us to create and express ourselves, but our Balance allows us to enter into awareness and experience without becoming immersed in either.

This is the process of transition in its simplest form. There are many variations of the process, and many different experiences can arise during it. The steps usually happen in the order given even if they are not recalled, but there are exceptions in the reports given. We all have different paradigms. The requirement, regardless of what appears, is the same. If it appears separate, limited or with meaning, it is not in Balance. Gain Balance and merge with it. In all things that present Maya, observe both, and choose neither.

We have now come full circle, from our birth into the physical world to our birth into The One in Balance. We have not left our mind behind, for it is a part of our nature. Rather, we have learned to Balance our attention between experience and awareness. We have discovered that The One is always with us, and that it is available in us through our attention. We walk the earth, or any experience we choose, with a lighter step. We are of The One. Welcome home, Sky Hero.

We have continually used the terms Mind and the mind. It is easier to understand the constant pulling between immersion in experience and immersion in awareness this way. But we know now that there is not the mind and Mind. They are One. The mind is The One immersed in experience—yet The One is fully present. Mind is The One immersed in awareness—yet The One is fully present. Balance is the full presence of both the mind and Mind. This my Master calls the Heart. The Heart is the center—the Balance. And as you will discover, the Heart is the center throughout the hologram. From the beginning, which contains the end, to the end, which contains the beginning, there is only Balance.

Unit Three

Return of the Sky Heroes

The Transpersonal Realm

Student: What happens when we no longer desire experience and become fully aware of The One?
Master: It begins again.
Student: But if we are already perfect, if we're already of The One, it seems that all this isn't necessary, that it's all a mistake.
Master: Mistake? A child is born perfect, with all the abilities of an adult, yet the child must grow. This is because the child has chosen the experience. This is not a mistake. It is a choice.
Student: But is it necessary?
Master: It is not necessary. It is the choice of the child. Your experience is not necessary, but you have chosen it.
Student: Then there is no purpose in it, no reason for it?
Master: There is only the purpose that you have chosen, only the reason that you give.

Of all the teachings of my Master, this one was the most difficult for me. There were two reasons for this. First, the idea that there is not a built in purpose for life, that all purpose and reason comes from us, gives us the final responsibility for what happens not only to ourselves, but to the whole world. I have always been taught that there is a plan somewhere, and that some day we would find out what that plan is. It took me a long time to accept the fact they we are the creators of our reality, and that we alone hold the outcome in our hands.

Secondly, I did not like the answer: It begins again. It gave me the feeling that we are stuck in a loop. I did not care for the concept of heaven that I was taught as a young child. The thought of being completely satisfied without ever experiencing a desire to do anything, never again to desire self-expression, was not to my liking. Neither did the thought of being immersed in awareness without ever having experience. Both gave me the impression that there was something missing.

It took me two full years to resolve this inner conflict. Resolution came, as always, when I found Balance. It gave me the greatest freedom a spirit can know, and the power within experience that the Masters speak of. I did not understand the answer my Master gave to my question because I did not understand the question I had asked. So I asked it again.

> Student: I once asked you what happens when we become fully aware of The One. You said that it begins again. How does it begin again?
> Master: I do not recall that question.
> Student: We were talking about experience being unnecessary. You said that experience is not necessary, that it is a choice.
> Master:. The choice of either experience or awareness is the choice of Spirit. Balance is in the Heart. The desire for experience is the nature of Spirit. The desire for awareness is the nature of Spirit. The Heart is the center. It is without beginning and without end.
> Student: Then why did you say that it would begin again?
> Master: Your question asked what happens when you no longer *desire* experience. When you no longer desire experience, you are no longer in Balance. The desire for experience is the nature of the creative Spirit. The desire for awareness is the nature of the creative Spirit. The Heart is the center. The One is all. You are in The One always, but you experience The One only when you are in Balance. When you do not recognize your desire for experience, you have left the Heart, where there is no beginning or end, and created a beginning for yourself.

We have been applying our lessons of Knowledge, Integrating them into our lives, and gaining Balance as our Path arises before us. We know that this process brings us freedom from the illusion, but freedom when, and to what end? Those questions are answered in this final unit. We will begin by taking a closer look at the transpersonal realm.

We began our exploration of the transpersonal realm when we discussed the process of transition. We know that at the time of physical death, the mind expands to include the awareness of a world of energy beyond our consensus reality. That is why we can say that we will all arrive there sooner or later. Our movie of reality will end. And we know why, from a holographic standpoint, we are there now.

Our physical reality is surrounded by layers of energy. These layers of energy are in harmony—in Balance. Although all is One and energy cannot be divided, we will divide them for the purpose of discussion only. There are seven layers of energy to discuss. I have chosen to use the term "layers" because, again, the concept of levels causes us to think of some as higher or lower than others.

Think of the energy layers around you as an extension of a concentric spider web with seven rings. Place yourself in the middle of your web and focus your attention on the very center. As you do so, you are unaware of the seven rings of your web. But as your awareness expands, it moves outward to include those rings.

Now, leave the center of your web and move to the first ring but, as you move, allow the center of the web to move with you. When you arrive at the first ring, what was your center now becomes another ring, and the ring you are now on becomes your center. You are, therefore, always in the center. In this way, all the layers of your web are always available to you. You are not really moving on the web. You are simply changing the focus of your attention.

This example is much like awareness in the layers of the transpersonal realm. When your attention is focused in the physical aspect of your reality, your awareness is limited to it. You are focused on the center of your web. As your attention expands beyond the confines of your physical world, so does your awareness, but you remain in the center. It is a simple matter of a change in the focus of attention that gives the appearance of movement. But wherever your attention is, you remain in the center.

The layers of energy that we call the transpersonal realm appear in religious tradition throughout the world. They are reported as spontaneous occurrences by those who experience NDE's, traumatic or life threatening situations, severe illnesses, and as a result of starvation and vitamin depletion, to name a few. And they have been actively sought in all cultures throughout history through the use of drugs, fasting, prayer, ritual, sensory deprivation, sensory overload, self-mutilation, and a vast number of other methods. All these layers are accessible through the focus of attention, just as the rings of your web.

Those who have traveled these layers and returned have described them through their own paradigm. This is why we find reports of a different number of layers as well as different descriptions of them. We will consider seven because it is the most often reported, and because a reflection of the seven transpersonal layers is mirrored in the physical body.

We understand that all is energy, and that energy is holographic. It is not surprising, then, to find seven centers of energy located in and around the human body. These energy centers are called "chakras," and are found in a line upward from the base of the human spine to just above the head. As we discuss the transpersonal realm, we will compare its seven layers to the seven chakras, or energy centers, found in the human body.

As we discuss the layers of the transpersonal realm, remember your spider web and keep in mind that all layers are accessible to anyone at any time. They are all a part of our Magic of Agreeing and are all accessible to us. There are, however, self imposed limitations on what layers we are able to access and what experience results when we do. These limitations are a product of our paradigm and the focus of our attention. For example, an individual highly focused on a belief in an external creator usually experiences the energies of the transpersonal layer associated with the archetypes without experiencing a progression through other layers. They describe the experience of this layer according to their paradigm; they experience the god they believe in.

As you continue your practice of Integration and your awareness naturally expands, you may gain access to these various layers. It is important for you to know that you are not accessing a *higher* awareness. You are still traveling *your* Path through *your* mind to *your* intrinsic Knowledge of the holographic energy of The One. Although it may appear so at times, there is nothing external in this experience. All experience is a projection of your mind. You are traveling your "spider web" of awareness. You are always at the center.

The first transpersonal layer is our own consensus reality. Some traditions have labeled the seven layers "heavens." That's why we have terms such as, I'm in seventh heaven. What most of us don't realize is that the earth, or our physical movie of reality, is the first layer, or first heaven. And we are correct in labeling it a transpersonal layer for, as we shall see, it is beyond the personal experience of many individuals still involved in The Magic of Agreeing.

We have a natural ability to perceive the energy of The One, and this includes all the energy beyond our consensus reality. But we have learned to rely on our physical senses while participating in the first transpersonal layer. Our paradigm is structured around sensory information provided by it, and it is our paradigm that filters and refines this energy to meet our physical expectations. This is why we are not aware of the vast world of energy around us. We have a tendency to relate everything to the earth on which we stand.

We interact with our perceived reality in response to sensory information from it. This interaction began in the acts of gathering food and water and building shelter, and expanded to include our social and technological world. The physical interaction with the energy of the first layer is *not necessary* in order to maintain the physical body, but we have learned to rely on it and our paradigm is structured around it. This interaction now provides the physical body with the basic needs of survival.

The first chakra is located at the base of the spine and is called the root, or base chakra. It is in harmony with the energy of our physical earth, gives vitality to the physical body, and is the seat of what is known as "vital life force." This life force is an energy that is refined from The One, through our paradigm and the activity of the physical body, in response to attention. Vital life force is a refined energy of The One, yet a product of the physical body in response to attention. It is unique to the first level because the physical body is part of the refining process. The energy of physical survival vibrates in the base chakra. These include those basic needs of food, water, shelter, and procreation.

Again, although we have learned to rely on the interaction of the first chakra with our physical environment by gathering food, water, and shelter, the actual participation in the process eating, drinking and seeking shelter is not necessary. The first chakra, when in Balance with the rest of the energy centers, has the ability to assimilate food and water directly from the energy of the first layer. But we have made the basic needs of the physical body a major part of our experience, so the drive for physical survival requires, for most of us, the actual act of gathering food and water and building shelter.

The second transpersonal layer is inhabited by entities who, at the time of physical death, have left the first layer while *focusing their attention on the activity of it.* The second layer is, in most respects, an extension of the first layer without the physical substance of it. It is easily accessible because it *vibrates in harmony* with the attention of many of the residents of the first layer. Remember, paradigms in harmony attract. Because of this, it is the most often described layer beyond the first. The second transpersonal layer is accessible with just a slight shift of attention.

The power of the paradigm in presenting reality is as evident a force in the second layer as it is in the first. Entities residing there are *emotionally focused* on a physical portion of the movie of consensus reality. They carried their wants, needs, and desires with them when they left at the time of physical death. This layer is often called Hades or hell, and is said to be a place of suffering and torment.

But it is *not* a place of punishment. It is simply a place where its inhabitants cannot satisfy the earthly desires that are still the focus of their attention. Inhabitants of the second layer maintain their energy in the "form" of a physical body, experience the needs of the physical body, and have a sense of time. But, because they can no longer produce the vital life force of the physical body, they can no longer satisfy themselves with experience as they did while here. This is the cause of their "suffering." They are still are emotionally committed or tied to the activity of the first layer, and are attracted to the energy of vital life force that is produced in it. Individuals emotionally committed to a spouse, family, position, cause, or possession are still focusing their attention on them. We find greed, lust, emotional love and hate, and addiction to physical substances wherever we travel in this layer.

We also find entities unintentionally residing in the second transpersonal layer. There are those who, at the time of physical death, were focused intently and emotionally on an activity of the first layer. These includes soldiers in the heat of battle, law enforcement officers involved in a fight, or other individuals involved in a life-and-death struggle. Their attention, at the time of death, was focused on the energies of the first chakra with the intention of remaining physically alive. Remember, our movie of reality is the result of our focus of attention and the programs of our paradigm, and all experience is a product of our mind. Their attention was so focused on the first chakra at the time of death that they did not perceive the process of transition. It was fully filtered from their mind and, for them, virtually did not happen. They are sometimes found long after transition took place, still acting out the intense movie that was played in their mind at their time of death. Included in this category are those who have died suddenly, not having experienced the programs for physical death. They simply don't know that they are no longer in the first layer.

All the individuals residing in the second layer share one thing in common. Their *attention* is still focused on the first transpersonal layer and their *paradigm* is functioning as if still in it. This focus of attention includes both extremes of the positive and negative interpretations our paradigm has assigned to the first layer. We find entities focused on "good" as well as "bad" in the second layer. As an example, we might encounter an individual who is still focused on building a home for his family, as well as one who is intent on ridding the earth of a specific race of people. This is an extreme example, but it serves as a reminder that the focus of attention, not an interpretation of right or wrong, is that which limits our experience.

Residents of the second transpersonal layer are attracted to those individuals in the first who share the same vibration in the mind and produce the energies of vital life force they still desire. They may also be attracted to the physical location in the first layer that is still the focus of their attention. These locations often contain the energies of the first chakra that are held in place by The Magic of Agreeing of all those still remaining here. Intense emotional energy, especially when shared with a group of individuals, leaves a lasting imprint on the holographic energy of The One as long as the minds of the participants are still focused on it. Extreme examples are battlefields and places of religious worship. But they may include the house that an individual spent a lifetime building, the location of the remains of their physical body, or the buildings and icons that are still the focus of their religious conviction, to name a few.

Although a few are highly focused on the first layer and refuse to turn their attention to the Light of Mind, most of the residents of the second layer continue on after a short period of time. They are held there *only by their attention*. They soon recognize their situation and complete the process of transition. If they do not do so on their own, there are many from the first layer who enter the second to assist them, as well as some from the third layer who enter the second to encourage them on. All that is necessary for transition is for them to realize their situation and turn their attention to the ever-present Light of Mind. Having done so, they quickly continue the process of transition as their Path arises before them. There are exceptions, but transition usually takes them to the next layer where they may go on or return again to the first.

Residents of the second layer may find ways to interact with the energy of the first through places, situations, or the individuals still in it. But most will not return to the first layer from the second. With very few exceptions, they must go on through transition in order to re-enter the first layer.

The second chakra is located at the navel. It is the seat of the energy of emotional desires, and physical power. They include physical pleasure, lust, greed, position, possessions, emotional commitment, working harmoniously in groups, and the activity of changing the physical environment. Again, it is the focus of attention, not an interpretation of good or bad, that drives the energies of the second chakra. The energies of the second chakra vibrate in response to our attention and manifest through our paradigm. Any interaction with the first layer, at either end of the emotional spectrum, that becomes a need in the paradigm, results in an attraction that remains with us when we leave it.

The second chakra, when in Balance, is able to participate in the emotional interaction of the first layer without developing a need for that interaction. This Balance does not eliminate the extremes of emotion, but tempers emotions so they may be quickly returned to their source and not become a lingering part of the paradigm.

The third transpersonal layer is often called heaven, or paradise. It is here we find the place of reward and punishment and, in a truer sense, the hell spoken of in the second layer. Holographically, and in Balance, the words "heaven" and "paradise" include the opposites of their commonly held connotations of reward; they include the place of punishment. Entities in the third layer have gathered themselves together in "places" or "communities" that support their belief and reality structures. The place of reward, as well as for punishment, is found here. Remember, Balance is. In the first and second layers, Balance is found in the interaction between the two. In the third layer, balance is found in the fact that both reward and punishment exist there.

Residents of the places of reward are not aware of those in the place of punishment, nor the other way around. Neither are they aware of the other communities within their layer. Their paradigm filters from their awareness the fact that there is much more activity taking place in the energy around them—just as ours does here in the first layer.

Entities in the third layer of reward believe that they deserve the reality they are in. They usually maintain a discernible human form. Most belief structures include a "physical" paradise, and many others accept existence in some identifiable form. They are, however, not bound to the physical substance of form. Although they can still eat, they do not "need" to. Although they can walk from place to place, they can also move about their reality with just a thought. They may present themselves in a replication of the physical form they took in their physical movie of reality, or take on any form they desire. But they can do so only if they have developed a paradigm to support it, and that must be accomplished in the first layer. They spend their time enjoying the "pleasures" of their expectations—and going to school.

A desire for Knowledge is intrinsic in the third layer, and its residents possess a childlike curiosity. Individuals may seek any form of Knowledge, from the science of the first layer to an understanding of The One. The desire to learn is predominate here, and teachers abound. The residents of the third layer of reward have found an experience that meets their expectations and they share it with others in agreement with them.

Those in the third layer of punishment have also found an experience that meets their expectations. They, too, share it with others in agreement with them. Their punishment is the opposite of reward. They maintain a form, but it is often a degenerated replication of the worst physical form they can recall. It may still contain their memory of pain and suffering while in the first layer. They are hungry and thirsty, but have no satisfaction. They yearn for Knowledge, but there are no teachers. Everything they accomplish is done with a *struggle of attention*. Even moving about takes a great effort of attention. Unlike the residents of the second layer, they are not emotionally driven to the pleasures of the first layer, but they honestly believe they deserve to be punished. They have accepted self-judgment. They believe they have lived a "bad" life, have not lived up to the expectations of their belief system, or should be punished for things they did or did not do.

In addition to the religious communities and belief systems in the third transpersonal layer, there are also communities of unfinished desire. These are not the personal desires of self-gratification found in the second layer. Here we find scientists still working on their projects, artists still painting or creating, composers still composing, and dancers still dancing. These entities, when confronted with self-judgment, held little or no paradigm of reward or punishment. They did, however, hold a deep desire to continue doing what they were doing in the first layer. They were unfulfilled, and their attention still focused on their "work." Most are more loving and giving than many of those who inhabit the places of reward in the second layer, and usually not at all interested in self-gratification. They are now in a "place" where they continue their efforts of attention with others of the same mind. These are happy and highly energized communities and, because their focus of attention is still on the challenges of the first layer, are in harmony with many of us here.

A notable quality of all the residents of the third transpersonal layer is the childlike nature mentioned. All of its residents are fully committed to their experience, and they continue without questioning it. They have no sense of time. They believe that their experience will go on forever. Their desire to learn is childlike. They accept any answer that fits into their paradigm, and immediately reject any that does not.

Residents of the third transpersonal layer function in the same logic. They possess little or no ability of cognitive thought—the ability to give thoughtful consideration to other possibilities. And they are like children in a school yard at recess. The emotional love and joy they experience and project is childlike. No one is waiting for the school bell. Those in the areas of punishment are the same. They can be compared to a child experiencing the punishment of standing in a corner. Their entire world is self-centered.

And they believe, even though they have been sent to the corner for a short time, that it is lasting forever. Their corner is empty, they are alone, and are filled with sorrow and self-pity.

The third transpersonal layer is the place of *Ego fulfillment*. It is here that individuals fully experience the results of a lifetime of expectation based on Maya. They experience their reward or punishment through the judgment of their Ego. And they experience it in exactly the way their Ego rewarded or punished others physically, mentally, or emotionally during their movie of consensus reality. Their mind retains their paradigm and supplies an experience founded on it. Like us here in consensus reality, they share it with others through the power of The Magic of Agreeing. Whether it is reward, punishment, or the simple expectation that the attention given to their work will go on forever, the movie of reality played out on the view screen of awareness in the third layer is the final product of Ego.

The vast majority of the residents of the third layer return to the first to gain another experience. All projections of the mind are self-limiting—all dreams have an ending. After a time, they simply lose interest in their movie and "fall asleep." This is not actually what happens, but it is the closest we can come to describing it. But remember, their paradigm is still with them. Because of this, they still desire experience. Their attention now focuses on the energy of the hologram that vibrates in harmony with their attention. They are attracted, once again, to the first layer. They again choose an experience that meets their expectations. They awaken into their new dream in the first layer in a physical body, in the physical conditions, with physical limitations, and surrounded by supporting actors. This does not happen by chance. It is not an accident. It is a choice made by the focus of attention. It is their Path arising before them.

The third chakra is located at the solar plexus. Its energy vibrates in harmony with attention given to self-evaluation and the evaluation of others. The third chakra is the energy center for the Ego. As with all the chakras, this energy is fully filtered and refined by our paradigm before energizing the third chakra. The vibration of this energy is often the result of the limited principles of Maya that are developed through emotional interaction in our movie of reality. What we experience is usually a feeling or conviction rather than an understanding. We do not often know why we believe or feel the way we do. It is usually the result of something we were taught by others, but learned through *emotional experience*.

Our system of evaluation and judgment is evident in the solar plexus. The emotional energy of the second chakra is often held captive in the third by the Ego. We can actually feel it there. It is also the seat of energy for self-control, will power, authority, and humor. The energy of the third chakra is emotionally challenging to work with. Our ability to judge ourselves and our part in the movie of reality resides in the Ego of the third chakra. Again, this ability is a product of our paradigm and its programs that result from emotional experience. To accomplish judgment for ourselves, we continually judge others and their part in the movie.

A major function of the Ego is to externalize experience. The feeling that what is happening, good or bad, is the result of external conditions created by others, and that we are not in control of it, resides in the Ego energies of the third chakra.

The third chakra in Balance is able to participate in experience without judgment. It holds no expectations and places no blame on external conditions. This Balanced energy results in acceptance of full responsibility and self-control. Again, this is manifest in a feeling rather than an understanding.

Let's pause for a moment to identify some commonalties we have discovered this far. The essence of Maya—the sense of separation, limitation, and meaning—is a part of the supporting paradigm of *all three layers*. There are qualities available in the first layer that are suppressed or missing in the second and third. The second and third layers are without the physical body, and both are almost *free of cognitive thought*—the ability to give thoughtful consideration to other possibilities. Remember, all that is, is of The One. Experience is of The One. Full immersion in limited experience is found in the first transpersonal layer, as well as the ability of cognitive thought. But cognitive thought is virtually absent in the second and third transpersonal layers. Although it is not impossible to do so elsewhere, the easiest place to work on the paradigm and gain Balance is in the first layer.

The first three layers of the transpersonal realm, as well as the first three chakras, are interwoven into our consensus reality through the power of The Magic of Agreeing. Because of this, interaction on a mental level between these layers is not difficult. It requires only a slight shift of attention. Those who are aware of the energy of our being report that the energy patterns of those in second and third layers of the transpersonal realm differ little from those of us who reside here in the first.

Now, on again to the next layer. There is said to be a great division between the third layer and those beyond, and that those who cross it cannot return. This is, of course, a limitation. It is unlikely that anyone having gained the Balance necessary to make the crossing would desire to return in a physical form, but to say it is impossible is not correct.

While the first three layers are a result of immersion in experience, the fourth layer is without limited experience. It does contain experience, but of a different form. It contains *experiential awareness*—the ability to be involved in experience while remaining fully aware of the nature of it. This awareness is viewed by the mind through its paradigm, but the mind has no method of explaining or defining it. It simply is.

In the fourth transpersonal layer, cognitive thought, the ability to thoughtfully consider all possibility, is predominant. It is Maya appearing in the mind that gives us the impression of division in the first three layers. This division exists *only in our mind*. As we enter the fourth layer, the illusion of separation, limitation and meaning is transcended. The presentation of Maya now comes under the mastery of our attention. Maya does not disappear. All that is, is of The One, and the Maya produced by the mind is still present in the fourth layer. But even though Maya is still present, it is held in place by the attention to Balance between the mind and Mind. This is Balance. It is a state in which both the mind and Mind are fully active. This is the ability to focus attention both on the experience and the potential for experience. We could say that experience expands to contain awareness, or that awareness expands to contain experience in the fourth layer. With Maya under the mastery of attention, we are able to maintain our sense of identity and self-expression, or experience, while remaining aware of the full potential of The One. This Balance is manifest as experiential awareness.

As an example, you are a member of a *race* of people. Identification with a race of people is a possibility that can result in limited experience when you become immersed in it. This occurs when you allow your mind to attach separation, limitation, and meaning to the experience. When you allow your attention, while in Balance, to hold that awareness concerning your race, you access the fourth transpersonal layer and experiential awareness. Your mind is filled with the possibilities for any and all experiences concerning that potential separation in the form of that race of people. You fully participate in the experience of the people without separation from the source of the experience. In addition, your perception is holographic. The physical senses are manifest as your innate holographic sense and encompasses them all. You see, hear, and feel in every "direction" throughout time and space as we know it; you are without restriction. You *know* every individual who is a member of your race, as well as your part of it. You have *awareness* of the total potential experience of each individual as well as the entire race. You *fully understand* the holographic whole as well as the individual parts. This awareness arises with unconditional Love and total acceptance. There is no judgment in the fourth transpersonal layer.

This experiential awareness exists for every aspect of our reality, each and every "piece" of our movie. It is accessed through attention. When we place our attention on a grain of sand, a bird, or a tree, the same experiential awareness arises. When we think of nations, governments or the entire world, our Balance contains all experience as well as total awareness of them. It is a state in which both the mind and Mind are fully active. It is *the state of Balance.*

The fourth transpersonal layer is not a place. It exists everywhere and through all time. It is both the beginning and the end. The fourth layer is the Balance of The One. The fourth transpersonal layer is the Heart.

Again, entities in experiential awareness of the fourth layer are in a state of Balance between experience and awareness. They exist nowhere—yet everywhere. They are able to fully comprehend the "meaning" given to experience while remaining totally "aware" of the full potential of The One. They are able to experience the results of separation, limitation, and meaning without losing themselves in it. They are also able to focus their attention on the full potential of The One without losing themselves in it. They are in Balance.

The fourth chakra is located at the Heart. It vibrates in harmony with unconditional Love and understanding. The focus of attention on the Heart chakra is free from emotion and beyond the intellect of consensus reality. It is in full harmony with the energies of the first three layers, yet vibrating in Balance in The One. The Heart chakra contains the fullness of expression as well as the vastness of potential. The whole of this energy is held in Balance in the Heart, and it is gained only with attention to Balance. One will not access the Heart while holding to a paradigm of separation, limitation, and meaning.

The Heart is Balance, and because of this, is the energy from which Balance is expressed in thought, word, and deed. Balance is not a static state. Some think that the Heart in Balance feels none of the needs or desires of the first three chakras and holds no dreams or expectations of the potential of The One. This is not true. The Heart, because it is Balance, is alive with the vibrations of all the chakras, with all the layers.

The Heart does not contain a specific quality of good or bad, right or wrong, positive or negative. Again, the Heart, although we have called it a transpersonal layer, is not perceived as an individual layer of energy. The Heart has no state other than Balance. The Heart is Balance, and encompasses all the transpersonal layers. When we enter the Heart, we enter The One in Balance.

Beyond the fourth layer, there is only energy. Location is not an issue here. The thoughts of individual entities are combined through attention in these layers. Ideas come into possibility here. It is here where we participate in agreement with the various possibilities held in the potential of The One. Our combined attention results in any possible movie of consensus reality—or not. The dreamed possibilities of all entities in the first three layers, as well as those in the remaining layers, are vibrating here.

The fifth transpersonal layer is commonly called the place of the gods or archetypes, and it is, indeed, a place of powerful creative energy. All the thoughts and desires of every entity in the previous layers are summed up and exist here as a single driving force. Possibilities not yet in expression, possibilities held in Mind of those in the layers yet to come, are vibrating here. It can be thought of as the combination of all paradigms in energy form. The entire potential of The One exists here, as everywhere, in its fullest. But so do the limiting thoughts of every entity that is.

This is the creator of which we are a part. This is the creator of which all entities experiencing limitation in any form are a part. The creator is constantly changing, flowing and growing in response to the attention of those in the first three layers as well as those in the remaining. Although one will not enter the energies of the fourth layer while holding Maya in the mind, a strong belief in an external god can lead to awareness of the fifth.

Remember, all is energy and interconnected. If we enter the fifth transpersonal layer with our paradigm in place, our mind interprets this energy as an experience and we perceive it through our physical senses. Because of this, holding a strong belief in an external creator can result in a limited awareness of the fifth transpersonal layer. It is presented by our mind according to our expectations. The creator is an archetype and, by its very nature, appears in whatever form is held in the paradigm of the observer. The god of our belief is created by our mind in response to our attention and the energies of the fifth transpersonal layer. This is one of the reasons why we have so many different teachings on the nature of an external god. When this creative force of our combined minds is viewed through a paradigm of separation, limitation, and meaning, we are presented with the god of our expectations.

Our perception of an external god is often of a being with his or her mind made up. There is no negotiation with the archetypes. As we shall see later on, the combined attention the archetypes give to creation is without consideration for other possibilities—without cognitive thought.

The idea that a god would like to see good things happen, or that a god is rewarding good and punishing evil, is an evaluation resulting from a limited paradigm. The concept results from our belief that there is an external creative force. The creative force of the energies of the fifth transpersonal layer responds directly to the attention of all entities anywhere. It is here that all our paradigms are added together, and our combined creative energy is given to the sum. It is our own creative energy and The Magic of Agreeing, not that of the archetype. The archetype itself is our creation. It has no power of its own. This creative force is without any sense of good or bad, right or wrong—and we are the source.

The creative force of the fifth layer is thought made manifest through intent. In our consensus reality, intent is given through the spoken word. The fifth chakra is located at the throat. It is the center for the energies of creativity through speech, writing, and the arts. It vibrates in harmony either with the energies of any of the chakras, or the energy of the Heart, depending on our individual attention. This is why, throughout all major religions, the power of the spoken word is held in high regard.

We can give voice to a thought with or without including cognitive thought. It can be an expression of the energies of the first three chakras given in intense emotion, an expression of the unconditional Love and understanding of the Heart, or an expression of a possibility held in the energies of the remaining chakras. The act of carefully choosing the words we speak and the thoughts we hold in our attention has a tremendous impact on the vibrations of all the layers. And as we know, our movie of reality and our actions within it respond to our attention and are manifest through thought, word, and deed.

The fifth chakra in Balance speaks, acts, and thinks from the Heart. Every word spoken, every action given, and every thought arising is held in total, unconditional Love. The fifth chakra in balance is without judgment of others or self.

The sixth transpersonal layer lies just this side of The One. Here we find the possibility for all experiences, including alternate realities—realities that are not directly tied to our Magic of Agreeing. All that exists within our physical universe is contained within our Magic of Agreeing, even if we are not physically aware of it. The transpersonal layers we have been discussing to this point are *not alternate realities*. Alternate realities do exist in dimensions beyond the confines of our physical movie of reality. Yet there is only The One, so these alternate realities are interwoven into the hologram of our consensus reality and are a part of it. Because of this, they are accessible from our reality and, in some cases, our reality overlaps with alternate realities. It is not the purpose of this book to discuss this, but you should know that this earth and its life forms as well as the transpersonal layers we are discussing are of one reality, and are only one of many realities we have created—one of many movies we may attend.

The sixth transpersonal layer is the "place" where experience, or creative energy, begins. It can be compared to standing outside a building containing an unlimited number of cinema theaters. Each one has a poster displaying the highlights of its intended presentation. These are just presentations, just combined thoughts of potential creations. They are not yet manifest in any "form." They are in the creative state—they exist as possibilities but do not yet contain the fullness of limited experience. They are laid before us in unlimited number, but we are "seeing" holographically at this point, so we are able to view them all.

We choose our experience in much the way we choose which movie we will attend in the cinema. It is a matter of personal choice and is driven by the focus of our attention. And our choice is, as you recognize, influenced by the experience of previous movies we have seen. Once we have made our choice of experience, we become involved in our new reality in much the way we become involved in the cinema. Our mind begins the process of filtering and refining our awareness of the holographic world around us to provide an experience for us.

The sixth transpersonal layer is rich in mental activity, and is sometimes referred to as "divine mind." It is here where we imagine the potential of The One into possibility. It is the place of birth for creative thought, just this side of unlimited potential. It can be thought of as a giant "think tank," where any and all possibility is open for exploration. And this possibility is considered without limitation. There are absolutely no restrictions on creative thought here. It is like the mind of children involved in play, dreaming reality as they participate in it. To children, it makes no difference if their play is consistent with consensus reality. If they can imagine it, it becomes so.

The sixth chakra is located at the brow, in the center of the forehead between the eyebrows. This chakra vibrates in harmony with the imagination. It is here we mentally leave the world of consensus reality and create "impossible" movies in our mind. We call these alternate movies "fantasies," and usually believe that they are not possible within the confines of consensus reality. Even so, most of us enjoy them and will even attend cinema presentations that have been created around them.

The sixth chakra is the center of *imagination*. Remember that the focus of our attention is the driving force for all the chakras. Imagination is our ability to access the possibilities of The One and allow them to manifest in our awareness. The combination of imagination and attention can create the beginning of a movie. Imagination and attention without Balance results in full immersion in either experience or awareness. Imagination and attention in Balance results in freedom from the limitations of Maya. Imagination and attention in Balance is the essence of cognitive thought.

The seventh transpersonal layer is the full *potential* of The One. It is here that the limitless potential for all exists. Unlike the sixth layer, no single thought of limited possibility has been given the energy of attention. Because of this, no experience exists. But the potential for experience exists without limitation here, and as we shall see, limited experience has its beginning here.

There is no manner in which this vast potential can be described—at least not from our perspective. We have attempted to give examples but, in the final analysis, there are simply no words to describe it. It is true, though, that although it contains the potential for all experience in its energy, it is void of any *limited experience*.

The seventh chakra is the crown chakra. It lies just above the top of the head, beyond the physical body—void of limited physical experience. The crown chakra is the holographic "mirror" of the potential of The One. It is pure energy and is, from our holographic model, only potential. It can be felt, beyond thought or description, just beyond the top or your head.

The seventh chakra is the place beyond thought where full awareness lies. As this awareness is viewed by our mind, it is given attention and the filtering and refining process begins. The potential is then structured to fit within our individual paradigm and eventually makes its way into our consensus movie.

The energies of the seventh chakra contain no qualities of good or bad, right or wrong. These energies are simply potential. But when they make their way into our awareness, they are met by our paradigm. When our Balance is in the Heart, the potential of the seventh chakra is experienced in freedom from separation, limitation, or meaning. When the energies of the seventh chakra are experienced away from Balance, they are the harbinger of a movie containing separation, limitation, and meaning.

Recall again your spider web and remember that all the layers of awareness are accessible to anyone at any time. The focus of attention in the crown chakra is without thought, without emotion, and without expression. The focus of attention on a potential experience held in the energy of the crown chakra results in the possibility of that experience being made manifest through the imagination and into the mind. Further attention, especially when shared by many individuals, brings the potential experience, the energy of the hologram, within the powers of The Magic of Agreeing. From that point, it is a simple matter of continued attention until the experience is fully manifest in our consensus reality.

The seventh chakra in Balance is aware of all potential, all possibility. When accessed through the Heart, this potential can become manifest in the physical movie of reality with just a thought.

When we discussed the first layer, I said physical interaction with the energy of the first layer is not necessary in order to maintain the physical body. Attention focused on the potential in the crown chakra can result in phenomena such as the ability to survive without food and water. These manifestations are, however, not the evidence of Balance, nor does Balance necessarily result in such phenomena. An individual in Balance has access to the full potential of the crown chakra, but the very act of Balance, and the individual's Path, may preclude them from making a physical display of this potential.

Full immersion in awareness is also accessible from the first layer through the practice of stilling the mind. As mentioned, stilling the mind is thought to be a form of meditation. However, immersion in awareness is the same as immersion in experience. This is not Balance. As you know, in Balance, both the mind and Mind are fully active.

The ability of cognitive thought is available to entities in the seventh layer. By comparison, entities immersed in awareness are like those in consensus reality who are so involved in the world around them that they "never give a thought" to anything else. Even though other possibilities may "pass through their mind," they never give them their attention. The moment they do, they are considering other possibilities. And with that attention, consensus reality is changed for them. The same is true in the seventh transpersonal layer. The moment another possibility is considered, immersion in awareness ends and transition begins.

We have now developed a map of the transpersonal layers and the chakras. We have seen Balance in them all. We have also seen a progression toward

Balance from the first transpersonal layer to the Heart. If Balance is, as the Master says, we should see the same progression appearing in the other direction, from the seventh layer toward Balance in the Heart. This involves the last three transpersonal layers of the our web, from The One toward the center.

Entities immersed in potential are alive in awareness. Once again, recall our spider web. When our attention is focused on the first layer, our view screen is filled with experience. We are immersed in *experience*. Experience is a function of the mind, and the paradigm of the mind filters the fullness of awareness from our conscious view screen. Likewise, when our attention is fully focused on the seventh layer, our conscious view screen is filled with potential. We are immersed in *potential*. Awareness is a function of Mind. The paradigm, now residing in Mind, filters experience from our conscious view screen. Balance is found only in the Heart.

The fullness of Mind is timeless, presenting all potential in a single, eternal, holographic instant. The fullness of Mind is without emotion. Emotion is a function of the mind, and it remains in the background for those immersed in potential. Although the potential for experience is there, no limited experience exists in Mind. Experience is a function of the mind, and the filters of Mind do not allow it to arise on the view screen of *their* awareness. Those immersed in potential have *separated* themselves from experience and *limited* themselves to awareness. And because they are totally aware of all potential meaning, they are *meaningless*. They are without self-expression.

But separation, limitation, and meaninglessness are functions of Mind. Just behind the filters of Mind, the mind is calling to express itself, calling to create. Because of this continual calling of the mind, they find themselves aware of a possibility held within the potential of which they are a part. It lasts for just a moment—just the slightest thought arising from the mind. They give no attention to it. Their attention remains immersed in the limitless potential of The One. But they have *become aware of an experience*. And it has an effect on the filters of Mind.

Entities immersed in potential dream. Remember, we are holographic. The creative impulse, the desire for self-expression, is always with us. Our imagination does not suddenly disappear at some time in our development. There is no time as we know it in The One, so we are at a loss for words to describe what happens there. But we know that they can only participate in total awareness "for a period of time" before the desire for self-expression surfaces. It is then that they "go to sleep and dream."

And they dream as we do. What is in their imagination, in their mind, is played out on the view screen of their dream awareness. They dream those thoughts that passed the view screen of Mind while they were immersed in potential. They create.

Their dreams are real and valid experiences, just as ours are. No Magic of Agreeing has an effect on their dreams, nor do the limitations of immersion in potential. Their mind, free of constraints, is producing an experience. They are personal dreams. Cognitive thought is not a part of their personal dreams. They are having an experience, and thoughtful consideration of other possibilities is simply not a part of their dream reality.

The dreamers awaken from their dream much as we do. The memory of their dream, of their experience, quickly fades into the background as they become immersed again in potential.

Thoughtful consideration of other possibilities, or cognitive thought, is most evident in the *two extremes* of the transpersonal layers, the first and the seventh. We can compare an entity immersed or awake in the seventh layer to an individual immersed or awake in the first. We can say that they are awake, but it is subjective. They are awake in potential, but have little or no experience. And they possess the very same ability of cognitive thought that is evident in the first transpersonal layer. Entities in the seventh transpersonal layer are able to give thoughtful consideration to other possibilities. Cognitive thought is the impetus, while immersed in awareness, that transforms potential into possibility. From immersion in awareness, potential becomes more a possibility and less a potential as attention is given to it. It is the same process of filtering and refining the potential of The One that is found in the first layer. It is the very act of giving attention that creates a paradigm.

The Heart is always with us. Balance is our nature, and those in the seventh transpersonal layer can, with the focus of attention in Balance, gain the center and move to the Heart just as those in the first can. But they are experiencing immersion in awareness and are without self-expression. Even though they are timeless, this state of imbalance will not continue forever.

Any immersion in separation, limitation, or meaning has an end. Our nature is Balance, and our intrinsic drive is for it. The Master tells us that if we do not recognize our desire for experience, we are not in Balance. Here in the first layer, our mind is presenting our movie of reality, and the full awareness of Mind lies in the background. For those immersed in awareness of the seventh layer, Mind is presenting all potential, and the creative impulse of self-expression—the mind—lies in the background. The mind desires self-expression. It is the creator of experience, and we are creators. Those immersed in potential do not recognize their desire for experience. Because of this, for them, it begins again.

Their movie of awareness, displayed on the view screen of Mind while the mind lies in the background, ends much the same as ours does. They experience transition. For us, it takes a lifetime of practice for the death of awareness. For them, without time, it is an instant—the instant they focus their attention, without Balance, on other possibilities. In that moment, the death of full awareness—and transition—begins. They follow their attention as we do. Their attention is toward experience, and they begin the experience of the presentation of the mind.

The sixth transpersonal layer is the energy of attention to possibility. Most of the entities leaving the seventh layer pass right through this layer. They have already developed expectations for an experience. But entities who have not developed expectations for experience arrive in the sixth layer while still *focusing their attention on the potential of the seventh*. The sixth layer is, in most respects, an extension of the seventh without the full potential of it. It contains the possibility for all experience in its earliest form, as pure creative thought. It is the Light of the mind of every entity in the seventh layer who has dreamed that possibility. It is easily accessible because it vibrates in harmony with the attention of the seventh layer.

The power of the paradigm in Mind that is limiting experience and presenting potential is as evident a force in the sixth layer as it is in the seventh. Although a few are highly focused on the seventh layer and refuse to turn their attention to the experience of the mind, most of the entities experiencing the sixth layer continue on after a short period of time. They are held there only by their attention. They soon recognize their situation and become aware of the process of transition. All that is necessary for transition is for them to realize their situation and turn their attention to the ever-present experience of the mind, and the possibility for experience that has been the focus of their attention. Having done so, they quickly continue the process of transition as their Path arises before them. Transition takes them to the next layer.

Remember, those in transition from the seventh layer are without time or distance, and not separated as we appear to be here in the first layer. With the focus of attention, they instantly join with "others" in agreement, in harmony. With the experience of "others," they experience the creative self of their mind. They are beginning to realize self-expression—and begin making comparisons. They are experiencing the mind as their Path arises before them.

Their desire is for self-expression, and they are in agreement on the chosen theme. It is the one they gave a moments attention to, the one they dreamed. They are drawn, by their attention, to all those minds that vibrate in harmony with them. They think it would be a great idea to participate together in an illusion, in a dream. It will be like making a movie, but it will only exist in their minds. Most of them just want to create and direct their dream movie. They do not all want to be actors.

Combining their efforts of thought and creativity, they begin to build the set and write the script for their movie. They create it from the energy of which they are a part. The set they create is beautiful, with plants and animals, majestic mountain ranges, vast oceans, and great plains. They are having a wonderful time, and think they have created the best dream movie ever. They select, from among themselves, actors that will follow a script. The actors will rely upon each other to make the movie whole.

You remember the creators. They are The Sky Heroes of Dream Time.

As they focus their attention on one possibility, they relinquished their ability to give thoughtful consideration to others. They join the attention of the archetypes. They are in the fifth transpersonal layer. Although still timeless and without "place," they gather together in thought and begin giving attention to their creative abilities. They are like little children in a school yard at recess. Vibrating in harmony with the common attention of all entities anywhere in any time, they become more and more involved in creating and expressing themselves through experience.

They quickly learn that limited experience requires a special combination of energy, and that this combination must be held in place by attention. This combination allows them to experience opposition. They do not call it positive or negative, good or bad. That will come later, after the Sky Heroes have gotten into their costumes and become immersed in the first layer. For now, it is just energy combined through an agreement and the focus of attention so that limited experience can happen.

There are many experiences happening in the energy of thought here in the fifth layer. But each group of entities in agreement is unaware of the others. The mind, in providing them with this wonderful new outlet for creative expression, is already filtering and refining their reality for them. They have to focus their attention, and continue to agree, in order to hold their creation together. They cannot consider other possibilities. If they did, their dream would fade away and return to The One.

All limited experience has an end. The majority of the entities in the fifth transpersonal layer return again and again to the seventh layer to become immersed in awareness. But their paradigm, the focus of their attention during experience, goes with them. Again they answer the internal call to self-expression, and again they return to experience. They are on their Path. Many of them begin to desire more experience in their parts in the movie. When this happens, they pass fully through the fourth layer during transition, through Balance, and become immersed in limited experience. It is unlikely that they will stop at the third layer. It is filled with entities having form but no costumes. Nor is it likely they will pause at the second. From the second, the light of experience in the first layer shines ever so brightly.

The ability to give thoughtful Balanced consideration to other possibilities was not with our Sky Heroes in the sixth and fifth layers. They did not exercise it while immersed in potential. But it surfaces again now, in its fullest, while they are immersed in limited experience. Balance is the only truth. And even though they have forgotten that they are the creators of their dreamed reality, the Sky Hero's Mind is ever in the background. Fortunately, their Path remains with them in their experience. It arises ever before them—calling them to Balance.

We have come full circle. The beginning is the end, and the end is the beginning. This is as it should be. This is what all Masters teach: Balance is.

We have looked at the layers of the transpersonal realm and seen their relationship to the chakras found in the human body. In doing so, we have found a model of the holographic nature of reality reflected in the very physical form we have taken. But where is Balance for us? At which layer of transpersonal awareness, at which chakra, does it lie?

We know it is in the Heart—in Balance, but let's look at it again.

There is an impulse built into our nature, an impulse for Balance. While we are involved in our movie of consensus reality, this is identified as the "spiritual impulse." Consensus reality in the first three layers is rich in limited experience but virtually empty of awareness. Even so, we are holographic in nature, so the longing for awareness becomes manifest whenever our "movie" experience diminishes or becomes less desirable. When we are not in Balance, we are drawn to it.

The One is rich in potential but empty of limited experience. Even though all experience exists in potential while we are floating in full awareness, we are without self-expression. But all that is, is of The One. As we were without awareness while immersed in our movie, we are without expression while immersed in The One. Here, while totally immersed in the potential of The One, we become aware of the same impulse for Balance, and we may recognize it as our "experience impulse." Even though we are drawn to Balance, we are void of self expression, and it may seem to us that we are drawn to experience. This is because immersion in experience is the opposite of our immersion in awareness. But we are drawn, as always, to Balance.

Home is where the Heart is—literally. The Heart chakra, the fourth layer, is the center. Remember, all that is, is of The One. This includes the first three layers of consensus reality as well as our creative force, imagination and The One—the last three layers. We are not in Balance while we are involved in our limited movie of reality because we lack awareness. But neither are we in Balance when we are immersed without expression in full awareness. We are entities in Balance—and Balance is in motion. It is from the Heart that we are able to move freely about our holographic world.

Look at it another way. We did not "leave" The One when we became involved in consensus reality, in our limited experience as Sky Heroes. The One is evident in the energy of our crown chakra. It is only the awareness we lack. Likewise, we do not "leave" the mind behind when we become immersed in The One. It would be silly to think that a holographic being would suddenly lose his or her creative impulse simply by becoming immersed in awareness. We are holographic. It remains with us, and results in the opposite of a spiritual impulse. It results in a desire for self-expression. We are creators. Again, our Balance is found in the very center of our web. In the Heart.

We have labeled the layers and discussed them as layers in order to understand them from our perspective, yet we know that there are no layers. They just appear to exist because of our limited awareness. We will continue to call them layers but remember, we are holographic energy, and all the "layers" of our holographic reality are available to us always. The limitation exists only in our mind. In Balance, the layers disappear and we become fully aware of our holographic nature.

And we have constantly found ourselves out of Balance, yet know that Balance is. We are always in Balance, but our paradigm withholds this from us.

Imagine yourself again at the center of the spider web, and let's call the center consensus reality. You are immersed in limited experience. Mind is only a vague concept that you are relating to what is now your center. Your attention is not in Balance, yet Balance is.

Now, imagine yourself immersed in Mind. You are still in the center of your web, and all those layers of awareness are still accessible to you. But you are immersed in potential. Experience, or the mind, is only a vague concept that you are relating to what is now your center. Your attention is not in Balance, yet Balance is.

Now, imagine yourself in Balance in your Heart—still in the center of your web. From here, you are able to fully understand and relate to *all experience* in the first three layers while remaining totally aware of the driving force and *potential for* experience in the remaining layers, from here the concept of layers has fallen away. You are able to imagine, express, and participate in your innate ability as a creator without becoming immersed in the Maya that is a part of self-expression. Both the creative drive of your mind and the full awareness of Mind are active. You are in Balance as always, your attention and your paradigm are in the center, and are free to explore the entire transpersonal realm. You have found the Heart.

We have looked deep into the transpersonal realm. To many, the thought of expanding awareness to include these layers seems overwhelming. How would we ever feel comfortable enough to freely explore the holographic world that is ours? And yet, it is our nature. It is even built into the movie of reality we have created. Our movie will end. Sooner or later, transpersonal awareness is ours. Balance is a wonderful concept, but how do we know it will remain when we leave this movie?

Take comfort. Nothing is hidden in the hologram. All that is, is of The One. The very state of awareness we require to explore the transpersonal realm appears right in our movie of consensus reality. It is here for us to identify, and to practice.

States of Awareness

We will look at *states of awareness* in the same way we looked at Mind and the mind, and the layers of the transpersonal realm, remembering that our breakdown is for the purpose of discussion only. As always, we will remember that all is holographic energy and cannot be divided. Knowing this, we will say that there are three states of awareness available to us in consensus reality.

The state of awareness available while awake in consensus reality is called *conscious awareness*. We call ourselves awake, but we know it is subjective. We are really awake in conscious awareness and under the influence of the problem solving activity of the mind. We are sleeping in relationship to our dreams and the transpersonal realm and, even though we can draw comparisons in our mind, we have little or no awareness of The One.

There is a specific ability available to us in the first transpersonal layer while in a state of conscious awareness. We are able to access our ability of cognitive thought. Again, cognitive thought is thoughtful consideration of other possibilities. For an entity in Balance, cognitive thought is thoughtful *Balanced* consideration of *all* possibilities. Any consideration given without Balance is *creative* thought. Creative thought adds the *energy of attention to the possibility* of the thought, and begins the filtering and refining process. Cognitive thought is the impetus, in the first and seventh transpersonal layers, that transforms potential into possibility. We have, while immersed in experience, the potential to become Balanced. But without cognitive thought and the focus of attention, it is not yet a possibility.

Another state of awareness that is evident in consensus reality is *sleep awareness*. This is the awareness available to us when we are involved in our personal dreams, when we are asleep at night. During sleep awareness, our mind presents us with the reality of our dreams. Our dreams are recorded in our mind, as all experience is. They do not become a major part of our paradigm because they are not shared with the state of awareness we use in consensus reality. They are realities of self-expression without the constraints of The Magic of Agreeing. For the most part, what we limit ourselves to in our imagination, we limit ourselves to in our dreams. Children have highly imaginative dreams. As we grow and develop a paradigm, our imagination becomes limited by it.

During sleep awareness, we relinquish the ability of cognitive thought. Thoughtful consideration of other possibilities is simply not a part of our dreamed reality. Try as we might, our unlikely dreamscape continues even though we know it should not be so.

The final state of awareness available to us in consensus reality is *transpersonal awareness*. Transpersonal awareness involves information that is not consistent with consensus reality and is beyond the paradigm limits of conscious awareness—beyond our personal experience. It does not fit into our movie of reality.

As you recall, the mind naturally shifts from a state of conscious awareness to transpersonal awareness in transition during the process of physical death. Remember also that, without Balance, our ability to give thoughtful consideration to other possibilities escapes us during transition. Without practice, cognitive thought is simply not a part of our paradigm during transition into transpersonal awareness. Try as we might to give consideration to what is happening, we are either launched into another movie created by our mind or plunged into the limitations of immersion in awareness. These are the three states of awareness available to us in consensus reality. Conscious awareness is available when we are "awake" in our movie of reality. With the effort of attention, it allows easy access to cognitive thought. Sleep awareness is our time of self-expression beyond the confines of The Magic of Agreeing. Cognitive thought is usually not available in sleep awareness. Transpersonal awareness is available through the focus of attention and arises in transition. Without practice, cognitive thought is not available during transpersonal awareness.

The mind shifts from a state of sleep awareness to conscious awareness when we awaken from our nightly rest. In this way, the shift of our conscious awareness during transition is much like the shift of our dream awareness when we awaken into consensus reality. We are asleep and dreaming in our sleep awareness. We awaken, our dream reality quickly fades into the background as conscious awareness begins its presentation of our new reality. We are "awake" in consensus reality. During transition, we awaken from our consensus dream, conscious awareness fades into the background, and transpersonal awareness replaces it, through our paradigm, as our new view screen of reality.

The obvious result of this comparison is the fact that cognitive thought is most easily available to us during our state of conscious awareness. And even while awake in conscious awareness, it requires a focus of attention to activate cognitive thought. Unless we give our attention to the process of thoughtfully considering other possibilities, our mind presents us with the product of our paradigm and we remain immersed in experience.

You will also notice that we have used the term *states* of awareness rather than *levels* of awareness. And you may have noticed that the terms *greater* awareness or *higher* awareness have not appeared throughout this book. This is intentional. These terms imply that there is a progression of levels in the mind. You know that there are not. The mind is holographic. Because of this, conscious awareness cannot be thought of as a higher state than sleep awareness, and transpersonal awareness no higher than conscious awareness. There are no levels of awareness. Energy is holographic. There are just different states of awareness, and they are a result of our attention, where we are focused in the hologram. All states of awareness are always available to us.

This is why we often find things that are a part of our conscious awareness appearing in our dreams, or why we may awaken from a personal dream with the answer to a question asked during our waking state. We even access transpersonal awareness during both the sleep and conscious states, but our mind usually filters and refines this awareness to meet our paradigm. Why, then, does the paradigm of conscious awareness seem to pervade all states of awareness? Why do we maintain a physical form in our personal dreams and often carry it into the transpersonal realm?

It is because of our attention. Where do we direct most of the energy of our attention? It is usually into the state of conscious awareness. And it is usually into the paradigm of consensus reality rather than the Balance that is the Heart. The amount of time we spend focused on the movie of consensus reality becomes a part of our paradigm. We usually spend the major portion of our waking life focused on this movie, making little or no effort to apply our ability of cognitive thought to our natural state of holographic awareness. This is carried over into the other states. Indeed, the focus of our attention on this movie of reality, with all its limitations, has a tremendous effect on the paradigm of our mind.

Thoughtful Balanced consideration of all possibility is a place of Balance between Mind and the mind. While we express ourselves in consensus reality, we usually rely on the mind to provide us with an interpretation of sensory information and transpersonal awareness through its paradigm. The practice of cognitive thought requires our paradigm to expand its filtering and refining process. It is a process that requires the mind to consider Mind, the experience to consider the potential. Unless the process of cognitive thought is a full part of our paradigm—and a practice that is instinctive—we relinquish it when we shift from conscious awareness to another state.

Again, without the practice of Balance, our paradigm based experience remains with us into all transpersonal layers. Those in the second layer are still focused on the limited experience of the first. Their paradigm remains in place. The ability to give thoughtful consideration to other possibilities is not abundant there. Those in the third layer are experiencing the results of their expectations while in the first. They are having an experience, and they share it with those in agreement with them. And they display a simple, childlike curiosity and logic. The ability to give thoughtful consideration to other possibilities is scarce there. Those who have immersed themselves in awareness have accomplished the same limiting paradigm, but it resides in Mind.

The quality of thought, the very state of awareness that allows us to walk our Path as it arises before us, is cognitive thought. It is the ability to give thoughtful consideration to other possibilities that allows us to expand our awareness. It is the ability that is activated as we practice Integration and develop Balance. It is when we apply cognitive thought to the presentation of our mind that our paradigm becomes more flexible and allows greater perception. Cognitive thought is a place of Balance between the activity of our mind in experience, and the presentation of Mind in awareness.

And cognitive thought is most easily available in the first transpersonal layer—right here in consensus reality. Those who leave here without it return again to gain it. It is karma, but it is the result of personal choice. Those who practice it here are developing Balance, and they remain better able to complete the process of transition and gain the center.

In order to gain freedom, the process of transition must be completed in Balance. If Balance is not maintained throughout the process, we find ourselves without Balance in the direction of either experience or potential.

It is possible for us, just as for a child learning to walk, to become so focused on the object of our attention that we actually pass right through Balance and fall. In transition, when the Light of Mind is the object of our attention, we may fall from experience and become immersed in potential. This is why it is vitally important to find the place of Balance between the mind and Mind, between experience and awareness. Stilling the mind only causes the Light of Mind to become predominant. When the Light of Mind is predominant in transition, we are drawn to immersion in awareness.

It is unlikely that we will pause at the fifth layer of the archetypes when this happens. The presentation, while we are there in our mind, is one of external creative power. The extremes of good and evil, as interpreted by our mind, reside there as energy. It is likely we will pass right through it as we are drawn to the Light of Mind.

And we will not pause at the sixth. Here are unlimited possibilities for experience in thought form, and we have just come from limited experience. And from the sixth, the Light of Mind immersed in potential is ever so bright.

What happens most often is that we go from one extreme to the other. We pass from immersion in experience to immersion in awareness. And this is why the Master says: It begins again.

And, like the child, we arise and walk again. Fortunately, our Path remains with us. Balance still calls us. We are in The One always, but we do not realize The One without Balance.

When we have found Balance in the center, in the Heart, we are free to explore the entire holographic world we live in. Our Path has led us back, and the Master has returned to the Heart.

A Master

We have found that the transpersonal layers are accessible through the focus of attention. In doing so, we have also discovered that access to these layers, from our perspective in consensus reality, can produce different phenomena. We can know the crystallized future. We can interact with those who have left our movie of reality for another. We can alter our physical world through the focus of attention. And we know that these are not supernatural phenomena. They are a part of our very nature.

We have a tendency to equate spiritual growth with these phenomena. This is because they produce experience, and experience is something that our mind relates to in the first layer. These phenomena are evidence of transpersonal awareness, but what is the evidence of spiritual growth?

The evidence of spiritual growth is Balance. Look at it this way. Balance is. It is the only "law" in the universe. The hologram exists because every place is the center, and the center is everywhere. There is, therefore, nothing out of place. You are not out of place. You are in the center, on your Path. In Balance, I must meet you on your Path.

Student: Isn't there something I could do that would help my growth? I feel like I should be doing something.

Master: A master is still, yet there is always motion. The motion is the process of continual emptying.

Student: Well, I still feel like I should be doing something. How can we be emptying ourselves without doing?

Master: What would you do? You know that all is in Balance, and that you are, and always have been, in the very center of this Balance. Is there something that must be changed, something that must be corrected?

Student: No, I know that there is nothing of that sort to do, but I still feel like I should be doing something. Perhaps it is just my mind.

Master: There is something to do, something you do while you are in Balance. You reflect the Balance of The One, that is all. You do this right where you are, right now. Empty yourself of your awareness. Empty yourself of your experience. Empty your Balance into this thing your mind calls reality. This is the doing of the Master. To seek change by doing is the activity of the mind. There is nothing to change, nothing to do. To empty your Balance into The One is to *be*.

We will discuss "practices" later on, but for now, we should understand that the practice of Balance is not something that comes later in our development, nor is it necessarily associated with phenomena. The practice of Balance is the application of Knowledge to our movie of reality. It is an act of cognitive thought. It is a quality decision that is made when both the mind and Mind are fully active, and that happens the moment we place our attention in the center.

The One is not a place. The One is all-inclusive. We have named the seventh transpersonal layer The One, but have seen that the first layer—that in fact all layers—are also The One. We are not "going" anywhere. We hold, here and now, the very beginning of our movie as well as the very end in our hands. The total of all potential for both awareness and experience exists everywhere and throughout time as we know it. The One is holographic energy. It is fully present in all transpersonal layers. We are holographic energy. We have within ourselves the ability to be individuals, as we express ourselves in the first transpersonal layer, or to be One, as we express ourselves in the seventh. In either extreme, the whole exists. But it exists in Balance only when the mind and Mind are in Balance. It is only then that experience both is, and is not—and awareness both is, and is not. It is here that we have found the Heart.

Energy is holographic. Thought is energy. We have within ourselves the ability to give thoughtful Balanced consideration to *all possibility*. As you have seen, this ability exists in some form at both ends of the transpersonal spectrum. It is found in abundance only one other place, in the Heart. The ability to give thoughtful, Balanced consideration to all possibility and potential is a function of attention in Balance. Attention is the power of the human spirit. The power of the human spirit is the Heart.

The center is not a place. The center is Balance. Balance is in the attention we give to thought. There is no place to go in order to find the center. That "place" exists holographically whenever and wherever the Balanced thought is given. We carry with us, wherever we are, the whole of The One reflected in the chakras of our being—in our energy. We have within us, right here and now, the very *power of creation*. And when we exercise it, it is manifest *throughout The One*.

<u>We vibrate in harmony with all who share the same focus of attention. We vibrate throughout time and space.</u> We don't have to wait until we get

somewhere to realize it. In the Heart, here is nowhere else—and now is always.

It does not matter how important our mind tells us it is or is not. Balance is from the Heart, from the center. It is manifest throughout The One whether it is expressed with our child, our loved one, our cat, the clerk at the store, the president, or the Pope. It is the very act of Balance that *is the center* regardless of where or when Balance is performed. It carries the same power of attention to Balance every time it is performed.

And it is an act of the Heart made manifest through thought, word, and deed.

Master: You have questions?
Student: No, I don't have any questions.
Master: Ah! But there is a question on your Heart. Tell me about your question.
Student: Well, it feels like a question, but there is no way I could put it into words. It's more like a feeling than a question. It feels like a wonder—like an awe. Why does it feel like a question when it's a wonder?
Master: It is the mind understanding the Heart. What will you do with this question?
Student: I don't understand. What's there to do?
Master: What do you think of this question?
Student: There isn't any thinking, there is just the wonder of it all.
Master: You have no further need for me. Now you are the Master.

The dialogue was between my Master and myself. She had just announced that I was now a Master. And again, there was an immediate question in my mind. Shouldn't a Master be doing something? My mind was waiting for some new ability to arise in proof that I had made a transition. It is telling me that I still have the same aches and pains, still get up and go to work, still eat and sleep, still experience needs, wants, and desires. All that really happened is that my awareness expanded until all that I experience contains a profound feeling of wonder. To my mind, it feels like the Question; it is a prolonged *awareness* that begins in meditation and makes its way into every moment of life. As in meditation, it is not a question that can be asked. The Question is my mind's response to awareness beyond the limits of its paradigm. It is my mind's response to Mind. Even though it is not a question, the closest I can come to describing it is to call it "the Question." This wonder, this Question, is present in *all* of the "good" and in *all* of the "bad" that my movie of reality has to offer. No experience is without the presence of the Question, and this is not possible without Balance. Yes, I had gained mastery, but only over my own illusion. For my Master, this was enough. It must be so for me.

We tend to think of Masters as those who are doing great works, performing miracles, gathering followers, and establishing a name for themselves in the world. But for the most part, Masters exist in the background. They are found quietly reflecting the Balance of The One in everything they do. They are constantly helping others gain Balance in their lives. They are meeting people right where they are, here in the movie of reality, or anywhere throughout the entire transpersonal realm. We hear little of them, but they are always with us. Their eyes reflect the joy they have, and the warmth of their Heart radiates pure Love. And in their continual motion, Balance is manifest throughout The One. What greater act of "doing" could there be?

There are two principles that our Masters teach. One is Love, the other is Knowledge. The practice of either causes our paradigm to become more flexible and allows us more freedom of choice in our movie of reality.

Love and Knowledge are partners. Love is total acceptance of the holographic nature of our reality. It is the realization that Balance is—that all is as it should be. The Love we speak of is not without emotion but, because the experience of emotion is quickly replaced by Balance, it is freedom from emotion. We can, by giving careful thought to each word and action, empty this Love into The One. In doing so, Knowledge arises within us and Balance is manifest around us. This is the doing of the Master.

The Knowledge we speak of is beyond the intellect of consensus reality. It is a Knowledge that arises when our mind and Mind merge. It is a knowing so deep inside that it cannot be described. We gain Knowledge when we recognize that each emotionally filled interpretation presented by our mind is a product of our paradigm. We Integrate the activity of our mind and gain this Knowledge. When we do, Love arises within us and Balance is manifest around us. This is the doing of the Master.

When you experience Love and Knowledge arising in your movie of reality, you have Integrated the concepts that cause your Path to arise before you. But even more, you have given your attention, your creative power, to Balance. And that Balance is felt throughout The One.

The simple act of considering it and performing it is all that is required. You need no special belief in it, no special ritual to perform it, and no one need tell you when it should be done. It is the greatest power you have in your possession. It is a foundation concept— a concept that remains true no matter where you are in the hologram of The One. It can be applied, and is valid, anywhere in any time. This includes the physical world of our consensus reality as well as all the layers of the transpersonal realm.

This Balance gives you total freedom to move about within the hologram, within The One. The starting place is here and now. When you have learned to treat every individual and every situation arising in your movie of reality with Balance, there is no where you cannot go, nothing you cannot do. And you walk in Balance.

You are now the Master.

Your exploration, and your Mastery, began the moment you realized your Path—the moment you began Integrating Balance into your movie of reality. You know that your mind must respond to sensory information. It cannot simply set it aside. It must integrate it into your paradigm. You have gotten this far. You have consumed a lot of sensory information. And even as you began to read, the movie of consensus reality began to look different to you. Your experience began to fall under the influence of your Knowledge. The presentation of Maya began to come under your mastery of attention. And you may have had the awareness that you have always known of this Knowledge, that it is not something new to you.

Your awareness expands, and the limitations of experience lessen, as you continue to practice Balance and work on the limits of your paradigm. Love and Knowledge continue to cause your Path to arise before you.

But remain constantly aware that the only evidence of mastery anywhere is the evidence of Balance. There is simply no other test. Marvelous powers, wonderful works, or great mental abilities are no proof of the presence of Balance. We should never judge others, and never judge ourselves.

In whatever layer of awareness you find yourself, remember, you are a free creative spirit entity. There is no other entity, group of entities, god or gods anywhere that has the right to interfere with your freedom to choose. Freedom of choice is the foundation of creativity. The ability to question is the evidence of creativity. It is absolutely ridiculous to think that you have these abilities in your possession and do not have the right to use them. What god would give the eagle wings and tell him not to fly?

You are your own teacher. It has been said that when the student is ready, the Master will appear, and some believe this to be an external teacher or Master. They even caution against seeking spiritual growth without such guidance. But the original saying is intended to show that the Master each of us requires is *within*, and that Master must appear even if we have an external teacher. The Master within may be identified as The Higher Self, Mind, Christ Consciousness, the Heart—any title acceptable to your individual paradigm. I have chosen to call it the Heart. When your Heart is grounded in Love and a desire to become aware, Mind presents itself in Balance. When you have found Balance, your Master has arrived.

It is true that an external Master did appear in my quest, but that does not mean that I was more prepared or worthy than another. It may indicate that I was a slow student and needed special tutoring. My external Master came as a result of an honest seeking on my part, and not because of an established belief. And I held no expectations in regards to the appearance of a Master.

When she appeared, I was virtually without anything that I believed in. I had exhausted all of the questions I could ask, received no answers, and the remaining Question was deeper than thought could contain. Yet she would not release me to journey into the transpersonal realm while I held to the limits of my paradigm. She would not release me to freedom until the Master within had arisen.

An external Master may appear in your quest. Remember, again, the only evidence of mastery is Balance. The evidence of Balance arises when an external Master meets *you* on *your* Path. This Master explains your Path to you in terms you are familiar with. You receive guidance where you are. You are never ordered or directed by a Master, be it from within or without. The entities with which you share this experience are not here by accident, and the situations that evolve as a result of your relationships are your own creation. This is true anywhere you travel. It is not limited to the confines of consensus reality. A Master merely brings this to your attention. It is another opportunity for Balance, and for working through the patterns of limiting thought that you have created through many experiences. It is your Path, and you brought it with you. The teachings of a Master reflect this. The only purpose of an external Master is to lead you to your Master within.

Masters are entities in Balance. They are found in all the layers of the transpersonal realm. Masters have no need to be anywhere, and they are never found giving their attention to changing reality. Reality is in Balance, as they are. You know that changing the movie of consensus reality involves a focus of attention on the movie itself, and that the desire to change arises out of the illusion that there is something out of Balance. Why would a Master try to bring Balance to that which is already Balance? The

Master's "purpose," if you will, is to assist you in understanding that Balance is, and that your Balance, your Master, is within your very self.

Above all else, do not evaluate yourself in this movie of reality. Everything about this movie is in a constantly changing state. It flows from potential, to thought, to manifestation, and back again. There is nothing lasting here. Give it only your attention in Balance. Balance is the only thing that remains with you wherever you go.

Do not focus your attention intently on the transpersonal realm. It, too, is in a constant state of motion. There is nothing there that holds any meaning. Place your attention on your Heart, in Balance. Your Heart encompasses the whole of The One.

Be willing to listen to the advice and teachings of all, but rely on your own Heart, your own Master, as you travel your Path.

There is only one more step to take. We should learn to retain our ability to give thoughtful Balanced consideration to all possibilities, our power of cognitive thought, wherever we are. This means we should be able to take it not only into our personal dreams, but into the transpersonal realm as well. There are methods of practice, and this we will discuss, but first, we may want to consider agreeing with others of the Path.

Working Together

Master: Hello.
Group: Hello.
Master: It is good for you to gather together like this. There is much energy here. Much Love. Remember, you are of the Path, but all are on the Path. Honor those who know their Path, and join with them for fellowship. This is good.

Everyone is on the Path. The Path is created each moment by each individual. You are now *of the Path*. You have gained Knowledge of how you arrived in consensus reality and how your mind continues to build it for you. You continue to Integrate this Knowledge into every aspect of your daily movie, knowing that it is your Path arising before you. You not only welcome the death of your limited experience and the growth of your awareness as you practice Balance, you encourage it. Your Path is personal, yet it is energizing to interact with others of the Path. There is a tremendous benefit in joining others in the quest.

As an example, if I had never been exposed to Judo, I could get a book or two on the subject and read about it. I may even practice some of the discipline on my own. When I decide I really want to learn the sport, I join a DoJo and practice once or twice a week with others involved in the same sport. But, when I want to go on to national competition or perhaps to the Olympics, the practice of Judo becomes the focal point of my life. I seek out new people to participate with, and new places to practice. This is true of any developmental quest. And, although anything can be accomplished without the help of others, any such quest is enhanced by group participation, even if it is only one or two others. Remember the power of The Magic of Agreeing. Wherever two or more are gathered together for a single purpose, the power of The Magic of Agreeing is present. Should you decide to join with others in the quest, I offer a few suggestions.

Any group, however small or large, should agree that its primary purpose is that of spiritual growth, and spiritual growth is nothing other than Balance. It should do so without sacrificing the awareness that *everything is spiritual in nature*. It's easy for the mind to develop a sense of separation from the routine of consensus reality as a result of a group. When this happens, the mind develops a feeling of belonging to the group and begins the process of evaluating others. Do not allow this to happen. Continually remind yourself that you belong to The One, and The One belongs to you, and that all are of The One. There is no separation. All the actors in consensus reality are of The One.

One of the greatest benefits of having the support of a group is access to an objective opinion of the other members—feedback from their ability of cognitive thought. We often find ourselves deeply focused on the apparent "meaning" of the movie. During these times, our paradigm may not allow Knowledge to come to our awareness. Listening to the feedback from others as they observe the movie that is running in our mind can be a tremendous help, and we can be a similar help to others. Sharing experiences in an atmosphere of Love and fellowship is very rewarding.

We may have transformational experiences—experiences in which we find new meaning—while exploring the reaches of Mind. You know the origin of meaning is Maya, and that it is a product of the mind. But meaning can sometimes appear profound. As you recall, there are groups of entities that agree on meaning in the transpersonal realm. When we are confronted with this meaning, and it agrees with any lingering portion of our paradigm, it can appear as very powerful "truths" that can lead us off the Path to freedom and into another movie. We may forget for a moment that all is truth. In the transpersonal realm, a moment of thought is all it takes for the mind to begin a movie filled with meaning. This meaning is still a product of our mind, but sometimes it surfaces with such emotional conviction that it seems to come from outside us. As an example, my Path has taken me on one such side-road journey.

I was in the process of trying to live a "normal" life and had become involved in an organized belief system. My family and I were participating in a worship service. The services were well-conducted and stimulated a sense of emotional fellowship and belonging. Part of this particular service was dedicated to a family that had accepted a "calling" as missionaries. The couple, along with their two small children, had been taken onto the stage and presented to the congregation. The story of their calling was recited, and the family was "dedicated" by the church leaders. It was the paradigm of this group that the man is the head of the family, so his wife and two children were returned to their seats at the conclusion of this part of the ceremony. Special words were to be spoken over the man.

I was in a state of deep contemplation. Even though I was a part of an organized belief system, I was still struggling with Knowledge and Integration. But I know from experience that we cannot return to the past. This is one of the aspects of the Path that is most powerful. Our mind is holographic energy, and our Path is created with each experience. We cannot go back to an old paradigm. It no longer exists. So, even though I was involved in an organized belief system, my Path remained with me.

As I watched the woman and two children return to their seats, I was emotionally struck with the sense of the dedication and commitment that they displayed. I stepped a bit off Balance. In the next moment, I was taken into those feelings of emotional commitment and suddenly found myself drawn out of my body and floating nearly up to the high ceiling of the building. Although still aware in some way of my physical surroundings, my vision was filled with the presence of a shining being that emanated a feeling of power and emotional love. The sense of dedication that I had felt just a moment ago was amplified, and became overwhelming. All I could do was sob from deep within. A clear and audible voice asked: Would you do this for me?

At that moment there was no doubt in my *emotion filled mind* that the rest of my life would be dedicated to honoring this request. My mind presented me with visions of what it would be like. I knew how my wife would be pleased that I had finally made a commitment to something tangible. I could see myself teaching and preaching the concepts of this group, even though I did not fully agree with them.

My mind also presented me with the awareness of what I would have to give up. Any further work with hypnosis was out of the question. The paradigm of this belief system teaches that it is a tool of the devil. Meditation, if done at all, would have to be done in secret. It, too, is looked upon as a mystic taboo. Forget Shamanism and all forms of Eastern thought. I would have to keep my library very low-key. This entire sequence of thought, with all the associated mini-movies, flashed through my mind with perfect clarity, and it took only an instant. This experience was not something I was watching but something that I was a part of. I was accessing transpersonal awareness, filtering and refining it through the paradigm of my new belief system, and experiencing it holographically. It was about to become a *transformational experience*.

This transpersonal awareness was supported through the paradigm of the group I had become involved with. In this setting, and involved in the activities of it, I had become a part of this group's Magic of Agreeing. The group held a strong paradigm in common, but it was not one that I had fully accepted. Even though it was supported by The Magic of Agreeing of all those in the building, somehow I knew that I was off Balance. My Knowledge would not leave me. I could not go back. The paradigm I was about to agree to was replete with separation, limitation, and meaning. It was this internal struggle between the experience my mind was presenting me and the awareness present in Mind that allowed me to recognize my state. Even though my emotions were in charge, and my mind was more than willing to accept this new paradigm, Mind was still displaying its Light. I experienced a sense of Balance, and just the slightest attention to it caused me to become aware of Mind.

The best way that I can describe the presence of Mind is to say that it is an observer. It has always been with me, making itself known at the most inopportune times. It is filled with Love but empty of emotion. It is watching, waiting, calling, and encouraging me without ever actively doing so. Just knowing that the presence was there caused me to fully realize that I was decidedly off Balance. I was reminded of the words of my Master. She has repeated over and over: In all things that present themselves as opposites, in all things that appear without Balance, observe both, but *choose neither*. With an effort of attention, I pulled myself back into Balance, but I was still held in a transpersonal state of awareness. The initial presence asked again, this time in a more demanding and authoritative voice: Would you do this for me?

I must admit that at that moment I did not *want* to say no. My ability of cognitive thought was very fleeting. Every emotion in me said, go for it. But Balance is beyond emotion, beyond intellect, and beyond experience. I don't know exactly where the words came from, but somewhere in my being I said no. I was immediately returned to my seat, and again a part of consensus reality. But I sobbed uncontrollably for some time after. These experiences are often filled with lasting emotion.

You may, at some time in your quest, be confronted with a similar situation. You may even lose your Balance and commit yourself to separation, limitation, and meaning. It's here that the group can be a tremendous benefit. Once the decision to follow a "calling" is made—or a limited belief is accepted and integrated into our paradigm—the mind restructures our paradigm so we become virtually blind to any conflicting information. We lose our ability to consider other possibilities. The Love and support of a group are most helpful in resolving these side-road issues.

Remember, though, we are not dealing with issues of right or wrong. The support you give or receive should be in the Knowledge that all is Balance. An individual's freedom of choice should be honored above all else.

There is no doubt that the ability to remain fully aware of the fact that all experience is a projection of the mind on the view screen of conscious awareness during our daily lives is a challenging task. Even though we may take time to review it when we awaken, and perhaps even schedule periods of meditation to strengthen our attention, most of us become involved in the consensus movie for the better part of the day. This reality is supported by a well-established paradigm.

It would seem that the only way to maintain Balance is to sequester ourselves against the consensus dream and focus our attention fully on The One. But you know this is not Balance. This practice is followed by many Eastern traditions, but is not the way for us. Following such a practice requires us to forsake a way of life that is the product of our paradigm, and *our* paradigm holds *our* Path. Were our Path that of our Eastern brothers, we would have chosen that setting for our movie. Our Path is here, right where we are. This is an area where even two individuals working together can be of tremendous help to each other. Keeping in touch throughout the day with gentle reminders of Love and encouragement adds the strength of The Magic of Agreeing to the Path.

We may be pressed with a desire to change our *part* in the movie we find ourselves involved in. There are valid reasons for doing so, as long as we understand that we are not escaping a particular scene in our movie. The experience we are in right now is a result of our paradigm, and we do not leave our paradigm behind when we change our parts or our movies. The experience we are in right now is our Path rising before us. To justify change by saying that we do not want to participate in the *movies of others* is not valid. We are experiencing our own movie, not theirs. It is a result of our paradigm, not theirs. If we stop right now and start over with a new job, a new relationship, and a new belief system, we are soon confronted with the same challenges that we thought we left behind. Our paradigm remains with us—our Path remains with us—and follows us from part to part, scene to scene, in movie after movie. The perfect place and time to practice Balance and follow our Path is right here and right now.

This is not to say that change is not possible, but the reason for change should not be escape. Having others to discuss these issues with is encouraging. They may offer insight that your paradigm has filtered out, or you may offer the same to them.

A group can set up a calling schedule. Members can call one another during the day and give a gentle reminder of the nature of reality and encouragement along the Path. A combination of scheduled and unscheduled calls adds the feeling of participation and support during the day, and the mind responds very well to this ongoing activity.

The technology available today can also be utilized to assist us in our growth. The digital alarm watch is a good example. Most of them can be programmed to chime on the hour. This constant reminder gives us an opportunity to pause in the activity of our mind's involvement in consensus reality and reflect on the nature of the presentation. You will find that, after a period of time, your mind anticipates the alarm and begins reflection automatically.

The use of icons is helpful in offering us constant reminders of the Path. These icons can be anything of your choosing, but are most powerful if they are a creation of your own design. They can be anything from medallions or rings to wall paintings, plaques, desk ornaments, and necklaces. Taking the time to consider and create your personal icon requires the involvement of your mind. What you have chosen and created then holds a special meaning to your mind and your Path. It is true that this meaning is self-given, but it is your creation and your self-expression, and it serves as a reminder of your Path. The only caution you should take is that the icon does not stimulate past programming containing separation, limitation, and meaning. Your icon should remind you of the essence of consensus reality and your relationship to it. It should be a constant reminder that all that is, is of The One.

Joining together with others of the Path gives us a sense of participation and support, but the most vitalizing element of group participation is simply the joy of being together. In this, we should learn to take little steps. Take the time to simply enjoy the journey. Be together for fellowship. Have fun in the movie of consensus reality. Here is an example of what happens when we rush headlong into experience.

I was in Japan with a few close friends. We were in the process of climbing Mount Fuji, and our sights were on the goal—not the journey. We were passing most of the locals along the way. We smiled and nodded as we made our way past them, and they smiled and nodded in return. Most of them offered a phrase in Japanese. I did not recognize their words as one of the few phrases that I had learned, and I did not want to repeat it without knowing what it meant.

It did not take long before we needed a rest, and we found that some of those we had passed were now passing us. A Japanese student happened by and greeted us in English. In the course of the short conversation that followed, one of our party asked him what the phrase we were hearing meant. He smiled and said: Take little steps.

It's possible to climb the wonderful mountain without heeding these words, but you pay a tremendous price for doing so. Not only are you totally exhausted as we were when we reached the top, you have not enjoyed the experience that the mountain has to give. When someone asks you what it was like, you say it was a challenge, and one would not accomplish it without being in good physical condition. Your paradigm eliminates the fact that there were women and children laughing and playing along the way. You never wonder how an old couple had managed to make it to the top. Alas, and unfortunately, this was my experience. I recall only the struggle. I have little recall of the beauty of the mountain. But I did learn a lesson from it: Take little steps.

Those who charge headlong into the Path may return from their journey the way I did from the mountain. They have no appreciation for the Path. There is no recall of how they arrived there, and there is a deep longing to go back. They have had a life-changing experience, but have no way to relate to it. They have no Balance. Taking little steps allows us to enjoy the journey as well as the goal.

Taking little steps means that we take time to enjoy the experience of our created reality and the Love of those around us. Remember always, all that is, is of The One. Experience, when enjoyed in Balanced Love, is vitalizing to both the mind and Mind. We create our own fantasies and participate in them without fear. We enjoy the company of others, even those that do not appear to be on the same Path. Taking little steps means that there is no hurry, that all is as it should be, that it's just a dream and no harm can come to the dreamer. Others may appear to be going faster than we are, but perhaps the speed at which they travel is normal for them. Go only as fast as you feel comfortable with—only at a speed that allows you to enjoy your journey. Taking little steps brings joy, and joy is a quality that conquers all.

Taking little steps includes working with what you are comfortable. As an example, I am a decidedly analytical individual with a strong technical background. Sensory information is processed easily in my "left brain." It's natural for me to work with this tendency. It would be unnatural for me to do otherwise. The paradigm that I developed in my early life would have it no other way. Although I enjoy fellowship with all, the most stimulating for my mind is fellowship with those who speak the same language I do. These are the scientific explorers. I would not be as comfortable in a temple surrounded by serious, robed figures. Perhaps you would.

In your participation with others of the Path, involve yourself only with those practices where you are comfortable. Never tell your mind that it is wrong. We have already discussed right and wrong, and have agreed not to judge others. Let's not judge ourselves either. What your mind is presenting to your awareness is the result of the paradigm that you share, and you have had an active part in developing it. It does not matter what movie runs as your Path arises before you. What matters is that you maintain Balance throughout the course of it.

Again, the company of others who are of the Path makes our journey more enjoyable, and gives us the support we sometimes require.

We are prepared now to take a look at methods of practicing and improving our ability of cognitive thought, and of making more choices on our Path.

Lucid Dreaming

There are quick and easy methods of transcending the paradigm of our mind but, as you have learned, without Balance these journeys often result in yet another movie. Each of us has given a lifetime of attention to the development of our programs, and they are the foundation of our "reality." It is for this reason that I do not encourage practices that are designed only to gain access to the transpersonal realm. This awareness may arise naturally as we gain Balance, but is not necessary for full Balance to evolve. And transpersonal awareness is not something we should seek without Knowledge and Integration, and the resulting Balance.

There is, however, an active method of gaining access to a hidden potential in our mind that is available to almost everyone. This is the state of lucid dreaming—the ability to become awake while remaining asleep and dreaming. It is one of the most powerful tools available to us in our development. Lucidity gives us an opportunity to explore reality from an entirely different prospective, one that is beyond many of the limitations we accept in our consensus dream. Our Path remains with us, even in our dreams. Because of this, lucid dreaming can be a useful aid in walking our Path.

It's possible to achieve the state of conscious awareness, to gain cognitive ability, while you remain asleep and involved in a personal dream. When this happens, you become aware that what you are experiencing is nothing more than a personal dream. You could say that you "wake up" while you remain dreaming, or that you arouse your conscious awareness while in the personal dream state. Remember, the active state of awareness when you are involved in a personal dream is normally sleep awareness, and that sleep awareness is replaced with conscious awareness when you awaken. During the lucid dream state, both sleep awareness and conscious awareness are active.

To become lucid, your conscious awareness is aroused *while you remain asleep and dreaming*. It is then that the sleep awareness that provides your dream as well as the conscious awareness of the waking state are both active. The whole of the movie of the personal dream is then projected onto the view screen of conscious awareness. You have a feeling of becoming wide awake and alert while you remain asleep and dreaming. You are awake, yet you know that you are dreaming. This is an exhilarating experience, and it is filled with an immediate sense of total freedom from the dream. This is the lucid state.

One of the first things that you notice when you become lucid is that the reality of a personal dream varies little from that of consensus reality. Many proclaim: It was so real! Solid objects remain solid as long as we accept the projection of our mind. A cool dip in a stream will give us all the sensations of "reality." When someone touches us, we feel it.

The next thing that impresses the lucid dreamer is the flexibility of the dream. The reality of the dream remains only as long as we accept it as real. While lucid in the personal dream state, your projection of thought is not supported by The Magic of Agreeing. You, the dreamer, are the only one holding the dream reality together. You may look at a scene, look away, and return your attention to the scene only to find that it has changed. The scenes are the product of your mind only, and your attention is drifting. Because of this, you can manipulate the dream in any way you desire. Having realized that what you are experiencing is a creation of your mind, you can now walk through walls or even dissolve them completely. You can fly through the air. You can learn to change the course of your dream, change dreams, and even move from dream to dream at will. This sounds a lot like what the Masters call Dream Time.

You can learn to become lucid by applying your knowledge of how your attention effects your paradigm. You know that the focus of your attention is the driving force in creating your paradigm, and that your paradigm follows you wherever you go. This is the knowledge that you will apply in developing lucid dreaming. You will develop an aspect of your paradigm, while in the state of conscious awareness, that follows you into your dream awareness.

The first step in accomplishing this is to make dreaming a more important part of consensus reality. You should begin now to make an effort to recall your dreams in as much detail as possible. To accomplish this, keep a record of every dream you have. When you awaken in the night, ask yourself: What was I dreaming? And record it then. It is not necessary to recall the entire dream at that time. Just make notes of the highlights of the dream. Keep a pen and pad at your bedside, and a light to write by. When you awaken in the morning, ask yourself the same question, and record your dream immediately before it slips away. Again, it is not necessary to record your dreams in detail as they happen. Just make notes about the things you recall at that moment. This practice lets your mind know that you have assigned importance to your dreams. Your paradigm now expands and includes more and more memory of your dreams presented in your conscious awareness.

Now, some time during the day, assign a time of *attention* to your dreams. Review your notes and expand them, this time in as much detail as you can recall. Make this a daily discipline. Assign time for attention to the process, and take the time to do it. Tell yourself that this is important to you. Give it attention. Work on your paradigm. As you perform this task, your paradigm begins to accept the importance that your attention is giving to dream recall. This practice improves your ability for dream recall, but you still need a method of bringing conscious awareness into the dream world.

This may seem like a simple task, and it is. But it takes practice and must be performed properly to be effective. For this reason, we will break it down into two steps and combine them into one process.

First you must become consciously aware, while you are dreaming, that you are dreaming. This can be accomplished by identifying a specific characteristic of your dream reality that is not consistent with consensus reality. And the task is simple.

In your dream reality, you have no recent past. Stop right now and ask yourself: How did I get here and what was I doing half an hour ago? Your mind is able to recall events leading up to your present experience. When you ask this same question while in a personal dream, your mind is not able to recall the events leading up to your dream experience. There are none. You simply arrive in an experience that is created by your mind for this moment in your personal dream state. Your mind may attempt to construct a recent past for you, but it does not matter. As long as you have asked the question, you are in a position to determine if you are dreaming or awake. But how will you know to ask this question while you are asleep and dreaming? Again, you can work with what you already know about your mind.

Anything that is the focus of your attention during conscious awareness has a good chance of appearing in your personal dreams, as well as anything that you do habitually. When your attention is highly focused on your work, it often surfaces in your dreams. Planning a vacation, which is an experience filled with excitement, has a good chance of appearing in your dreams. For this reason, the practice of recalling the recent past throughout the day is an excellent method of stimulating lucid awareness in your personal dreams.

Recall of the recent past should be a constant practice throughout the course of your consensus movie. You do not often pause and allow your mind to drift back to the events that lead you to your current experience, but this constant reflection serves as a reminder that you are not involved in a personal dream. When you have made it a habit and practiced it properly, it happens in your dreams. It becomes a part of your paradigm that follows you into your personal dreams.

You may schedule times for recall, but performing it during specific sensory situations is the basis for our method.

Sensory situations that are the most beneficial are those that require your mind to search for different programs. Remember, your mind has different programs for different situations in consensus reality. You have programs for different social situations and for different physical situations. These situations arise during conscious awareness as well as during sleep awareness.

Sensory situations in which to initiate recall should include any major change of location. Each major change of location forces your mind to reach for different programs. You have different programs for home, work, sports, driving the car, and even for sitting and watching television. Your personality, as your paradigm adjusts to your new experience, undergoes a subtle shift with each change of activity. As an example, when you leave the house and get into your car, your mind begins your "Driving the Car" program. The moment you are seated, recall how you got there. Ask yourself: How did I get here and what was I doing half an hour ago? Take a moment to reflect and recall the events leading up to your current experience. When you arrive at your destination, recall again. When you find yourself in the bathroom, ask the question. When you open the door and go from one room to another, or from indoors to outside, recall your recent past. When you learn to practice this in your consensus movie, it soon surfaces in your personal dreams. The fact that you have developed the habit of recalling your recent past, and that you attempt to recall it in your personal dreams, is an opportunity for you to gain lucidity.

Sensory situations that initiate recall should also include any emotionally charged event. This includes emotions that your mind has labeled either positive or negative. Each emotionally charged event causes your mind to search for different programs. The moment you feel your emotions undergoing a change, recall the recent past. Ask yourself: How did I get here and what was I doing half an hour ago? Every time you answer the phone, you are confronted with a different individual. Ask the question. When you see your lover, your children, or your pet, recall the recent past. Each time you feel upset, at a loss, aroused, or depressed, perform the task. Take the time to reflect on your recent past and recall the events leading up to your current experience.

Once you have learned to perform this task throughout the day, and have made it a habit, you have a very good chance of doing the same thing in your personal dream. When you perform this task while in your personal dream, you have an opportunity to gain a state of lucid dreaming.

This seems like an easy task, but it cannot be taken lightly if it is to be effective. You may recall your recent past any time the thought crosses your mind, but be sure to perform it during changes in your environment as well as during changes in emotional situations. These very same conditions arise in your personal dreams. Practice it until it becomes a habit. I apologize for the redundancy, but I cannot overstate this: The amount of attention you give to the process while awake is carried over into your dream state. Without a good focus of attention, you will not know you are dreaming.

Do not let it become just a moment's reflection. Remind yourself as you recall that this is the process you will perform in your dreams. Take time to pause and reflect. Give it cognitive thought. Never skim over it. Recall events leading up to each daily experience in detail. See yourself doing the things that led up to your experience. Recall things that were said, the names and faces of people that were there, the feelings you had, and details of each situation. Resolve firmly in your mind every time you perform the task that you will do the same thing in your personal dreams. Developing this habit follows you into your personal dream state. This is the first step in our process.

Secondly, develop a test that will prove to you that you are in a personal dream. The reason for this is that lucid dreaming is a subtle state. When you attempt to recall your recent past in your personal dream, your sleep awareness is still quite active. Your mind may attempt to tell you that it is not important, or that you can do it later when you have more time. Your mind wants to continue the dream, and conscious awareness is not a part of its dream program. Your personal dream is filled with experience, and reflection on the question of your recent past is not much of an experience. It is at this point that you will perform your test.

Your test should be something that you actually perform while in a state of conscious awareness during recall but, when performed in the personal dream, serves as proof that you are dreaming.

We know that the personal dream is not held together by the laws of The Magic of Agreeing. Because of this, certain qualities in the dream are very unstable and flexible. To develop your test, we will use these unstable qualities of a personal dream. One of the flexible qualities of personal dreams is mechanical devices.

Mechanical devices do not function well in personal dreams, and oddly enough, the newer the device, the less well it functions. One of these devices is the digital watch. Digital watches do not keep time in the personal dream. Analogue watches—the ones with hands—seem to do far better at keeping dream time. They have been around longer.

When you look at a digital watch in a dream, record the time in your mind, look away for an instant and look back at the watch, the time changes tremendously. It may not even appear as the same watch you saw just a moment ago. Or, it may be a different watch than the one you know is yours.

Knowing this, simply add the process to your recall of the recent past to prove you are or are not involved in a personal dream. Once you have completed the recall process, whatever the outcome, look at your watch, record the time in your mind, look away for a moment, and then look back at your watch. The proper time on your watch serves as proof that you are not in a personal dream. Changing time or conditions of the watch proves that you are, and an opportunity to become lucid presents itself. Of course, to perform this test, you must have a digital watch.

Remember, when you are involved in a personal dream, your mind will attempt to continue the dream just as it does while you are involved in the consensus dream. You may not find your watch and think that you have forgotten it. Or, you may be convinced that it is broken and that's why it will not keep time. For this reason, the practice should be a part of your recall process each and every time. You must know that your watch is there and that it should be accurate. To insure that it is an effective test, take the time to do it every time you perform your recall in consensus reality. And again, don't skim over the process. The amount of attention you give the process in conscious awareness is the amount of attention available in your personal dream.

Another flexible quality of personal dreams is written text. When you read something in a dream, look away for an instant and look back again at the text, it changes. Knowing this, you can add the process to your recall. Make a small card for pocket or purse with a different phrase or saying on each side. Keep it with you and, when you perform recall, take it out and read one side, hold that phrase in your mind, and read the other side. Now, turn it back and read the first side again. The text on both sides remains the same each time you read them in consensus reality. When you are in your personal dream, the text changes every time you turn the card and read. It does not matter if you have memorized the text. Your mind must create it on the card while you are involved in your personal dream, and written text is very unstable in the personal dream state.

Remember again, your mind will attempt to continue the dream. You may not be able to find your card, or it may be a different card than the one you carry with you in consensus reality. The text on your dreamed card may be unreadable and confusing. It may even appear to be in a foreign language. For this reason, the practice should be a part of your recall process each and every time. You must know that there is written text on your card, and that it is with you. Perform the process each time you recall the recent past during consensus reality. Read one side of your card, turn it over and read the other, and turn it back to read the first side again. Perform it as if it really matters. Tell yourself that this is the same process you will perform in your personal dreams. The attention you give to the process while in conscious awareness follows you into your personal dream reality.

These two tests are effective because the laws of physics are held together by The Magic of Agreeing and, even though the laws are in your paradigm, the other actors giving attention to them are not. You can develop other tests. For instance, if you jump into the air in a personal dream and attempt to hold yourself there, you will overcome the "laws" of gravity. If you walk up to a door in a personal dream and will yourself through it, it will happen. You can change any aspect of a personal dream with the slightest amount of cognitive thought and the focus of your attention. But your daily practice should be something you will be comfortable performing while other actors in consensus reality are present. Walking into doors to prove that you are not involved in a personal dream would not be considered one of them. But you can do it when you are alone, just to prove to yourself that you are not dreaming. Or, you can jump into the air and attempt to hold yourself there. Anything you do to add a sense of importance and the energy of excitement to the daily test follows you into your personal dreams.

Now, here is the entire method. With each major change of location and each emotional change, take a moment to recall the recent past. Do not just skim over it and let it go. Make an effort to recall specific events that led up to your current experience, and satisfy yourself that you have a congruent recent past. Next, regardless of the results of your recall, perform your test of proof. Again, perform it consciously and give attention to it. This is the very act that will, while you are involved in a personal dream, give you proof that you are dreaming. Continue this practice whenever the thought crosses your mind throughout the day, but be sure to do it with each major change in location and each emotional change. Practice until it becomes a habit.

When you find yourself in a personal dream, and your test proves to you that you are dreaming, you immediately experience total freedom within the dream. As mentioned, it is an exhilarating experience, and one you will want to continue. But, like any new experience, it takes practice.

Lucid awareness is a very subtle state between the *awareness* that you are dreaming and *experience* in the dream. It is a state of balance between sleep awareness and conscious awareness. In order to continue the dream, you must remain involved in the dream. Reach out and touch something. Look around. Find your voice and give a shout. But you must not become too involved in the dream. When you become too involved in the personal dream, you lose awareness of the fact that you are dreaming and sleep awareness takes control of your dream. When this happens, you simply go back to sleep and continue your dream. But when you do not participate in the experience of the dream, you either awaken into conscious awareness or drift into a different dream. Does this scenario sound familiar, like Balance?

Many people practice lucid dreaming to enhance their abilities in consensus reality. While in a lucid state—while you are awake yet asleep and dreaming—your conscious awareness and cognitive ability are activated *along with your paradigm.* In the lucid state, you are using the same energy pathways in the mind that are active in consensus reality. These energy pathways are the same pathways that the physical body uses while awake. Therefore, anything that you practice in the lucid state effects your abilities in consensus reality. You can practice physical skills in a lucid dream without the limits of your physical body. Because of this, your skill level in the state of conscious awareness improves.

You can improve any aspect of your life by practicing it in the lucid state. As an example, when I practice the piano, I notice a marked improvement in my performance in consensus reality. I actually play as if I had practiced more. I have. I have practiced in my lucid dream, using the same energy pathways in the mind that are active while I am awake in consensus reality. Remember, while lucid, you are using the same patterns and pathways that you use while awake. You are in a state of conscious awareness even though you remain asleep and dreaming. You can even solve problems and improve your memory. If your desire is only to enhance the aspects of the consensus dream, this is a wonderful place to practice your skills. It is not the purpose of this book to discuss these techniques, but they are well covered in *Exploring the World of Lucid Dreaming*, by Stephen LaBarge and Howard Rheingold.[1] The book includes a wealth of techniques for gaining and maintaining the state of lucid dreaming that are not discussed here.

It is a good idea to fully enjoy the lucid state before you go on to the task

---

[1] *Exploring the World of Lucid Dreaming*, by Stephen LaBarge and Howard Rheingold, along with full training course in lucid dreaming and electronic aids that can assist in its development are available through: The Lucidity Institute, Box 2364, Stanford, CA 94309.

of applying it to development. Your mind still wants to present you with experience during your lucid dream, and it will cooperate with you if you are having fun. Begin by simply enjoying the state of lucid dreaming. As mentioned, flying is an excellent idea. Another may be visiting a favorite area of the country, or enjoying the company of a close friend. You may have any experience you desire, and all fantasy is available.

For most, the first experiences in the personal lucid dream are pure fun and fantasy. You can do things in your personal dreams that you feel uncomfortable doing in consensus reality. There is a benefit in this. In expressing your desire for experience while dreaming, you find that your sense of limitation is overcome. Full enjoyment of the state of lucid dreaming is the same as taking little steps. And you are practicing Balance while doing it. You are maintaining the ability of cognitive thought in a state of awareness where it is not normally found.

Although called by other names, many Shamanic practices include lucid dreaming as a part of their teachings. There are also established belief systems based entirely on the practice of lucid dreaming. For our purposes, lucid dreaming is an opportunity to practice Balance and walk our Path.

One of the most beneficial experiences you can have in lucid dreaming is the experience of your Path. You know that your Path is always before you but, when you focus your attention on it, it arises to fill your view screen of reality. In the personal dream, this can be quite an experience. You can develop an intention to experience your Path and include it in your daily recall practice. While in a state of conscious awareness, and after you have fully performed your recall test, simply add the experience of your Path. Imagine that your Path is arising before you. You can imagine it any way you are comfortable with. Some may want to stand alone before the tunnel of transition, while others may be more comfortable in a classroom with a teacher. Whatever method you choose, you should develop an intention to do it. Take a few moments after your daily recall and test to actually daydream the experience. Close your eyes and imagine it in your mind. That is where it is presented during lucid dreaming. Develop an intention to experience your Path in your dreams. Tell yourself that the next time you realize that you are dreaming and become lucid, your Path will arise before you.

In whatever you choose, remember that your mind is presenting your Path through its paradigm. Therefore, you may develop expectations of the manner in which you wish to experience your path, but you should never develop expectations of the Path itself. Allow your Path to arise naturally, as in meditation. And remember that Balance is the only requirement throughout the presentation, just as it is in consensus reality.

You know that your Path includes emotionally charged landmarks. These landmarks, when they arise in your personal dreams, may be so overwhelming that they cause you to lose your state of lucid awareness and become deeply involved in the experience. This is not a setback. You have learned Balance—both in standing and falling. And you have developed an ability to recall your dreams. Recall your experience, write it down, and review it in the light of Knowledge and Integration. Do not assign meaning to it, simply acknowledge it as a landmark on your Path. Then, travel your Path again. Do this consistently, and you will travel your Path to freedom from the limits of your paradigm.

Although it is possible to do so, I do not recommend the use of lucid dreaming as a method of entering the transpersonal realm. As you have learned, entering into transpersonal awareness without Balance results in yet another movie being played out on the view screen of our awareness. Use your ability of lucid dreaming only to explore the possibilities within consensus reality, and as a means to fully enter your Path. Transpersonal awareness is a natural result of an evolving spiritual being. Allow it to come naturally to you.

You can see how this practice in your personal dreams can integrate itself into your movie of consensus reality. You begin to recognize, as you travel your Path, that all experience is dreamlike in nature. Eventually, you gain freedom not only from the personal dream, but from the dream world of consensus reality.

My Master was once asked: Why do we need to sleep? Her response started a dialogue that continued off and on for some time over a number of meetings. Her teachings are in agreement with the concept of dream time and the Sky Heroes.

We created our body to live forever, and it does not need sleep or rest. Our physical body is energy. It is a projection of our mind, and when our mind and Mind are in Balance, so is our body.

We are spirit—unlimited, holographic energy. Immersion in an illusion, any illusion, is not our natural state. We can spend about three hours in a cinema before we start feeling the need to express ourselves. We can spend about sixteen hours in our illusion of reality without feeling the same need. Our consensus reality is like a cinema. While in a cinema, we are experiencing an illusion within an illusion. Our abilities of self-expression are very limited there. We must follow the paradigm of the creators of the movie. While in consensus reality, we are also limited. We must follow the restrictions of the laws of The Magic of Agreeing. We must limit our self-expression to an agreed upon paradigm.

Sleep is our outlet for self-expression without these restrictions. We are actually awake in our dreams. Even though we carry many of our limitations with us into sleep, we are able to create and express ourselves in our dreams any way we wish. This freedom of self expression is our natural state as spirit.

As we learn Balance, we require less sleep. In Balance, we are able to free ourselves from the restrictions of consensus reality and express ourselves as the spirit we are.

Dreaming, it seems, is a natural outlet for our creative energy. Perhaps that is why the old ones call the beginning of consensus reality *Dream Time*.

A Shaman's Way

In the beginning of the section on lucid dreaming, I mentioned that the ability is available to almost anyone. There are those who, for one reason or another, have difficulty achieving the lucid state of awareness through dreaming. Some are in continual pain, others are unable to function in consensus reality without medication, and many simply sleep so deeply that gaining a lucid state is very difficult. But lucid dreaming is not the only method of gaining a state of lucid awareness. Lucid awareness becomes available any time you transcend the limits of your paradigm and, while retaining Balance, remain aware that you are doing so. You are, little by little, becoming lucid as you apply the lessons of Knowledge and Integration to your consensus movie.

In addition to lucid dreaming, Shamanic cultures throughout the world utilize sensory deprivation, sensory overload, psychedelic substances and sleep deprivation as the four major methods of gaining a state of lucid awareness. These methods are often combined and applied in a specific ritual. A lesser known Shamanic method of a focus of attention combined with deep, focused breathing is very effective in clearing the matrix of limiting thought that is the paradigm. These practices are found in chanting that is designed to force an individual to breathe at a certain rate, and drumming and dancing does the same. Focused breathing, while maintaining Balance, causes our Path to reveal itself. The process, like lucid dreaming, is simple to learn but must be understood and applied properly in order to be effective.

As you know, the mind and the body are holographically one. It is those vibrations held in our mind that result in our physical being. You know that all energy is holographic—and that you are an energy being. Because the body is a reflection of the mind, your paradigm and your Path are manifest *in the energy of your physical body*. Each and every part of our paradigm, every pattern of limiting thought, is reflected in our physical being. The body can be thought of as a reflection of our mind in denser form.

Recall the grid discussed in the section: The Path in the mind. Remember how each new experience is linked to all past experiences. This grid is like a map, and this map is mirrored in our physical body. The physical body, then, holds a map of the development of our paradigm. It is a record of the course we have taken as we applied our attention to our reality. This map in our physical body is a mirror of our Path. It includes every memory we have accumulated, as well as a record of all the emotional energy we have applied in the development of our paradigm. As you recall, the memories that have resulted in landmarks are highly charged with emotional memory. The purpose of focused breathing is to allow our Path to rise before us and experience each landmark we have created. All memories that arise on our Path, including the landmarks, are treated with the same discipline we use in meditation. We acknowledge them for what they are, gently return them to their source, and merge with them as we allow our attention to brush lightly over the Question.

The Shamanic method of focused breathing applies the energy of attention to our Path. Prolonged deep breathing creates a surcharge of vital life force in the body and, when the mind is focused properly, this map is vitalized and our Path arises. Those places in the map of our paradigm that have received a great deal of the energy of our attention in the past, the landmarks, now surface and are manifested in our physical body. They may manifest as pains, cramps, tics, tingling sensations, or hot spots, to name a few.

Remember, the mind and body are holographically connected. With the manifestation of each landmark, our mind is usually filled with memories related to it. As with any method of accessing our paradigm and clearing the matrix of limiting thought that results from it, a specific process should be followed and cautionary measures taken.

As is the case with meditation, we cannot tell in advance which landmark on our Path will be vitalized first, nor can we know the order in which they will arise. The map is holographic and cannot be understood with the logic we have learned to apply to consensus reality. For this reason, we should never decide in advance what outcome we expect from any focused breathing session. We should never decide to "work on" a specific problem we think we are dealing with. Predetermining the course or outcome of a session by giving our attention to it causes our mind to run the program we have focused on rather than the next step on our path. We create another landmark rather than accessing the one just ahead on our Path.

Our paradigm is being created as long as we are actively giving attention to our experience. This process began before birth, when we made choices concerning the experience we desired. But, as we have learned, our mind became fully involved in the process when we experienced our physical birth. Physical birth is the mechanism that allows us to participate in our new reality. For some, the process of physical birth is highly energized in the paradigm and appears as a landmark. It is possible, but not necessary, for our mind to follow its pathway all the way back to our actual birth experience. Again, we cannot know in advance what course our mind will follow through the matrix of limiting thought that is now our paradigm. But we should be prepared to follow the Path, and learn to trust the map without attempting to understand its course or determine its outcome. We should enter each session of focused breathing without expectation. Recall the words of my Master: You cannot have *expectations* without *limitations*.

The practice of meditation is a steady application of Balance to the Path created in the development of our paradigm. By the time an individual has worked through all the landmarks that it has resulted in, they are prepared to meet all illusions in Balance. The practice of focused breathing, however, offers more immediate access to the transpersonal realm. It is possible to enter with patterns of limiting thought still firmly in place. Again, without Balance, these patterns are only reinforced and made stronger. It is for this reason that I urge you to practice focused breathing as a means to travel your Path without giving any thought to the transpersonal realm. Your awareness will expand to include it naturally. This is accomplished, once again, by having absolutely *no expectations* prior to participation in focused breathing. Any expectation you hold in your mind is energized by the process and presented by your mind as a reality. Again, you cannot have expectations without limitations.

In order for focused breathing to be effective, you should be willing to fully participate with the energy in each landmark, and then let it go completely. You may, as you travel your Path, be presented with memories that contain extremes of the emotional spectrum. These emotions may even be more intense than those that occurred during the actual incident in your life. Occasionally, seemingly meaningless landmarks arise with astounding emotion, while those you thought held a great deal of meaning are given a passing review. You cannot know in advance how the energy of your mind is linked to each landmark. Again, the map is holographic and cannot be understood with the logic of consensus reality. When the deep feelings of love arise, you should become fully involved in them, actually experiencing them again. When deep sorrow surfaces, you should be willing to cry openly. In anger, you should be prepared to actually act out your emotions. This is not to say that each session will be filled with deep emotional experience and, again, you should not form expectations. It may sound redundant, but singularly, expectations result in more limitations than any other factor. The very act of forming them automatically limits your awareness.

Your practice will often include simple, but to your mind, meaningful connections to people, places and events that you can give no logical reason for. This is yet further evidence of the holographic nature of your mind. Remember, it is recording and running programs for all sensory information, even that information that you are not consciously aware of. Letting go of each landmark and every experience should be total. Your mind may attempt to assign separation, limitation, and meaning to each landmark you pass, each experience you have. Remember, the experience is a product of your mind. All meaning comes from within. Never assign meaning. Simply recognize it for what it is, return it to its source, and merge with it. In attaching meaning, your mind tries to fit your experience into your belief structure. It may give you the impression that each landmark is the result of an external experience.

You know better. All experience is within. Each experience, as well as the words and actions of every actor in your movie of reality, is given its meaning by your mind. You must recognize it for what it is and return it to its source. Do not dwell on your landmarks, and talk of them to no one. Others will only listen and assign their interpretation of separation, limitation, and meaning. Your Path is internal; keep it so.

Continued practice brings us to the same state of awareness that is accomplished in the discipline of meditation or the practice of lucid dreaming. It brings us to Balance. But again, that state of awareness should be neither a goal nor an expectation.

Focused breathing is best accomplished with someone to assist you. You may be involved in the process for some time. Your attention may drift from the process just as it does in meditation. But you have an advantage in focused breathing. Your attention in the process is directly related to *your rate of breathing.* When your attention drifts, your breathing changes. An assistant monitors your process by observing your breathing and gives you a gentle reminder when your mind strays from the task.

In addition, focused breathing is an intense process that requires a great deal of resolve and, on occasion, can result in the expression of emotions held deep in your paradigm. Although not necessarily a result of every practice session, you may even become disoriented or physically ill. For this reason, it should not be attempted alone. Have someone present who fully understands the process and is willing to assist you through it.

Someone with whom you have developed strong emotional ties can assist only if both of you are fully committed to the process. Remember how your Ego has developed programs for different individuals and situations. Be aware that, with someone emotionally close to you as your assistant, your mind may not be as free to express your feelings as it would with someone else. On the other hand, when you and someone close to you do agree to follow the process and participate openly, it is a rich and rewarding experience for both. Discuss this with whomever you choose, and commit fully to the process. Your partner will observe and assist you as your mind is exposed. You will share emotions, feelings, and knowledge about each other that is very personal. Your partner should commit to the same rules concerning separation, limitation, and meaning that you have. It is from within. It is personal. Resolve together to keep it so.

A group of participants may perform the practice together, but there must be enough room to allow personal space for each pair. And, as with your partner, a group should respect the inner personal development of each member. One would think that a group of individuals practicing focused breathing would interfere with each other, but this is not the case. Members of a group share qualities of The Magic of Agreeing. Rather than being distracting, the awareness and energy of a group is encouraging and supportive.

You require a minimum of conditions for focused breathing, and all are easily attainable. The process is performed in much the same setting as meditation. Allow at least two hours for the entire process. During this time, you should not be interrupted by the routines of consensus reality. The process should not be attempted if you are excessively tired or have just consumed a large meal. Arrive rested and refreshed, and ready to go to work on your paradigm.

Locate yourself in an area where there is little or no sensory information associated with the world around you. Auditory information gathered by your mind while you are practicing focused breathing is energized just as your own thoughts are. You do not want the influences of consensus reality to effect your attention. As with meditation, you may use white noise to mask any unwanted auditory information. Do not use meditation tapes, music, drumming or any form of audio masking other than white noise. With the exception of white noise, each of these produces a specific response, and the response is different for each individual, depending on his or her paradigm. As you recall, your mind must process incoming sensory information. It is filtered and refined through your paradigm to fit in with your current sensory experience. The key word here is "quiet."

Eliminate any outside visual information. As with meditation, Gansfield glasses are excellent. If you prefer, your visual environment may be dark—like the womb. If this is your choice, a sleep mask may be used and can be constructed easily. Whatever you use should completely block visual information from your eyes and be light and comfortable. Your environment during the process will not be completely darkened. The lighting should be dimmed only enough to allow your partner to monitor your progress without difficulty. This means that he or she must have enough light to see you clearly.

Make your environment free of religious icons, incense, and reminders of any established belief and reality structure. Remember, all is energy. These items often hold an energy given by an individual or group of individuals that remains through the power of The Magic of Agreeing even in the absence of the individuals. As your awareness expands, it may encounter this energy. Remain as free from it as possible. For the same reason, do not perform any rituals in conjunction with the process of focused breathing. Opening statements, prayers, dedications, and the like should be eliminated. They are all interpreted by each individual in a different manner. You know this from experience. The simple solution to the mind's interpretation of sensory information is to eliminate it.

Lavatory facilities should be readily available. The length of time involved may necessitate the use of them. They should be conveniently located so the participants can gain access them without being exposed to outside stimuli.

The only additional necessities are pillows and blankets. Pillows are used for comfort as well as a target for emotional releases. Blankets are necessary because the body often becomes chilled during the process.

This last condition exists only in group situations. In this case, there should be a separate room at hand where partners who have completed their practice can meet without interrupting those still in the process.

Having met these conditions, you are ready to begin. Come together with your partner or your group at a predetermined time. It is not necessary to be solemn, but your greetings should not include idle talk of consensus reality. Your words carry the creative energy of your mind. Greet each other with Love and joy. Convene with resolve and intent, and begin your practice in earnest. At first, your mind may give you the impression that there is something missing in the process. Your mind thrives on expectations, and you have provided none. This is just as you want it. As you continue practice, your mind will become accustom to these proceedings and even look forward to them.

Assume a comfortable position on your back with your hands resting at your side. It is not necessary for you to remain in this position throughout the session. You may, later on, feel more comfortable on your side but, if possible, begin on your back.

When you are comfortable, begin breathing deeper and faster than normal. A rate of one breath for six to eight heartbeats is fast enough. Inhale for three or four heartbeats and exhale for the same. Breathe just a little faster and a little deeper than normal. You will be breathing this way for some time, so choose a comfortable rate. If possible, breathe in through your nose and force the breath out of your mouth, as if you were blowing out a candle. The breath should not be taken deep into the lungs but should distend the stomach. This method of breathing in through the nose and out through the mouth, although desirable, is not absolutely necessary. You may find it more comfortable to breathe entirely through your mouth. What is important is that you breathe just a bit deeper and faster than you normally would. You are vitalizing the body with a surcharge of energy.

Focus your attention on your breathing and become aware of what is happening in your body and your mind. Your focus of attention should be on your breathing, and your awareness should include your physical body. You will experience thoughts much the same way you do in meditation. Treat them the same. Acknowledge them, and return them to their source. Return your attention again to your breathing, becoming aware again of the activity in your body and your mind.

Your rate of breathing during the process is directly linked to your attention to it. When your mind begins to wander from the discipline, your rate of breathing slows down. Your assistant monitors your rate of breathing and signals you when this happens. Except for conditions discussed later, no words are to be spoken by your assistant. As your Path arises and becomes charged, any words spoken may be filled with the emotional energy you are experiencing at that moment. It is for this reason that the signal should be nonverbal. The signal may be a tap on the forehead, a squeeze of the shoulder, or a light shake of the arm. Anything that you have agreed upon and are aware of as a signal for you to return your attention to your breathing is acceptable, as long as it is nonverbal.

Agree on how many signals your assistant will give each time your rate of breathing slows. Plan to give at least one signal, and no more than three, each time your breathing slows. You may be so deeply involved in a landmark that you are not aware of the signal. You may have intentionally changed your rate of breathing. Or, you may have entered the transpersonal realm and are not in contact with your physical body. Regardless of the reason, your assistant will give the agreed-upon number of signals, and signal no more. Again, no words are spoken. The assistant will simply monitor your physical body from that point on and signal should your breathing again change from its newly established rhythm.

Continue breathing, focusing, clearing and returning your attention to your breath. As you proceed, your body and mind become energized. You may notice tingling, pains, cramps, or tics in different locations in your body. These are manifestations of your Path arising in your physical body, and your attention naturally focuses in these areas. Your focus of attention in these areas increases the amount of energy given to that landmark on your Path. As you become aware of these changes in your body and give attention to them, the associated memories arise in your conscious awareness. When you are able to experience them as well as continue giving your attention to your breathing, you are in Balance. When you are taken into one of the experiences, your attention drifts from awareness of the process and into the experience. This causes your rate of breathing to decrease and your assistant signals you again. You now have the opportunity to return once again to the process. Continuing this process causes the landmarks to release their energy and the corresponding limits of your paradigm to lessen. You are following your Path, landmark by landmark.

Energy release takes many forms. Many of your experiences will be a simple review with a recall of the emotions, if any, involved. In experiencing the greater landmarks, your breathing may increase with the emotions and you may want to laugh, cry, feel deeply saddened, or release anger. Now is the time to commit yourself fully to the process. The emotional energy you are feeling is holding your paradigm in place. Your full participation in it causes it to release into the hologram of your mind where it becomes balanced and resolved.

You may discontinue your focused breathing while these landmarks are released. Your assistant is there to care for you. He or she may give a quiet shoulder for comfort, hand you a pillow, help you to the lavatory, or adjust your blankets. When the emotions have been released, your assistant will help you to your position so that you may continue. This should be accomplished without speaking a word—*unless you decide to quit.*

Feelings of defeat may arise during the process. You may get the impression, from your mind, that it is senseless to go on. Feelings of unworthiness are not uncommon, and are often accompanied by a lack confidence or commitment. Anger and frustration, without conscious awareness of an accompanying landmark, can arise without warning. Emotions without conscious awareness of an accompanying landmark are *imbedded landmarks*—landmarks so deeply ingrained that the associated memory is held behind the paradigm. The fact that you are not consciously aware of the memories related to the feelings is of no consequence. The process should still be followed through. You should continue focused breathing or your release until the emotions are resolved.

But they are often overwhelming, and can lead an individual to want to get up and walk away from the process. It is here that your assistant may intervene with words of encouragement, telling you that you should continue, that you are very close to accomplishing a great achievement. Reminding you of your desire for freedom, the assistant should make every effort to get you to continue the process. Words of encouragement are to be continued until you resume the process or leave the facility. Once you begin the process again, your assistant returns to the agreed-upon nonverbal signals. If you decide to quit, do not remain. Do not give the energy of defeat to those still involved in the process. It is very helpful if you have resolved yourself fully to the process before it is begun. Your assistant can then give you a reminder of your commitment.

Establish a time limit of one and one half hours for focused breathing. This time may be shortened or extended to meet your needs, but let it be the maximum for the beginning sessions. Nor is it necessary for you to perform focused breathing for the whole time. If you become fatigued or start to drift often, you may discontinue the process. Do not, however, stop in the middle of a landmark.

When you have completed your session, allow another half hour to relax and center yourself. During this time you may lightly review the session in your mind. Do not give it too much thought, and do not attach meaning or develop expectations for your next session.

The position of monitor, or assistant, is one of great responsibility. As an assistant, you must have a full understand of the process. You must also be willing to hold in confidence all that transpires during the session. This is a total commitment for both you and the participant, and cannot be taken lightly. Remember, all is energy. Two of you have agreed to share an experience together, and it will have an effect on both of you. Your sense of commitment and dedication is available, in the connection of your minds, to the one you are assisting. You must maintain a constant, caring vigil over the body of your partner. If you have to use the lavatory, do so as quickly and quietly as possible. Do not consume large quantities of liquids before the session. Provide yourself with water, only sipping to quench your thirst. Do not eat during your vigil.

As a monitor, you should be aware that the energy of the mind of your partner expands into the space around the physical body. During the practice of focused breathing, this area becomes energized. Quick movements can cause a disturbance in this energy. Be aware of this, and move slowly.

Know that when the mind expands into transpersonal awareness, breathing may totally stop for as long as three to five minutes. Rather than slowing down as it does when the mind is drifting from the discipline, it will suddenly stop. Allow at least this amount of time to pass before you attempt to arouse your partner.

You will become aware that the rate and method of breathing are directly related to the experience. As your partner experiences feelings of love, breathing concentrates in the lower abdomen and may even sound like sighing. When feelings of anger or frustration occur, breathing rises to the upper chest and becomes concentrated there. And when your partners mind begins to drift from the discipline, breathing becomes slower and more shallow. Your position as assistant, and the attitude with which you perform it, is as much a part of the process as that of the participant. When you both take it seriously and apply your attention to it, you both reap the benefits of it.

Practice focused breathing no more than once a week, on average. A weekend retreat dedicated to focused breathing is often beneficial, but should be done only occasionally. Allow yourself time to Integrate the achievements you make in creating a more flexible paradigm into your consensus movie. Continue your practice of Knowledge and Integration. Take little steps, and enjoy your journey.

As with lucid dreaming, the practice of focused breathing is to be used strictly for the purpose of traveling your Path. Do not develop expectations concerning the transpersonal realm during your practice. Again, transpersonal awareness arises naturally as you develop Balance.

Remembering

We have discussed the difference between recall and memory. You know that you have, in Mind, memory of all your experiences as well as full awareness of The One. You have learned that your paradigm limits not your memory, but your ability to recall this memory. Your memory cannot be limited. It is holographic, as you are.

You also have access, through Mind, to all experience that could ever be and all awareness that is. Again, you are spirit; you are holographic energy. But in traveling your Path while experiencing the movie of consensus reality, your mind may question: Am I sure that this is the truth? Am I on the right Path?

All is truth. Truth is achieved by each individual by extracting from the total of all truth, the truth that fits their paradigm. Although metaphorical, this is accomplished with a sword.

The sword of truth has two edges, and everyone holds the sword of truth in hand. A man locked into the movie of consensus reality, perhaps in prison, experiencing each day in physical suffering and limitation, has lowered his sword to the ground. One edge is cutting into the physical matter of the movie of consensus reality, but the other is directed toward the unlimited awareness of The One. And he is in the center. It is he who holds the sword. He may not be aware of his balance, but Balance is.

A man immersed in the holographic potential of The One has buried his sword in the void. One edge is cutting into the energy that is the foundation for all experience, but the other is directed toward that experience. And he is in the center. It is he who holds the sword. He may be lost in the hologram of awareness and void of all experience, but Balance is.

You are holding your sword of truth in your hand. Truth is not something you must question. It is not something you need to seek. All is truth—and all is not.

The question of truth is a question of the mind. The concept of truth applies only to experience. Have no fear of the question or the concept, but swing your sword in Knowledge.

Your sword of truth is directed by your attention. As you place your attention on experience, your sword begins to slice the unlimited potential of The One. As you place your attention on awareness, your sword begins to slice the unlimited experience of The One. When your sword is resting at your side, in its sheath, you are in Balance.

As you place your hand to the hilt, be aware of your attention. When you draw your sword of truth, draw it in Knowledge. Allow your mind to hold this image as you travel your Path, and allow Balance to present you with your memory.

Your very nature is Balance, and this Balance is in your memory. The memory of Balance does not appear on your conscious view screen in a way that your mind or Mind can understand. The memory of Mind gives you the impression of absolute knowing, but is not able to show the mind how you know. Your mind gives you the impression of total experience, but it is not able to show Mind how experience is. The memory of Balance is without thought. It is as if the thoughts arrive after the memory. It is filled with Love, but this Love can not be compared to any earthly love.

As you travel your Path, you begin to recall and you begin to remember. A Knowledge beyond knowledge arises. There is nothing more you must learn. These are the things of Mind. There is nothing more you must do. These are things of the mind. Yet you continue to learn, and you continue to do. You are a creator. But you are creating without the need to create. You are in Balance. Balance is your nature.

You are remembering. Your intrinsic Balance is arising within you. You see every actor holding the sword of truth. You see every actor in Balance. And you allow your sword of truth to remain at your side.

Occasionally, your mind gives you the feeling that you must draw your sword as you travel your Path. You place your hand lightly on the hilt, just to know that it is there. But you do not draw your sword.

You remember.

The Quality of Faith

The Path has given you Knowledge, but as stated in the introduction, this Knowledge is not new. All Masters, throughout time, have been giving us the same message. In the ninth century Shankara wrote in Viveka-Chudamani (The Crest-Jewel of Wisdom);

The Atman is that by which the universe is pervaded, but which nothing pervades; which causes all things to shine, but which all things cannot make to shine....

The nature of the one Reality must be known by one's own clear spiritual perception; it cannot be known through a pandit. Similarly, the form of the moon can only be known through one's own eyes. How can it be known through others?

Liberation cannot be achieved except by the perception of the identity of the individual spirit with the universal Spirit. It can be achieved neither by Yoga, nor by Sankhya, nor by the practice of religious ceremonies, nor by mere learning.

Disease is not cured by pronouncing the name of medicine, but by taking the medicine. Deliverance is not achieved by repeating the word "Brahman," but by directly experiencing Brahman.

Caste, creed, family and lineage do not exist in Brahman. Brahman has neither name nor form, transcends merit and demerit, is beyond time, space and the objects of sense-experience. Such is the nature of Brahman, and "thou art That." Meditate upon this truth within your consciousness.

Supreme, beyond the power of speech to express, Brahman may yet be apprehended by the eye of pure illumination. Pure, absolute and eternal Reality—such is Brahman, and "thou art That." Meditate upon this truth within your consciousness....

Though One, Brahman is the cause of the many. There is no other cause. And yet Brahman is independent of the law of causation. Such is the nature of Brahman, and "thou art That." Meditate upon this truth in your consciousness....

SHANKRA

And the same truths are echoed among the early Christians and Sufis;

My Me is God, nor do I recognize any other Me except my God Himself.

St. Catherine of Genoa

In those respects in which the soul is unlike God, it is unlike itself.

St. Bernard

I went from God to God, until they cried from me in me, "O thou I!"

Bayazid of Bistun

The knower and the known are one. Simple people imagine that they should see God, as if He stood there and they here. This is not so. God and I, we are one in knowledge.

Eckhart

These truths can be known and understood in the mind, but they must be Integrated into the Heart for true freedom. This requires faith, the kind of faith that can move mountains.

But faith has been misunderstood of late. It has been altered from its original meaning of an in-depth understanding that has Integrated itself into the whole being to an emotional conviction not based on logical proof or material evidence. This has led many to believe that if they question, they have lost faith. This is not so.

The ability to question is a part of our nature. It is not something that suddenly appeared when we "fell from grace" or "lost our way." It is a quality of the human spirit that remains with us always. Why, then, would anyone ask us to set it aside and rely on our feelings? You have learned the answer to that question. It is easier to live with our old paradigm than to walk our Path. But the Masters have been asking us to upgrade our paradigms for at least two thousand years.

The teaching of Jesus follow the principles presented in this book. These principles still remain in the Bible, even though it has been edited to conform to the organized religious teachings and political preferences of His time.

The stories of the healings Jesus performed were allowed to remain in the Bible. Even before the New Testament was written, leaders of the rapidly growing religious communities were already arguing among themselves about their beliefs. A group of believers that had never been schooled in Jewish teachings—the gentiles—was growing in size and strength at an astounding rate. The political power that is inherent in such large groups was in a fine balance. Both the converted Jewish believers and the gentiles needed a leader that displayed power. Jesus' power was displayed in His ability to heal the sick. A record of the miracles He performed remain in the Bible, while many of the esoteric teachings were set aside as unimportant or controversial.

But Jesus is a man in Balance. He knows what is happening as well as what the crystallized future holds. Jesus knew that by the time those new believers became involved in arguing about good and bad, right and wrong, they would have forgotten the lessons of Knowledge, Integration, and Balance. Knowing this, He included the lessons in His very actions; He imbedded them in the stories that would be told about Him.

Most of the healings performed by Jesus involved men and women that were not of the Jewish faith. It is easier to work with a limited paradigm than one that is well-established. And most of the stories contain teachings on the quality of faith necessary to overcome our movie of reality. One of the best teachings on this quality of faith is found in the story of the Centurion in the Gospel according to Matthew.

Matthew: 8:5 And when Jesus was entered into Capernaum, there came unto him a centurion, beseeching him,

8:6: And saying, Lord, my servant lieth at home sick of the palsy, grievously tormented.

Note: A centurion is a Roman army officer over 100 men. This centurion is not a Jew, does not attend religious services, believes that the highest authority in his movie is Caesar, and his uniform includes a medallion of the graven image of Caesar. To the Jews of Jesus' day, displaying such a graven image was anathema. He may have stuck out in this crowd.

8:7: And Jesus saith unto him, I will come and heal him.

Note: Jesus knows of the man's faith, but takes this opportunity to impress the crowd and give a message on faith.

8:8: The centurion answered and said, Lord, I am not worthy that thou shouldest come under my roof: but speak the word only, and my servant shall be healed.

8:9: For I am a man under authority, having soldiers under me: and I say to this man, Go, and he goeth; and to another, Come, and he cometh; and to my servant, Do this, and he doeth it.

Note: The centurion knows that Jesus will be criticized for coming to his home, and is letting him off the hook. But in doing so, he explains the foundation of his faith. The faith of the centurion is founded in Knowledge, the Knowledge of authority. And he relates it to something he already knows, he relates it to his authority. This is just what Jesus wants him to do.

8:10: When Jesus heard it, he marveled, and said to them that followed, Verily I say unto you, I have not found so great faith, no, not in Israel.

Note: Develop this scene in your mind. There is a crowd of followers gathered around, watching and listening to this discussion between a powerful Jewish teacher and a Roman soldier. They had backed away and become quiet as the centurion approached, as they always did in the presence of Roman officers. But they were now listening intently to hear Jesus' response to the centurion's request. He now tells the crowd that this soldier has displayed the greatest faith He has seen, and He doesn't stop there.

8:11: And I say unto you, That many shall come from the east and west, and shall sit down with Abraham, and Isaac, and Jacob, in the kingdom of heaven.

8:12: But the children of the kingdom shall be cast out into outer darkness: there shall be weeping and gnashing of teeth.

Note: Jesus goes on to tell them that their emotional conviction will do them no good, and in fact, will get them into latter difficulty if they do not find a way to apply it through their mind. He let's them know it is an application of Knowledge in everyday life that results in faith.

8:13: And Jesus said unto the centurion, Go thy way; and as thou hast believed, so be it done unto thee. And his servant was healed in the selfsame hour.

To most who read the Bible, this is a story of the healing power of Jesus. It is not just a story of His healing powers; it is a lesson in the foundation of faith. When you look up the word "faith" from this text in your concordance, you find that it means "a multitude of understanding," not an emotional conviction. The centurion had given his faith some cognitive thought, some attention. We know this from the way he was able to explain not only that he believed, but why and how he believed.

When Jesus was confronted with this kind of faith, the results were always miraculous. When the necessary quality of faith was not present, He often took steps to bring it about, as he did with a woman from Canaan in Matthew 15:

15:22: And, behold, a woman of Canaan came out of the same coasts, and cried unto him, saying, Have mercy on me, O Lord, thou Son of David; my daughter is grievously vexed with a devil.

15:23: But he answered her not a word. And his disciples came and besought him, saying, Send her away; for she crieth after us.

Note: Again, we should take a good look at the scene. Jesus is sitting with his disciples, and another "unbeliever" approaches Him. She is not a Jew, she is a woman, which is also a strike against her in the Jewish paradigm of the day, and is decidedly not of the inner circle. Remember, Jesus is aware of all this, yet he ignores her. He says nothing, knowing that she will get the attention of His disciples. When they can stand her begging and pleading no longer, they finally ask Him to send her away. After hearing his disciples plea, Jesus finally addresses the woman and appears to be following their advice.

15:24: But he answered and said, I am not sent but unto the lost sheep of the house of Israel.

15:25: Then came she and worshipped him, saying, Lord, help me.

Note: Begging and pleading some more, she still has made no connection in her mind. She emotionally "believes" Jesus can heal her daughter, but has not Integrated this belief in her mind. And she is still making quite a fuss, no doubt holding the attention of the disciples.

15:26: But he answered and said, It is not meet to take the children's bread, and to cast it to dogs.

Note: Did I just hear Jesus call the poor woman a dog?

15:27: And she said, Truth, Lord: yet the dogs eat of the crumbs which fall from their masters' table.

Note: Allow this movie to run in your mind. This woman has just been put down in the worst way. Her emotions are in a shambles. She is not at Jesus' feet for herself, she is there for her daughter, and He just compared her to a dog. But a movie is now running in her mind. It is a movie that Jesus just implanted there. The movie is of a master's table, the children seated there, and the dogs at the children's feet. She sees the dogs eating the crumbs that fall from the table. She makes the connection in her mind—Integration and an upgraded paradigm are the result. Until she realized that she could have what she was asking for, she could not have it. Jesus, in making the analogy, encouraged her to change her way of thinking. And it shows in her attitude. No longer pleading, with a different look on her face and perhaps a bit of a twinkle in her eye, she looks up at Jesus and says: Truth, Lord: yet the dogs eat of the crumbs which fall from their masters' table. If they can get something, so can I.

15:28: Then Jesus answered and said unto her, O woman, great is thy faith: be it unto thee even as thou wilt. And her daughter was made whole from that very hour.

What happened to the woman that caused her faith to become great? What quality did she possess in turning to Jesus with the confidence that was not there while she was pleading? She had made the connection in her mind. Jesus helped her upgrade her paradigm.

These stories are not about healing powers or miracles. They are stories designed to demonstrate a quality of faith, a multitude of understanding necessary for us to walk our Path.

In the two thousand odd years since these teachings were presented, our world has changed—but our movie has not. The concerns of individuals, cities, countries, and nations is the same as it was back then. The problems confronting families are still those of earning a living, having a home, raising children, and retirement. We have the same good and evil in our world today, it is just a little more sophisticated. We have the same struggle between belief and reality structures, it is just on a larger level. We are experiencing, in our "modern age," the very paradigm of separation, limitation, and meaning that has pervaded our movie of reality throughout history. The teachings of the Masters are as valid now as they have ever been.

The principles we have presented in this book must be applied, not just believed. This is not a movie that you can sit back and watch. You are either creating your Path, or walking it to freedom. It is through the *application* of your faith that you cause your Path to rise before you. There will always be questions. There will always be challenges. You will always be upgrading your paradigm. And you will find yourself continually questioning your paradigm as you walk your Path. This is nothing less than growth. Take joy in it.

You Are

The story of the prodigal son is given in a parable taught by The Lord Jesus as recorded in the Gospel according to Luke. As with most teachings of the Master that are presented in parables, a twofold message is presented. One message is given to those locked into the movie of consensus reality. It is designed to give them hope and an awareness of the Love of The One. The second message is presented to those who are more aware of the holographic nature of reality and our relationship to it, and are able to comprehend the inner teachings of truth. To paraphrase, the story of the prodigal son goes like this:

A rich man had two sons. The younger son decided that he would like to have his inheritance now, while he could enjoy it. He asked his father—and his father consented—giving his younger son his inheritance and allow him to leave home.

The young man squandered all of the money and ended up as a hired hand feeding swine for a farmer. He felt sorry for himself, but knew that he was responsible for his actions. Thinking about his lowly position and what he had done, the young man realized that even the servants in his father's house were better off than he. He resolved to return home and ask to be given a position, not as the son of a great household, but as a servant.

The young man's father saw his son on the road home and was overjoyed. He told his servants to prepare a feast for the boy. Upon his arrival, the father welcomed his son with open arms, had him cleaned and clothed as royalty, and even placed a royal ring on his finger. The young man's father welcomed him home with total forgiveness and fully reinstated him as a member of the family.

The young man's older brother was working in the fields during his arrival. He did not know what all the commotion was about, and asked the servants what was going on. Upon hearing what had happened, the older son became upset and quiet. His father confronted him and asked what his problem was. The older son told his father that he was upset because of the way his brother had been welcomed home. He mentioned that his father had never thrown a party for him, and that he felt that he had been slighted. His father replied:

Luke 15:31: Son, thou art ever with me, and all that I have is thine.

Both sons had developed a sense of separation and limitation; the younger son's as a result of his actions, the older son's because of his attitude. The older son had remained home working and serving his father as he thought a good son should, but he never had a party. When his father welcomed his younger brother home with unconditional Love, he was upset and felt slighted.

The story of the younger son is for those in the world who feel they are lost, separated and alone. It is presented in a manner that includes unconditional Love and forgiveness. It lets us know that we are never separated from The One.

But the father, when he turned to his older son, gives a message to those who are of the Path. His fathers words are strong and clear: You are with me always; all that I have is yours. *You can have a party anytime.*

We, when we involve ourselves in the rigors of consensus reality with a sense of obligation, may make the same error. We may forget that all that is, is of The One. We are always in the center. All that is, is ours to enjoy.

Our mind sometimes questions why others get to enjoy a party while we continue without. But all that is, is ours to enjoy. We need only take the time to enjoy it. This is the greatest party we can have in the world—knowing always that we are of The One.

All that is, is of The One. Love is the greatest expression of The One—the highest expression of its energy. Love is Light. God is Light. You are Love. You are Light. Holding Love in your Heart and in your mind makes the world a place of Love and Light for you and for those around you. This is your greatest gift to the world—and to yourself. Love is yours now and always. You are ever within Love.

You are free. You are the creator of your reality right here and now. Although it may seem limited to you, it is only your perception of it. It is all yours, to have and do with as you please. Each and every scene in your daily movie is of your creation, and it is your Path rising before you. To treat your Path with the same perspective and energy that you gave to create it causes it to extend from you and into the illusion—remaining the same.

To hold your Path in Love and understanding—in Balance—causes your Path to return to you as enlightenment. And, like the younger son, you begin your journey home.

You can not lose. The younger son in the story was never separated from his father's Love, never without all his father had—except in his mind. He began to *realize* this in his mind when he turned his thoughts to home. He began to *expect* a portion of it when he began traveling the Path back. He *experienced* it in its fullest when he arrived, but still—it was all in his mind. The words his father spoke to his older brother are the truth of The One: *You are ever with Me, all that I have is yours.* Call home. Hold the Love of The One in your Heart as you travel your Path.

You are One. Your relationship with every entity that is, is of The One. You may meet them again in another movie—in another reality—as you travel your Path, but we are all of The One. Our existence remains totally and without separation in the absolute Love of The One.

It has—does—will happen. There is no time. Love is eternal. The One is eternal. You are an eternal spirit being. No matter where you are on your Path, this remains true always. Hold Love in your Heart and allow time to be a thing of your mind—a thing of Maya. Love causes the illusion to fade away until all meaning is gone from it.

The Lord Jesus made a statement that caused much controversy in the minds of his listeners. He said: I and The Father are One. He did not make this statement to separate Himself from us. His message throughout His teachings is clear. All that is, is of The One. You, and all your brothers and sisters, are of The One. You are, right here and now, able to fully enjoy the fruits of your relationship to The One. Do not allow the limiting paradigm of your mind to stand in your Path. Learn to say, as the Lord Jesus said: I and the Father are One.

All are on the Path but, when you can speak these words with understanding—you are *of* the Path.

Be free to express the most powerful words a human spirit can voice;

I AM

And you shall know the truth, and the truth shall make you free. John 8:32

Raissa Publishing
P.O. Box 295, Dept. H
Port Angeles, WA 98362

$16.95, S&H included

Visa & MC accepted.

Call toll free:
1-888-423-5270

Email: Raissa@Tenforward.com

ftp://www.tenforward.com/raissa/index.htm

Network

Share The Path with your friends.

Walk in Peace